James Perrin Warren

Culture

of WITHDRAWN

Eloquence,

Oratory and Reform in Antebellum America

The Pennsylvania State University Press
University Park, Pennsylvania

Library of Congress Cataloging-in-Publication Data

Warren, James Perrin.
    Culture of eloquence: oratory and reform in antebellum America / James Perrin Warren.

        p.   cm.
    Includes bibliographical references and index.
    ISBN 0-271-01900-X (cloth: alk. paper)
    1. Speeches, addresses, etc., American—History and criticism. 2. American prose
literature—19th century—History and criticism. 3. Oratory—United States—
History—19th century. 4. Peabody, Elizabeth Palmer, 1804–1894—Oratory. 5. Simms,
William Gilmore, 1806–1870—Oratory. 6. Emerson, Ralph Waldo, 1803–1882—
Oratory. 7. Fuller, Margaret, 1810–1850—Oratory.   I. Title.
PS407.W37   1999
815'.309—dc21   98-41327
                                                                                              CIP

Copyright © 1999 The Pennsylvania State University
All rights reserved
Printed in the United States of America
Published by The Pennsylvania State University Press,
University Park, PA 16802-1003

It is the policy of The Pennsylvania State University Press to use acid-free paper for the
first printing of all clothbound books. Publications on uncoated stock satisfy the mini-
mum requirements of American National Standard for Information Sciences—
Permanence of Paper for Printed Library Materials, ANSI Z39.48–1992.

To the members of the A.Y.P.W.B.C.

Contents

Acknowledgments

It has taken me more than ten years to write this book. I drafted an essay on Emerson's theory of language during the summer of 1988, when I had the good fortune to attend Hans Aarsleff's NEH Summer Seminar at Princeton University. That work seeded many summers of research and writing, all supported by Washington and Lee University's John M. Glenn Faculty Grant program. In addition, sabbatical leaves came at two crucial points in the writing and revising of the book. A Class of 1962 Fellowship allowed me to take a full year's leave in 1990–91, and during the fall of 1995 the Lewis Law Center of Washington and Lee provided quiet office space and excellent staff support. As dean and now as president, John Elrod has personified the unflagging generosity of my home institution.

Personal debts are a pleasure to acknowledge, in particular when they stretch back so far. Ward and Peggy Allen have discussed the figures in this study and influenced my thinking about them more than even they realize. My senior colleague Severn Duvall guided me toward the work of William Gilmore Simms and has kept up a running conversation on Emerson for some fifteen years now. Richard Brodhead and Marie Borroff got me started many years ago, and their critical writings have served as exemplary models to follow. Philip Gura and David M. Robinson provided excellent advice in their critical readings of the manuscript. My colleagues in the English Department at Washington and Lee, junior and senior, have listened to me even at my least eloquent. Monika Eaton and our four girls have listened to me even at my most vehement. To all of these people I extend my deepest gratitude.

Several libraries provided resources and support in large measures: Washington and Lee's Leyburn Library; University of Virginia's Alderman Library; Princeton University's Firestone Library; Harvard University's Houghton Library and University Archives; the Boston Public Library;

University of South Carolina's South Caroliniana Library; the Library of Congress. I thank the libraries and their staffs for their help. My thanks go to Harvard University and the University of South Carolina for permission to quote from manuscript materials consulted in their libraries.

For expert copyediting and indexing, I am grateful to Romaine Perin. For support for the indexing, I wish to thank Dean Larry Boetsch and the Glenn Grant Publications Fund. For editorial support, I thank Cherene Holland at Penn State Press.

Finally, my special thanks to Philip Winsor, Senior Editor at Penn State Press, who saw both my books through the publishing process with unfailing grace and expertise.

1

Culture of Eloquence

1

On 30 June 1881, Wendell Phillips addressed the centennial anniversary meeting of Harvard University's Phi Beta Kappa chapter. The audience included such dignitaries as President Charles W. Eliot of Harvard, President Daniel Coit Gilman of Johns Hopkins University, and Justice Oliver Wendell Holmes, and literary figures such as James Freeman Clarke, George William Curtis, and Thomas Wentworth Higginson. Delegations from seventeen of the twenty existing Phi Beta Kappa chapters marched in the procession to Harvard's Sanders Theatre. In addition to marking a public anniversary, the ceremonial occasion marked Phillips's return, after fifty years, to the speaker's platform at Harvard, for he had last addressed a Harvard audience at his own commencement exercises in 1831.[1]

During those fifty years, Phillips had become one of the most famously eloquent speakers in America. And he was still, in 1881, one of the most controversial. The innocuous title of his address, "The Scholar in a Republic," conceals Phillips's wide-ranging call for social change, a call that in effect summarizes important themes from his fifty-year career as a public speaker and reformer. More important, however, is the fact of his public performance itself. For Phillips, the scholar in a republic must be an independent, moral, social agitator:

> I urge on college-bred men, that, as a class, they fail in republican duty when they allow others to lead in the agitation of the great social questions which stir and educate the age. . . . The freer a nation becomes,

1. James Brewer Stewart, *Wendell Phillips: Liberty's Hero* (Baton Rouge: Louisiana State University Press, 1986), 322–24.

the more utterly democratic in its form, the more need of this outside agitation. Parties and sects laden with the burden of securing their own success cannot afford to risk new ideas. "Predominant opinions," said Disraeli, "are the opinions of a class that is vanishing." The agitator must stand outside of organizations, with no bread to earn, no candidate to elect, no party to save, no object but truth,—to tear a question open and riddle it with light.[2]

Phillips's definition of the agitator provides a retrospective, idealized view of his own career, a view that defines a particular position the agitator occupies in American culture. Phillips begins by appealing to the "college-bred men" of his audience and labeling them a "class" with a "republican duty" to lead in the active consideration of "the great social questions which stir and educate the age." The proper role of the scholar, according to Phillips, is to educate the republic in its responses to those social questions, and the proper position of the scholar-agitator is "outside of organizations." But where would such an "outside" be? Phillips's figure of the agitator "stands" outside all institutions in order to "tear a question open and riddle it with light." The image implies that the agitator can also stand outside the "great social questions" themselves, tearing them open and riddling them with the light of truth. But this assumes that the scholar-agitator is somehow outside the stirring and educating of the age— a teacher rather than a student, an answerer rather than a questioner.

Standing before the audience of "college-bred men," Phillips embodies the figure of the scholar-agitator in the act of speaking. He occupies an independent, unentangled space, defined as utterly necessary for democratic freedom. But his embodiment of the figure is also laced with a palpable nostalgia. The possibilities for standing "outside of organizations, with no bread to earn, no candidate to elect, no party to save, no object but truth" reside more vividly in Phillips's personal version of antebellum Boston than they could in the Cambridge, Massachusetts, of 1881. Phillips speaks from the privileged position of Beacon Hill, and his moral authority stands side by side with his family wealth, but the cumulative rhetoric of the agitator disguises his tendency to universalize his personal history. In other words, the figure of the scholar-agitator closely follows the outlines of Phillips's own fifty-year career of agitation, especially in his role as a leader of the American Anti-Slavery Society.[3]

The nostalgia in Phillips's address arises from the distance between his own experience as an agitator and the likely experience of the college-bred men

---

2. *Speeches, Lectures, and Letters: Second Series* (Boston: Lee and Shepard, 1891), 349–50. Subsequent quotations from the address will be cited parenthetically.

3. For Phillips's family background and early life, see Stewart, 1–96; for the role of class and race in the "Boston clique" of abolitionists, see Stewart, 97–116; for Phillips's leadership in the "Garrisonian"

listening to him in 1881. There are many ways of measuring that distance, but I would point to the structures of incorporation that define America in the Gilded Age.[4] One of the most significant of those structures is the "culture of professionalism," which was institutionalized in postbellum research universities such as Harvard and Johns Hopkins and effectively embodied by the two university presidents, Eliot and Gilman, who shared the platform with Phillips. There may be a certain attractiveness in the figure of the agitator—independent of corporate structures, professional careers, middle-class wages and aspirations—but for the majority of Phillips's audience, then and now, that figure must remain chimerical.[5]

Despite the distances, Phillips speaks with abundant power and authority. His contemporary Edward G. Parker described the "mainspring" of Phillips's oratory as "deep, impassioned moral conviction."[6] And Phillips's moral authority depends, in part, on his position as an independent outsider, with no personal interest in the social questions he proposes to the audience. In "The Scholar in a Republic," he represents himself as a college-bred man, but he speaks in the interests of the larger class of citizens who are not college educated:

> A chronic distrust of the people pervades the book-educated class of the North; they shrink from that free speech which is God's normal school for educating men, throwing upon them the grave responsibility of deciding great questions, and so lifting them to a higher level of intellectual and moral life. Trust the people—the wise and the ignorant, the good and the bad—with the gravest questions, and in the end you educate the race. At the same time you secure, not perfect institutions, not necessarily good ones, but the best institutions possible while human nature is the basis and the only material to build with. Men are educated

branch of the American Anti-Slavery Society and in other abolitionist groups, see Stewart, 63–75. The American Anti-Slavery Society did not disband until the Fifteenth Amendment to the Constitution was ratified in 1870, and Phillips was instrumental in the society's continuing existence after the end of the Civil War. Still, the attitude he expresses concerning political parties is much more suggestive of his antebellum, Garrisonian abolitionism than of the postbellum career, when he himself ran for electoral office; see Stewart, 146–76, 270–319.

4. The best single-volume account of the new postwar America is Alan Trachtenberg, *The Incorporation of America: Culture and Society in the Gilded Age* (New York: Hill and Wang, 1982).

5. For a wide-ranging account of professionalism from the 1840s into the Gilded Age, see Burton J. Bledstein, *The Culture of Professionalism: The Middle Class and the Development of Higher Education in America* (New York: Norton, 1976), esp. 80–128. For three helpful views on more specific aspects of professionalism, see Gerald Graff, *Professing Literature: An Institutional History* (Chicago: University of Chicago Press, 1987); Thomas L. Haskell, *The Emergence of Professional Social Science* (Urbana: University of Illinois Press, 1977); Richard H. Brodhead, *Cultures of Letters: Scenes of Reading and Writing in Nineteenth-Century America* (Chicago: University of Chicago Press, 1993).

6. Edward G. Parker, *The Golden Age of American Oratory* (Boston: Whittemore, Niles, and Hall, 1857), 372.

and the State uplifted by allowing all—every one—to broach all their mistakes and advocate all their errors. The community that will not protect its most ignorant and unpopular member in the free utterance of his opinions, no matter how false or hateful, is only a gang of slaves! (344)

Phillips speaks in an axiomatic style, moving from one general proposition to the next with overwhelming confidence. The vexed questions of freedom of speech and universal suffrage are central to the passage, and he offers the same answer to both: "trust the people." The analogy underlying the series of axioms is that "free speech" is "God's normal school for educating men." Since a normal school trains teachers, especially elementary school teachers, the analogy implies that free speech and the vote are two elementary forms of education and expression. In effect, then, the figure breaks down the division between the "book-educated class" and the people, for Phillips's vision of free speech would transform the republic into a normal school, in which every citizen would be both student and teacher.

The problem with Phillips's generous view of the power of free speech to educate and uplift the human race comes in the last phrase of the passage. If any members of the audience disagree with the speaker's axioms, which assert the necessary progress of humanity through unbridled free speech, they become part of "a gang of slaves!" In the interest of trusting the people, Phillips betrays his distrust of the "book-educated class of the North." The utopian vision of free speech terminates in insult.

The insult also suggests that Phillips is once again speaking from an antebellum perspective, since the exclamation figures his opponents as the victims of a mental and moral slavery. Indeed, his seemingly contradictory rhetoric suggests the double bind of the "book-educated class of the North" before the Civil War. Daniel Walker Howe describes that double bind as a "double service": "Jacksonians were less concerned that statesmen should play a didactic role and tell people what was good for them; Democrats saw the orator as the people's spokesman. But for the Whigs, the orator performed a double service: he must not only defend the people's true interests but show the people themselves where those interests lay."[7] Although Phillips denied any allegiance to political parties, the role of the Whig orator is remarkably similar to the figure of God's normal school, for both emphasize the protection and education of

---

7. *The Political Culture of the American Whigs* (Chicago: University of Chicago Press, 1979), 27. The entire volume is of great value, especially in its treatment of political orators such as Daniel Webster, Henry Clay, and John Quincy Adams.

the people's "free utterance." Phillips's outburst betrays his desire to control the language and values of the community, even though it also clearly shows his passionate conviction that free speech is an absolute necessity for the progress of the republic.

If the source of Phillips's eloquence, as Edward Parker noted, lies in the speaker's "deep, impassioned moral conviction," it also resides in the mediating position occupied by the speaker. Most fundamentally, speakers mediate between their own moral convictions—the truth they seek to tell—and the audience's ability to hear and understand that truth. In "The Scholar in a Republic," Phillips effectively multiplies that fundamental role into several more mediations. Thus his moral conviction has much more to do with antebellum abolitionism than with the Russian nihilists he champions at the end of the speech (356–60), so that the address mediates between the two epochs marked by the Civil War. Likewise, he stands between the college-bred class and the "people," as if he could speak for and to both. Finally, the figure of the scholar-agitator mediates between inner conviction and outer action; the words of eloquence should educate the audience into moral action.

These several mediations come together in the following passage, in which Phillips narrates his own version of antebellum American history:

> These "agitations" are the opportunities and the means God offers us to refine the taste, mould the character, lift the purpose, and educate the moral sense of the masses on whose intelligence and self-respect rests the State. God furnishes these texts. He gathers for us this audience, and only asks of our coward lips to preach the sermons.
>
> There have been four or five of these great opportunities. The crusade against slavery—that grand hypocrisy which poisoned the national life of two generations—was one,—a conflict between two civilizations which threatened to rend the Union. Almost every element among us was stirred to take a part in the battle. Every great issue, civil and moral, was involved,—toleration of opinion, limits of authority, relation of citizen to law, place of the Bible, priest and layman, sphere of woman, question of race, State rights and nationality; and Channing testified that free speech and free printing owed their preservation to the struggle. But the pulpit flung the Bible at the reformer; law visited him with its penalties; society spewed him out of its mouth; bishops expurgated the pictures of their Common Prayer Books; and editors omitted pages in republishing English history; even Pierpont emasculated his Class-book; Bancroft remodelled his chapters; and Everett carried Washington

through thirty States, remembering to forget the brave words the wise Virginian had left on record warning his countrymen of this evil. Amid this battle of the giants, scholarship sat dumb for thirty years until imminent deadly peril convulsed it into action, and colleges, in their despair, gave to the army that help they had refused to the market-place and the rostrum.

There was here and there an exception. That earthquake scholar at Concord, whose serene word, like a whisper among the avalanches, topples down superstitions and prejudices, was at his post, and with half a score of others, made the exception that proved the rule. Pulpits, just so far as they could not boast of culture, and nestled closest down among the masses, were infinitely braver than the "spires and antique towers" of stately collegiate institutions. (350–52)

This lengthy passage gives a compact history of abolitionism. In the first paragraph, Phillips frames his history in scriptural terms, so that the history becomes part of a providential scheme of moral progress. And if "God furnishes these texts" and "gathers for us this audience," he then puts the scholar-agitator in the position of opening "coward lips to preach the sermons."

In the longer, second paragraph, Phillips focuses on abolitionism as the primary instance of such a "text," such an opportunity to speak. The "crusade against slavery" becomes an overarching reform movement, one that gathers all of the great issues of antebellum American culture into a single struggle. But in the second half of the paragraph, Phillips details the rejection of the reformer by those who control language and values, and he gives an accusatory litany of scholars and speakers who, silenced by faceless censors, "sat dumb for thirty years" until the Civil War broke through their paralysis. Given the context of the address itself, Phillips's sarcasm regarding Edward Everett, former president of Harvard University, is especially barbed. Everett could fairly stand for antebellum oratory, particularly of the grandiloquent type, and his lecture titled "The Character of Washington" was immensely successful and popular in the years of greatest abolitionist agitation, 1856–60. Phillips comes very close to accusing the filiopietistic Everett of moral cowardice, but a more moderate historian would argue that Everett modeled his moderate politics on the ideal figure of Washington, who "united all the qualities required for the honorable and successful conduct of the greatest affairs, each in the happy mean of a full maturity, and all in that true proportion in which they balance and sustain each other."[8]

8. "The Character of Washington," in Ronald F. Reid, *Edward Everett: Unionist Orator* (New York: Greenwood, 1990), 163. For a more general account of Everett as an orator, see Paul A. Varg, *Edward*

In the last of the three paragraphs, Phillips notes two exceptions to the broad and pointed accusations he has hurled at the audience. First, he alludes to Emerson as "that earthquake scholar at Concord," conferring titanic reforming power upon his "serene word, like a whisper among the avalanches." Second, he praises the "pulpits" that "nestled closest down among the masses," contrasting their bravery to the cowardice of "stately collegiate institutions." The final paragraph brings the audience back to their present position at the stately institution of Harvard, just a few miles away from the earthquake scholar at Concord. In bringing his narrative to the present, Phillips asks his audience to speak as he has been speaking, to do as he has been doing. By figuring history as an opportunity for moral struggle, and by figuring that struggle as a battle of words, he calls for his audience to join in preaching the sermons of agitation. The moral force of the address resides in the jeremiad rhetoric of bravery and cowardice, a rhetoric that seems to offer a stark choice but in effect affords the audience none.[9]

Phillips's bow to Emerson and the accompanying acknowledgment of Emerson's power as a speaker are in themselves interesting, since they accord with recent scholarship concerning Emerson's guarded commitment to the reform movement of antislavery.[10] But Emerson did not always think of Phillips on a like scale. In his journal of 1844–45, for instance, Emerson notes the controversies surrounding Phillips's antislavery lectures at the Concord Lyceum:

> I wish that Webster & Everett & also the young political aspirants of Massachusetts should hear Wendell Phillips speak, were it only for the capital lesson in eloquence they might learn of him. This, namely, that the first & the second & the third part of the art is to keep your feet always firm on a fact. They talk about the Whig party. There is no such thing in nature. They talk about the Constitution. It is a scorned piece of paper. He feels after a fact & finds it in the money-making, in the commerce of New England, and in the devotion of the Slave states to their interest, which enforces them to the crimes which they avow or disavow, but do & will do. He keeps no terms with sham churches or shamming legislatures, and must & will grope till he feels the stones.

Everett (Selinsgrove: Susquehanna University Press, 1992), 173–80; for the success of the Washington lecture in raising funds for the restoration of Mount Vernon, see 177–79.

9. The classic account of this rhetoric is Sacvan Bercovitch, *The American Jeremiad* (Madison: University of Wisconsin Press, 1978). For a pertinent discussion of the cultural work performed by filiopietistic oratory in the early republic, see the chapter "Ritual of Consensus" (132–75).

10. See Len Gougeon, *Virtue's Hero: Emerson, Antislavery, and Reform* (Athens: University of Georgia Press, 1990).

> Then his other & better part, his subsoil, is the *morale*, which he solidly
> shows. Eloquence, poetry, friendship, philosophy, politics, in short all
> power must & will have the real or they cannot exist.[11]

Emerson's sense of Phillips's eloquence accords with that of Edmund Parker
in *The Golden Age of Oratory*, although in this passage he ties the moral conviction of the speaker to the concrete analysis of economic realities. Both
Emerson and Parker recognize the dual fact that "all power must & will have
the real" and that Phillips wields a definite power of eloquence. A decade later,
however, Emerson's sense of power shifts:

> Of Phillips, Garrison, & others I have always the feeling that they may
> wake up some morning & find that they have made a capital mistake,
> & are not the persons they took themselves for. Very dangerous is this
> thoroughly social & related life, whether antagonistic or *co*-operative. In
> a lonely world, or a world with half a dozen inhabitants, these would
> find nothing to do. The first discovery I made of Phillips was that while
> I admired his eloquence, I had not the faintest wish to meet the man.
> He had only a *platform*-existence, & no personality. Mere mouthpieces
> of a party, take away the party & they shrivel & vanish. They are ines-
> timable for workers on audiences; but for private conversation, one on
> one, I much prefer to take my chance with that boy in the corner. (*JMN*
> 13:281–82)

The danger of Phillips's eloquence lies in the very moral conviction and public commitment that create the eloquence in the first place. Emerson reads that
danger as primarily aimed at the individual personality or self, which shrivels
and vanishes if there is no platform from which to speak, no audience to work.
He does not fear the powerful effect that Phillips's speech might have on an
audience; instead, he fears the effect of being eloquent on the speaker's "privacy." Thus Emerson appreciates Phillips's eloquence, but he implicitly admonishes himself to guard his privacy and personality in order to avoid becoming
a "mere mouthpiece."

Phillips in fact makes a similar distinction in a theme he wrote as a Harvard
undergraduate in November 1830.[12] The essay addresses the question "Your

---

11. Ralph Waldo Emerson, *Journals and Miscellaneous Notebooks,* ed. William H. Gilman et al., 16 vols.
(Cambridge: Harvard University Press, 1960–82), 9:136–37. Henceforth cited as *JMN.*

12. The essay is contained in a collection titled *Themes and Dissertations,* bound by Phillips himself

idea of what makes writing to be poetical, prose, or eloquent," and Phillips
focuses on the distinction between poetry and eloquence:"Is not poetry rather
that excitement of the feelings that ends in itself,—is it not affective, sublime
indeed, but somewhat abstract? While Eloquence is the same feelings urged forward to action, excited by intense, perhaps often personal, instinct." Phillips distinguishes between the two by distinguishing their respective ends or effects:
while poetry "ends in itself," eloquence ends in "action." This difference in effect
leads Phillips to consider audience:

> Poetry is addressed to man, Eloquence to men. The poets of Rome we
> read now in our proper character with the purest delight. The fire of
> their orators does not warm us, till we are Romans. Poetry then is based
> upon the common feelings of our nature, the same in all circumstances,
> and easily excited in every individual—Eloquence is addressed to men,
> in whom these feelings are centred with burning interest upon one object.
>
> Poetry is the language of the deepest feelings, never of the strongest
> *passions*. The faery or the spirit may be poetical consistently with char-
> acter. It requires man, in all the fulness and variety of his powers and
> complexity of his circumstances, to be eloquent.

The 1830 essay suggests that Phillips's sense of vocation is directly related to
his view of language as an instrument for effecting social change. Eloquence is
that instrument, and it acts upon the audience by engaging feelings and cen-
tering them "with burning interest upon one object." The essay also suggests
that Phillips's view of the scholar as an agitator and public speaker is already
formed during his own days as a young Harvard scholar.

Other themes and forensic exercises indicate that Phillips fully appreciated
the power of language to form and reform culture. The topics themselves, as
well as the fact that Phillips saved his responses and bound them in one volume, suggest the overwhelming interest in language that characterizes antebellum American culture:

> "Of forming a habit of extemporaneous speaking. Of the natural dif-
> ference of men as to this power."
>
> "Whether the invention of speech may be referred to the natural fac-
> ulties of man."

---

and now in the Harvard University Archives. The fact that Phillips saved these particular essays and forensic speeches is in itself significant. All of my quotations are from the manuscript, which is unpaginated. I
gratefully acknowledge permission of the Harvard University Archives to quote from the manuscript.

> "Whether a diversity of language be better for mankind than one universal language extending through all nations."
>
> "Whether the power of eloquence be diminished by the gradual progress of literature and science."

Phillips's responses to these questions blend eighteenth-century theories of language with elements of the new study of comparative philology. So, for instance, he argues that eloquence "owes little to natural endowments" and is most effective "when slowly acquired by habit," a view that accords with the Lockean theory of language as a system of conventionally accepted signs. But he argues elsewhere that the "invention of speech" should be "attributed to divine interposition" because "all languages are similar" and "were derived from a common origin." This response echoes the fundamental tenets of comparative philology, and Phillips points obliquely to the search for the Indo-European "mother tongue" when he asserts that "that origin must have been a grand comprehensive regular language."[13]

Phillips's youthful essays suggest that the subject of language exerted a powerful influence on his conception of himself, and they give a sense of his prospects as an orator. Phillips's long career as a public speaker on the lyceum circuit is already visible in his undergraduate views of language. Indeed, the undergraduate essays exemplify the oratorical culture of antebellum American colleges, a culture based on classroom performances such as forced recitations, theme writing, rhetorical analysis of passages, declamations, and forensic arguments. American colleges exerted additional oratorical influences on undergraduates through literary and debating societies, which sponsored a wide range of weekly debates on cultural and political topics. Moreover, textbooks such as Hugh Blair's *Lectures on Rhetoric and Belles Lettres* (1783), Caleb Bingham's

---

13. The best discussions of the history of the study of language, particularly in the relationship of French and German thinkers to Anglo-American philosophies of language, are by Hans Aarsleff: *The Study of Language in England, 1780–1860* (Princeton: Princeton University Press, 1967) and *From Locke to Saussure: Essays on the Study of Language and Intellectual History* (Minneapolis: University of Minnesota Press, 1982). See also Michel Foucault, *The Order of Things*, trans. Alan Sheridan (New York: Pantheon, 1970).

Several scholars consider the study of language in relation to antebellum American literature and culture. The seminal study by Philip F. Gura, *The Wisdom of Words: Language, Theology, and Literature in the New England Renaissance* (Middletown: Wesleyan University Press, 1981), has led to contributions by the following: Dennis E. Baron, *Grammar and Good Taste: Reforming the American Language* (New Haven: Yale University Press, 1982); David Simpson, *The Politics of American English, 1776–1850* (New York: Oxford University Press, 1986); Kenneth Cmiel, *Democratic Eloquence: The Fight over Popular Speech in Nineteenth-Century America* (New York: Morrow, 1990); and Michael P. Kramer, *Imagining Language in America* (Princeton: Princeton University Press, 1992).

Columbian Orator (1797), and John Quincy Adams's *Lectures on Rhetoric and Oratory* (1810) were formative influences on the generation that reached maturity between 1825 and 1860.[14]

There are, to be sure, several other important influences shaping antebellum America into a culture of eloquence. In New England, the Congregational focus on the sermon delivered by an educated minister relates directly to the training provided in the colleges, for many of the college-bred men of the early nineteenth century would become preachers.[15] In both North and South, opportunities for public speaking are legion: forensic, political, and celebratory speaking create three large and varied arenas in which the public address flourished.[16] On the national level, both houses of Congress feature some of the most renowned orators of American history, the most celebrated being the trio of Calhoun, Clay, and Webster.[17]

The most important innovation of the culture, however, is the popular lecture, which develops out of the lyceum movement. Modeled on the mechanics' institutions of England, the first American lyceum was started late in 1826 by Josiah Holbrook. The lyceum was a remarkable institution for popular education in communities of all kinds and sizes, and it quickly spread throughout New England and into the upper Atlantic states, the South, and the Midwest. In its first stage, it featured a series of public lectures delivered by the local intelligentsia, usually on subjects in the applied sciences. By the mid-1840s, as many as four thousand communities had a lyceum or some similar society for sponsoring public lectures, and the lecturers now included such celebrities as Phillips and Emerson. According to historian Donald Scott, the lecture "was expected

14. See Graff, *Professing Literature*, 19–51, for a concise account of antebellum college curricula and educational processes; for the role of literary societies, see Thomas S. Harding, *College Literary Societies* (New York: Pageant Press, 1971). It is interesting to note that Edward G. Parker dedicates his *Golden Age of Oratory* as follows: "To my alma mater, 'Yale,' whose great societies 'The Brothers in Unity' and 'Linonia' are nurseries of manly debate, I inscribe this volume, as a filial though humble offering." For a good account of the textbooks used during the period, see Ota Thomas, "The Teaching of Rhetoric in the United States During the Classical Period of Education," in William Norwood Brigance, ed., *A History and Criticism of American Public Address*, vol. 1 (New York: Russell & Russell, 1960): 193–210.

15. Lawrence Buell, *New England Literary Culture: From Revolution Through Renaissance* (Cambridge: Cambridge University Press, 1986), 137–38; the entire chapter "Oratory from Everett to Emerson" (137–65) is excellent. See also Buell, *Literary Transcendentalism: Style and Vision in the American Renaissance* (Ithaca: Cornell University Press, 1973), 102–39.

16. See Bower Aly and Grafton P. Tanquary, "The Early National Period: 1788–1860," in Brigance, *A History*, 1:55–110.

17. For individual treatments of the three celebrity speakers, see Brigance, *A History*, vol. 2 (New York: Russell & Russell, 1960), 603–733. Parker treats Congress at great length (14–153), focusing principally on Webster; he calls Webster, Calhoun, and Clay "the true Triumvirate of the Republic,—the triumvirate of transcendent talent" (120).

to incorporate the public, to embrace all members of the community, whatever their occupation, social standing, or political and religious affiliation. Useful to all and offensive to none, the lecture was an oratorical form deliberately and carefully separated from all partisan and sectarian discourse."[18]

Scott views the lecture system as a public ritual, a ceremony that "created and embodied an American public" and "was thought to be an embodiment of the entire democratic community" (808). That is certainly the ideal to which the lyceum aspired, and Josiah Holbrook's evangelical fervor for public educa-tion continually voices itself in just such ideal terms. In an 1829 pamphlet designed for town lyceums, for instance, Holbrook outlines the organization of the local association and envisions a worldwide network of "institutions for mutual instruction." He ends the list of practical, moral, political, and eco-nomical advantages with his educational ideal:

> There might even be established, under their patronage, institutions for
> qualifying teachers, and for giving practical instruction on the various
> subjects fitted to the employments of the farmer and mechanic, if not
> to those of the legislator, the physician, and the divine. From the sev-
> eral Boards of Delegates in various parts of the country, a general one
> might be formed, to be called the AMERICAN BOARD OF EDUCATION.
> Said American Board would, of course, be composed of gentlemen of
> the most liberal and enlightened views upon the subject of education;
> and, if they should meet annually, they would bring together a knowl-
> edge of the state and improvements of schools and common education
> in their several districts, and might recommend measures which would
> have the most salutary influence upon the interests of the rising gener-
> ation, and, of course, upon the highest and most lasting interests of our
> nation and the world.[19]

Scott's account of the public lecture system that evolved out of Holbrook's lyceum movement interprets the lecture system of the 1850s as, in a sense, the

18. Donald M. Scott, "The Popular Lecture and the Creation of a Public in Mid-Nineteenth-Century America," *Journal of American History*, 66 (March 1980): 793. This excellent essay is also my source for the statistics in this paragraph; see 791–93. Buell disputes Scott's picture of a neutral, expository, useful lecture in *New England Literary Culture*, 152–53. For a clear account of the lyceum movement, see Carl Bode, *The American Lyceum: Town Meeting of the Mind* (New York: Oxford University Press, 1956).

19. The pamphlet is reproduced in Kenneth Walter Cameron, ed., *The Massachusetts Lyceum During the American Renaissance* (Hartford: Transcendental Books, 1969), 45–47. A good source for reports on the lyceum movement, including Holbrook's promotional travels through the country, is the journal *American Annals of Education* (1830–39). See also Bode, *American Lyceum*, 19–59, 101–9.

embodiment of Holbrook's vision, for the system of the 1850s "was one of the central institutions within and by which the public had its existence. This public was not, of course, as inclusive as the mythology had it. By the mid-1850s it was almost exclusively a northern public, composed of what could be called the middle classes and overwhelmingly white Anglo-Saxon Protestant. Though it was believed to be the embodiment of an all-embracing national culture, the public lecture system was in fact an institution for the consolidation of the collective cultural consciousness by which this group came to assert a claim that it was the real American public" (808–9).

The lecture platform, in this view, becomes a theater of competing—often conflicting—interests and ideas. That dramatic quality is clear in the mediations attempted by Phillips in "The Scholar in a Republic." But it is even more dynamic in the culture of antebellum America, particularly as the local lyceum phase evolves into the public lecture system and, concomitantly, the lectures broaden in scope and "usefulness."

2

A salient example of this twin dynamism occurs in the history of the Concord Lyceum. On three occasions in the 1840s, Wendell Phillips addressed the lyceum in his lectures titled "Slavery," which raised questions among the lyceum curators as to the "usefulness" of inviting reformers to speak. Two days before Phillips was to deliver his first lecture, a conservative curator, the Honorable John Keyes, offered the following resolution: "Resolved that as this Lyceum is established for Social & Mutual improvement the introduction of the vexed and disorganizing question of Abolitionism or Slavery should be kept out of it" (*Massachusetts Lyceum* 156). The resolution was tabled, and Phillips delivered his lecture on 21 December 1842. By the time Phillips was to speak for the third time, however, Keyes had heard enough. At the meeting of the lyceum curators on 5 March 1845, a vote of 21 to 15 passed the motion to invite Phillips to lecture on slavery for a third time. Keyes and another curator resigned, and in the ensuing debate the president of the lyceum also resigned. Three curators were elected to fill the vacancies: Samuel Barrett, who had made the original motion to invite Phillips; Ralph Waldo Emerson; and Henry David Thoreau (*Massachusetts Lyceum* 159–60).

Both Emerson and Thoreau reacted quite strongly and intelligently to the controversy, and their responses evoke the dynamic nature of the lyceum and

the lecture platform. In *Journal V*, Emerson notes that he "pressed the accep-
tance" of Phillips's lecture on two grounds: first, that the lecture would be paid
for by certain "Ladies" who proposed it for the lyceum and that the lyceum
"should add to the length & variety of their Entertainment by all innocent
means, especially when a discourse from one of the best speakers in the
Commonwealth was volunteered"; second, "because I thought in the present
state of this country the particular subject of Slavery had a commanding right
to be heard in all places in New England in season & sometimes out of season." The entry continues in this same mocking tone, and Emerson reports that
he argued that "the people must consent to be plagued . . . from time to time
until something was done" (*JMN* 9:102). He also notes that "the proposition
was later made to have a Lyceum supplied by enthusiasts only" and replies with
a village metaphor: "We want a Lyceum just as much as a shoe-shop. It must
be boundless in its hospitality" (102–3). Emerson's humorous wit makes the
serious point that the lyceum must accept controversial speakers and subjects,
and his imagery suggests that the lyceum fulfills a fundamental moral and intellectual duty in creating or repairing the life of the community.

Thoreau's more public response to the controversy comes in the form of a
letter to the editor of the abolitionist newspaper *The Liberator*. As the editors of
this text point out, the letter is probably not a spontaneous response to Phillips's
speech of 12 March 1845; instead, it registers Thoreau's assessment of the controversy as it ran its course through three seasons of the lyceum. Thoreau begins
by summarizing the effects of Phillips's lecture on the Concord audience:

> We have now, for the third winter, had our spirits refreshed, and our faith
> in the destiny of the commonwealth strengthened, by the presence and
> the eloquence of Wendell Phillips; and we wish to tender to him our
> thanks and our sympathy. The admission of this gentleman into the
> Lyceum has been strenuously opposed by a respectable portion of our fel-
> low citizens, who themselves, we trust, whose descendants, at least, we
> know, will be as faithful conservers of the true order, whenever that shall
> be the order of the day,—and in each instance, the people have voted that
> they *would hear him*, by coming themselves and bringing their friends to
> the lecture room, and being very silent that they *might* hear. We saw some
> men and women, who had long ago *come out, going in* once more through
> the free and hospitable portals of the Lyceum; and many of our neigh-
> bors confessed, that they had had a "sound season" this once.[20]

20. The text is titled "Wendell Phillips Before Concord Lyceum" and appears in *Reform Papers*, ed.
Wendell Glick (Princeton: Princeton University Press, 1973), 59–62; this quotation is on 59. For the
textual introduction, see 303–7. This work henceforth cited as *RP*.

Thoreau strikes much the same chord of humorous wit that rings in Emerson's journal entry, and his sense of "the free and hospitable portals of the Lyceum" accords with Emerson's call for "boundless . . . hospitality." Like Emerson, Thoreau uses wit to mock the conservative, narrow-minded restrictions of his opponents. The sense of a dynamic, ongoing conflict pervades both responses, and Thoreau credits Phillips and the controversy with bringing former members back into the lecture room.

Thoreau describes Phillips's argument and style in terms that recall the figure of the scholar-agitator in "The Scholar in a Republic":

> He stands so distinctly, so firmly, and so effectively, alone, and one honest man is so much more than a host, that we cannot but feel that he does himself injustice when he reminds us of "the American Society, which he represents." It is rare that we have the pleasure of listening to so clear and orthodox a speaker, who obviously has so few cracks or flaws in his moral nature—who, having words at his command in a remarkable degree, has much more than words, if these should fail, in his unquestionable earnestness and integrity—and, aside from their admiration at his rhetoric, secures the genuine respect of his audience. He unconsciously tells his biography as he proceeds, and we see him early and earnestly deliberating on these subjects, and wisely and bravely, without counsel or consent of any, occupying a ground at first, from which the varying tides of public opinion cannot drive him. (60)

Thoreau figures Phillips as an heroic, solitary speaker, the "one honest man" who needs no institutional affiliation to give him the authority to speak. Like Edward Parker, Thoreau focuses on the "moral nature" of the speaker, which functions as the source of eloquence: the "command" of words bespeaks a moral authority beyond mere words. Thoreau also notes how "he unconsciously tells his biography as he proceeds," a view that accords with the ways in which Phillips uses his own "crusade against slavery" as the model for agitation in "The Scholar in a Republic." Thoreau's distrust of Phillips's affiliation with the American Anti-Slavery Society, opposed to his approval of the speaker's individuality, anticipates Emerson's comment, "He had only a *platform*-existence, & no personality" (*JMN* 13:281). Finally, Thoreau's analysis focuses acutely on Phillips's ability to win the admiration and respect of the audience without ceding his moral "ground" to the "varying tides of public opinion," and this point sharply recalls the function of Whig oratory in antebellum America.

Thoreau's appreciation of Phillips's integrity is so great that he reaffirms it toward the close of his letter: "It is so rare and encouraging to listen to an orator, who is content with another alliance than with the popular party, or even with the sympathising school of the martyrs, who can afford sometimes to be his own auditor if the mob stay away, and hears himself without reproof, that we feel ourselves in danger of slandering all mankind by affirming, that here is one, who is at the same time an eloquent speaker and a righteous man" (*RP* 61). With the word "mob" Thoreau betrays his contempt for the merely popular orator and his followers. When he proclaims the "danger" of "slandering all mankind," the irony lies most tellingly in the distance between the "mob" and the "eloquent speaker." By idealizing Phillips, Thoreau creates a sharp contrast between speaker and audience that effectively detracts from the potential eloquence and righteousness of the audience. Thoreau recognizes his "danger" precisely, and in that regard we should remember that slander is not necessarily the uttering of a falsehood.

For these reasons, Thoreau follows the praise of Phillips with an equal praise of the Concord audience: "Perhaps, on the whole, the most interesting fact elicited by these addresses, is the readiness of the people at large, of whatever sect or party, to entertain, with good will and hospitality, the most revolutionary and heretical opinions, when frankly and adequately, and in some sort cheerfully, expressed. Such clear and candid declaration of opinion served like an electuary to whet and clarify the intellect of all parties, and furnished each one with an additional argument for that right he asserted" (61–62). An "electuary" is a medicine mixed with water and honey or sugar; thus the eloquence of Wendell Phillips becomes a sort of medicine that is easy to swallow and causes immediate healing—even growth—of the "intellect of all parties." Thoreau redresses the balance between speaker and audience by registering, with apparent surprise, the intellectual "good will and hospitality" of "the people at large," but he clearly suggests that Phillips's eloquence causes this reaction in the audience.

The image of the popular lecture that emerges from the story of Phillips before the Concord Lyceum is fundamentally dynamic and relational. In delivering a lecture, a speaker such as Phillips engages the audience in a process marked by intellectual and emotional reciprocity. But the construction of such a dynamic cultural space is fraught with questions of balance, control, and authority. As Josiah Holland puts it in an 1865 article, "Most men of fine powers fail before a popular audience, because they do not fully apprehend the thing to be done. They almost invariably write above the level of one half of their audience, and below the level of the other half."[21]

---

21. "The Popular Lecture," *Atlantic Monthly* 15 (March 1865), 365. Holland is perhaps best known as the friend of his famous Amherst neighbor, Emily Dickinson, but he was also a popular lecturer from

Holland's comment raises a crucial aspect of eloquence—the *style* of the speaker's address to the audience. Thomas Wentworth Higginson concludes the 1868 essay "The American Lecture-System" by focusing on issues of audience and style:

> The different lecturers who have been named in this essay are persons of the most various gifts and training, with but this one point in common, that almost all of them are orators born, rather than writers; or at least reach the public through the oratorical gift. Subtract the audience, and their better part is gone. Emerson is probably the only one among them whose lectures, printed precisely as they are delivered, would be a permanent contribution to literature,—and it is, perhaps, this very fact which stands most in his way as a lecturer. Oratory and literature still remain two distinct methods of utterance, as distinct as sculpture and painting, and as difficult to unite. Their methods, their results, and their rewards, are wholly different. It is the general testimony of those who have tried both, that they put poorer work into their speeches than into their writings; but that, on the other hand, the very act of speech sometimes yields such moments of inspiration as make all writing seem cold. Thought must be popularized, execution made broader and rougher, before it can be appreciated in an instant by a thousand minds; but those thousand minds give you in return a magnificent stimulus that solitude can never supply. It is needless to debate which is best: it is the difference between light and heat.[22]

Higginson draws a sharp distinction between oratory and literature, which correspond to the spoken and written aspects of language. Speech, according to Higginson, is the "poorer work," but it also "yields such moments of inspiration as make all writing seem cold." The dynamic reciprocity of speaker and audience becomes the "magnificent stimulus" for new thought and expression. Moreover, Higginson recognizes the conflict in the relationship between speech and writing. The lecture can be written, but in delivery it must be "broader and rougher" than literature, and the lecturer's "better part" remains the audience that responds to and in turn stimulates the lecturer. Only Emerson, among the several lecturers Higginson discusses, does he find "literary" enough to pro-

---

the 1850s until his death in 1881; see *Emily Dickinson's Letters to Dr. and Mrs. Josiah Gilbert Holland*, ed. Theodora Van Wagenen Ward (Cambridge: Harvard University Press, 1951), 3–27 and passim.

22. *Macmillan's Magazine* 18 (May 1868): 56. Holland, Higginson, and Curtis are all cited in Scott, "Popular Lecture," whose essay led me back to these sources.

duce readable lectures, and that becomes a reason for faulting Emerson as a lecturer.

The stylistic contest between oratory and literature, inherent in the popular lecture as a form and as an event, bespeaks a parallel contest between two forms of culture. George William Curtis, yet another popular lecturer who, like Higginson, sat in Harvard's Sanders Theatre in 1881 and listened to Phillips's "The Scholar in a Republic," begins an 1856 essay, "Lectures and Lecturing," by making that point: "A few years since, when the steam-engine was harnessed into the service of the printing-press, we were ready to conclude that oral instruction would have to yield the palm, without dispute, to written literature. . . . Oratory would be doomed either to obsoleteness or to decay; authors would rise into the ascendant, and readers would far outnumber hearers."[23] But Curtis quickly notes that the two cultures have become "popular movements" that work "side by side . . . growing out of the same general state of society, governed by similar circumstances, and tending alike to the elevation of the masses" (122). Indeed, Curtis himself joins the two movements, for he edits *Harper's Monthly Magazine*, which advertises itself as providing high-quality, popular writing at a cheap price, while at the same time he performs regularly as a popular reform lecturer.

As the essay proceeds, however, Curtis does not remain content with the imagery of parallel "popular movements." Instead, he focuses on the particular benefits of the lecture for expression and education:

> But these lectures are valuable on another account. Literature and science are not equal to the demands of the times; they are not able to do the whole work of inward training. No; far from it. We need to know many things that talent hardly cares to write a book about, or, if put in a volume, would not answer the purpose half so well. We want them, moreover, in a talking style. A little more of elegant dishabille; a free, bold, Anglo-Saxon hittingness; a flavoring spice that tone and manner only can give; all that great something in original speech which rhetoric can not teach, and yet is often the finest, richest, strongest essence of an individual mind: these are qualities that may most aptly and effectively characterize the Lecture as distinct from the Essay, Narrative, Disquisition, and Review. (123)

---

23. The essay appears in Curtis's series "Editor's Table," in *Harper's Monthly Magazine* 14 (December 1856): 122–25. Edward Parker compares the young Curtis to Phillips in *Golden Age of Oratory*, 383. Curtis was active in several reform movements, notably as president of the National Civil Service

Curtis suggests that the lecture is not so high a form of language as "literature and science" and that "talent" in some ways "hardly cares to write" a lecture. But this formal hierarchy reverses when Curtis begins to use the plural pronoun "we," figuring himself as part of a popular audience that speaks its demands. At this figurative moment, moreover, the language of the passage itself becomes more direct, approaching the "talking style" and "Anglo-Saxon hittingness" that Curtis demands. Finally, this style of language is defined as "original speech," capable of delivering a "great something" that lies beyond rhetoric, beyond words.

In defining the "great something," Curtis identifies the lecture with "the spirit of the age," which he sees as "a strange impulse, deeper far than a mere love of money." The spirit is dynamic and sovereign, exercising "power over wind and waves never before possessed" and urging Americans "outward and onward to conquer this long-rebellious earth." Curtis's language evokes the dynamism of a Nietzschean will to power, and in his style he expresses an impatience with the printed word:

> Books are broken fragments. Books are products of insulated hours—dissevered nights—sundered years. Our life, and our life-time, and our life-capacity are not, and never can be, literary commodities. But the living speaker, commanding subject and audience by fullness of knowledge and potency of will—every muscle and nerve in the service of thought and emotion, every pulse obedient to the intellect—what is like it? The position of the speaker, as the most active, complete, vital force that can operate on mind and inspire heart, is but partially apprehended; and yet, society ought to be sagacious enough to see that, just now, his offices could be rendered tributary to its advancement. (123)

Although Curtis denigrates the role of rhetoric and books as secondary, his own prose style manages to create an image of "the living speaker," a figure of eloquence who exercises absolute command over the audience. From such a position of authority, the figure of eloquence bespeaks a desire for wholeness, both in the individual and in the culture at large. This is the sense of the speaker as "the most active, complete, vital force," one that operates on the mind and inspires the heart of its audience. In Curtis's view, such a speaker exercises power that is awesome enough to aid the "advancement" of American culture.

Reform League (1881–92); in "The Scholar in a Republic," Phillips makes seemingly biting remarks about Curtis and civil service reform; see *Speeches. Second Series*, 353, 363–64.

3

A specific attribute of the figure of eloquence is the Anglo-Saxon hittingness of original speech. Curtis develops this point near the end of "Lectures and Lecturing," in a paragraph devoted to the question of style:

> Remember what a speaking style is; viz., mind every moment forging a connecting link with other minds; mind in earnest motion and close contact; mind touching eyes and ears every instant, and receiving, as well as awakening emotions with inconceivable rapidity. Anglo-Saxon is the style. The sharp, clean-cut words—the words that ring and echo—the words that, instead of cumbering, heighten the elasticity of the idea, are your true vocabulary. For effect—straightforward, rifle-shot effect—nothing compares with it. You may look at the sweep of the wind over a ripe harvest-field, or watch the long roll of the billowy sea, if you are writing a fine essay; but if you are determined to be a real speaker, alive all through to subject and audience, you must master the language of the dogmatic will, the resolute purpose, the imperial soul—the noble, glorious, old Anglo-Saxon. (125)

As in the previous passage, Curtis here writes in a dynamic style to create the image of a dynamic "speaking style." He deliberately streamlines his syntax, employing simple parallelisms and repetitions, and he suggests the Anglo-Saxon vocabulary with concrete terms such as "sharp," "clean-cut," "ring," and "rifle-shot."

Just as important as Curtis's particular stylistic strategies is the vision of style he presents in the essay. "Anglo-Saxon is the style" because, for Curtis and most other Americans of Anglo-Saxon heritage, it embodies the dynamic "spirit of the age."[24] A particularly ironic example of the rhetoric of "Saxon spirit" occurs in Phillips's lecture "Toussaint L'Ouverture," in which he argues that "the negro race, instead of being that object of pity or contempt which we usually consider it, is entitled, judged by the facts of history, to a place close by the side of the Saxon." In making his case, Phillips first outlines the "three tests by which

---

24. For a useful introduction to representative statements from a variety of nineteenth-century discourses, see Cmiel, 94–122. A more wide-ranging but equally useful treatment of the phenomenon of "Anglo-Saxonism" is Reginald Horsman, *Race and Manifest Destiny: The Origins of American Racial Anglo-Saxonism* (Cambridge: Harvard University Press, 1981). For a discussion of popular theories concerning the English language in America, see my *Walt Whitman's Language Experiment* (University Park: Pennsylvania State University Press, 1990), 7–33, 109–38.

races love to be tried"—courage, purpose, and endurance—and concludes, "Of these three elements is made that Saxon pluck which has placed our race in the van of modern civilization."[25]

The connection between language and the "spirit of the age" is a commonplace of Romantic philology, and it appears, in a variety of shapes and places, throughout the culture of antebellum America. In an address to the sixth annual meeting of the American Institute of Instruction in August 1835, for instance, Emerson considers the topic named in his title, "On the Best Mode of Inspiring a Correct Taste in English Literature": "The Instructor should consider that by being born to the inheritance of the English speech he receives from Nature the key to the noblest treasures of the world in the native and translated literature of Great Britain and America."[26] Later that same year, Emerson delivers a series of ten lectures on English literature, the thesis of which he states in the "Introductory": "So is the aim and effort of literature in the largest sense nothing less than to *give voice to the whole of spiritual nature* as events and ages unfold it, to record in words the whole life of the world" (226; italics his). In the second lecture, "Permanent Traits of the English National Genius," Emerson presents translations of Old English poetry in order to enumerate traits of the "national character"—gravity, humor, a love of home, a love of utility, a love of truth and fair play, a respect for birth, and a respect for women—traits that, among others, he sees in the "English cast of thought" from Alfred to the present (233–52).

Throughout his career as a lecturer and essayist, Emerson maintains a double interest in the "English cast of thought" and the history of the English language. The mixture of ethnological and philological ideas represents the mainstream of nineteenth-century theories of language, to be sure, but even more important is Emerson's search for origins, the sources of original speech that "*give voice to the whole of spiritual nature.*" We can already see the search in

---

25. *Speeches, Lectures, and Letters. First Series* (Boston: Lee and Shepard, 1894); this is apparently a reprint of the 1861 edition. The text of "Toussaint L'Ouverture" (468–94) is from a lecture delivered in New York and Boston in December 1861. The quotations appear on 468–69. See also Stewart, 104–5.

26. *The Early Lectures of Ralph Waldo Emerson*, ed. Stephen E. Whicher, Robert E. Spiller, and Wallace E. Williams, 3 vols. (Cambridge: Harvard University Press, 1959–72), 1:211–12. Subsequent references to these volumes appear in my text cited as *ELE*.

The essential statement of comparative philology as a science both of language and of human spirit is Wilhelm von Humboldt, *On Language: The Diversity of Human Language-Structure and its Influence on the Mental Development of Mankind*, trans. Peter Heath (Cambridge: Cambridge University Press, 1988). Though somewhat unsympathetic, Hans Aarsleff's introduction to the volume (vii–lxv) gives an excellent account of Humboldt's theory of language, stressing Humboldt's intellectual debt to French philosophers of language such as Condillac and Diderot.

the "Introductory" lecture for the 1835 series on English literature. Several important passages form the core of the "Language" chapter in *Nature*. One among them:

> It certainly will not be alleged that there is anything fanciful in this anal-
> ogy between man and nature, when it is remembered that savages con-
> verse by these figures. In the writers in the morning of each nation such
> as Homer, Froissart, and Chaucer every word is a picture. As we go back
> in history, language becomes more picturesque, until its infancy, when
> it is all poetry; or, all spiritual facts are represented by natural symbols.
> The eldest remains of the ancient nations are poems and fables. And
> even now, in our artificial state of society, the moment our discourse
> rises above the ordinary tone of facts, and is inflamed with passion, or
> exalted by thought, it immediately clothes itself in images. (*ELE* 1:221)

Emerson clearly focuses on the philosophy of language as a foundation for his historical survey of English literature and culture. Thus he mentions Chaucer as one of "the writers in the morning of each nation," and Chaucer becomes the topic of the fourth lecture. He mentions the "eldest remains" as "poems and fables," and the third lecture is titled "The Age of Fable." Finally, he contrasts the present "artificial state of society" to the implicitly more natural, spiritual, and "picturesque" state of early cultures, and he asserts that "our discourse" becomes most like the earlier language when it becomes most "inflamed" or "exalted." The contrast functions as a motif throughout the series, but it comes out most strongly in the last lecture, "Modern Aspects of Letters," especially as Emerson closes the survey (380–85).

Emerson's idealizing vision of past writers and speakers shapes his represen-tations of eloquence in the early lectures. So, for example, he closes his first planned series, six lectures on biography, with a treatment of Edmund Burke, contrasting Burke's oratory to that of Demosthenes (*ELE* 1:197–99). In order to describe Burke's eloquence, Emerson distinguishes three kinds of eloquence—the natural, the practical, and the philosophic. The first "resides chiefly in cer-tain felicities of voice and manner" (199), felicities that Burke was known for not possessing. The second "awakens no emotion but extorts votes" (200). The third is a rough synthesis of the first two, although it also goes beyond them:

> There is still another sort grown up in modern times which aims to ele-
> vate the subject to its highest pitch; which takes of it a manly view such
> as the reason of nations might well consider; which strives to put the

subject into harmony with all particular and all general views and which draws arguments and illustrations from all regions of nature and art as if to show that all nature and all society are in unison with the view that is presented, which seeks to concentrate attention upon the facts but to consider them in accordance with the immense expansion in modern times of all the powers of society.

Of this school of philosophic eloquence whose traces are very visible even now in the British and American Senates Mr. Burke is the founder and head. (200)

In the turnings of relative clauses, Emerson's labyrinthine first sentence attempts to create the sense of "unison" that he finds in the third kind of eloquence. The four relative clauses lengthen, so that the sentence creates an effect of "immense expansion" that accords with the "modern times" and "powers of society" with which he begins and ends. In 1835, moreover, he is still willing to locate the school of philosophic eloquence in the Senate, although he qualifies that statement with the image of "traces."

The unison figures an ideal state, created by speech, in which speaker and audience, ideas and events, respond perfectly to one another. In the lecture "Art," delivered in the 1836–37 series *The Philosophy of History*, Emerson suggests that such power transcends individual identity: "In eloquence, the great triumphs of the art are, when the orator is lifted above himself; when consciously he makes himself the mere tongue of the occasion and the hour, and says what cannot but be said. Hence the French phrase *l'abandon*, to describe the self-surrender of the orator. Not his will, but the principle on which he is horsed, the great connexion and crisis of events thunder in the ear of the crowd" (*ELE* 2:49). The "unison" described here is paradoxical, verging upon the kind of mystic *Gelassenheit* Emerson admires in Swedenborg and Boehme, for it involves the speaker in a conscious, willful abandonment of conscious, willful control. In the apposite style of the last sentence, the speaker's will is abandoned to the dynamic "principle on which he is horsed," and that principle is transformed into "the great connexion" and "crisis of events." Further, these transformations are themselves transformed into sound, the sound of the speaker's words that "thunder in the ear of the crowd." By using the singular "ear," Emerson suggests that the self-surrender of the orator transforms both speaker and audience into a perfectly reciprocal unison of words and hearing.

Emerson develops significant versions of this unison in two other early lecture series. In "Genius," the fifth lecture in the 1838 series of ten called *Human Life*, he focuses on the "representative character of genius," which he finds instanced in "the rare fact of genuine eloquence" (*ELE* 3:82). Because the genius is representative, "he who can say without hitch or hindrance that which is boiling in the bosom of all men, is the poet and master of the crowd" (83). Emerson illustrates the orator-genius with an "analogous example" of eloquence in Boston's Faneuil Hall, but the prelude to the appearance of genuine eloquence is "slovenly and tiresome" speaking, which causes the audience to become restless and agitated: "The pinched, wedged, elbowed, sweltering assembly, as soon as the speaker loses their ear by the tameness of his harangue, feel sorely how ill-accommodated they are, and begin to forget all politics and patriotism, and attend only to themselves and the coarse outcries made all around them." By losing the "ear" of the audience, the slovenly, tame speaker allows the assembly to become a mere multitude and thereby loses the effect of unison. But then that speaker gives way:

> At last the chosen man rises, the soul of the people, in whose bosom beats audibly the common heart. With his first words he strikes a note which all know; his word goes to the right place; as he catches the light spirit of the occasion his voice alters, vibrates, pierces the private ear of every one; the mob quiets itself somehow,—every one being magnetized,—and the house hangs suspended on the lips of one man. Each man whilst he hears thinks he too can speak; and in the pauses of the orator bursts forth the splendid voice of four or five thousand men in full cry, the grandest sound in nature. (83)

The "analogous example" becomes, in Emerson's effective hands, an example of genuine, magnetic eloquence. The passage represents eloquence as a reciprocal relationship, in which the speaker both "strikes a note which all know" and "catches the light spirit of the occasion." Likewise, each member of the audience listens with a "private ear," but the entire audience answers the orator's momentary silence with "the splendid voice" of unison.

The second version of "unison" occurs in "Society," the seventh lecture in the 1836–37 series *The Philosophy of History*. In the second half of the lecture, Emerson enumerates seven forms of society, and he saves for last the society "of minds (eloquence)" (*ELE* 2:102). The sixth form of society is that of bodies only, "a fracture of society," the mob. The seventh is a direct contrast, and Emerson calls it "an example of a perfect society" that comes into being as "the effect of Eloquence, which makes that power so valued among men. Eloquence is the power which one man in an age possesses of piercing the superficial crusts of condition which discriminate man from man and addressing the common

soul of them all" (109). Emerson develops the figure of eloquence by contrasting the power of eloquence to the unassuming style of conversation. When
the eloquent orator addresses the audience, he no longer speaks the ordinary
language and is no longer the same person he was in conversation:

> He possesses the power of subordinating his personal nature to his
> higher faculties; he knows how to stand aside and let truth and reason
> speak for him, well knowing that the power of these is all piercing and
> irresistible. If out of the heart it came, into the heart it will go. By a few
> sharp and skilful statements he unites his various audience and whilst
> they stand mute and astonished, he touches their hearts as harpstrings
> until in the presence of the aroused Reason Good and Fair become
> practicable and the gravest material obstacles are swept away as the
> morning cloud. Under the dominion of a commanding sentiment
> Society becomes perfect, for individual interests, even personal identity
> melt into the swelling surges of the Universal Humanity. (110)

This is perhaps the boldest statement of Emerson's ideal, a unison of souls in
which the orator exercises the commanding authority of "the aroused Reason"
and "Society becomes perfect." Although Emerson calls this the society of
minds, he figures it here as a society formed by a unison of minds, hearts, and
souls. It is perhaps best to refer to it as a society of eloquence or, as I have been
calling it already, a culture of eloquence.

This sounds idealistic in the extreme, both on Emerson's part and on mine,
but the ideal serves as a point of contrast and "analogous example." That is, it
becomes a figure for both the possibilities and the failures of the culture of antebellum America. Nor does Emerson ignore the distance between the ideal of
eloquence and its actual embodiments. In "The Present Age," the eleventh lecture in the *Philosophy of History* series, he characterizes the age as one of deco-
rum and gentleness, finding these to be the great enemies of speaking the truth:

> The question with us is who is the most decorous man and no longer
> who speaks the most truth. Look at the orations of Demosthenes,
> Chatham, and Burke and how many irrelevant sentences, words, letters
> are there?—Not one. Go into one of our cool halls where sermons, ora-
> tions, and debates are pronounced, and begin to count the words that
> might be spared, and often the entire harangue will go. Sentence kept
> sentence in countenance, but not one, by its own weight, could have
> justified the saying of it. It is the age of parenthesis; you might put most

that we say in brackets and it would not be missed. We ring a few changes on the stereotyped parliamentary phrases and it serves the turn. Eloquence is an easy sum in the Arithmetical Rule of permutation and combination. Our orators have yet to learn that the thing uttered in words is not therefore affirmed. It must affirm itself, or no forms of grammar and no plausibility can give it evidence, and no array of arguments. The sentence must also contain its own apology for being spoken. (*ELE* 2:163)

In measured tones, Emerson weighs and counts the current sum of words, only to find the culture lacking altogether in eloquence. Rather than seeing antebellum America as a culture of eloquence, he figures it as "the age of parenthesis," constituted by words that "would not be missed." As he does in the series on English literature, Emerson creates a contrast between the present age and an ideal that he locates in figures from the past, and in both cases the contrast leads to a rigorous demand for eloquence.

The method of contrast and resulting demand for eloquence reappear strongly in the essay "Eloquence," first published in 1858 in the *Atlantic Monthly* and closely related to a lecture of the same title delivered from 1847 into the 1850s.[27] Emerson repeatedly defines eloquence in demanding, idealistic terms, calling it "a taking sovereign possession of the audience" (65), "a total and resultant power" (76), "the appropriate organ of the highest personal energy" (81), "a demoniacal power" (93), "the best speech of the best soul" (99). At the same time, however, he recognizes the distance between ideal and embodiment. Thus he concedes, early in the essay, that "this is a power of many degrees and requiring in the orator a great range of faculty and experience, requiring a large composite man, such as Nature rarely organizes; so that in our experience we are forced to gather up the figure in fragments, here one talent and there another" (66). In a journal entry from 1846, he makes a similar point: "I suppose we shall never find in actual history the orator; he is a fabulous personage" (*JMN* 9:430). And if the figure of eloquence is a "figure in fragments," in the same journal

27. The essay appears in the 1870 miscellany *Society and Solitude*, vol. 7 of *The Complete Works of Ralph Waldo Emerson*, ed. Edward Waldo Emerson, 12 vols. (Boston: Houghton Mifflin, 1903–4), 59–100. The *Atlantic* version is practically identical with the later version, except for minor differences in punctuation. The lecture and essay derive in large part from journal entries made in 1845–47; see *Journal O* (*JMN* 9:425–61), *Notebook Phi* (*JMN* 12:398–401). Also helpful is the foreword "The Lecture Notebooks from 1835 to 1862" (12:xi–xlvii); the editor notes the main sources for the lecture (xxxii) and the problematic dating of its first delivery—either 16 December 1846 or 10 February 1847 (xlvi). I quote from the 1870 version.

Emerson makes eloquence itself a chimera: "There never was an eloquence: it is a fabulous power, as I have said, concerning which men are credulous, because there is in them all a tantalizing picture, which they would fain verify on some personal history of Chatham or Demosthenes" (401).

I am far from arguing here that Emerson's idealism empties the figure of eloquence of significant power. Quite the opposite. The gap between the ideal figure and the concrete, actual embodiments suggests the dimensions of that power, for Emerson—like Phillips or Thoreau, and like other figures I analyze in this study—uses the gap as a "tantalizing picture" for himself. The sense of distance incites Emerson, as well as a host of other actual speakers of antebellum America, to study language as a means of creating a coherent, democratic culture. By recognizing the gap, Emerson takes the most significant step toward closing it.

4

By choosing *Culture of Eloquence* as the title of this book, I deliberately avoid defining antebellum America as the embodiment of Emerson's global ideal. The eloquence of Wendell Phillips creates a contested, shifting, dramatically dynamic scene, both in the Concord of the 1840s and in the Harvard University of the 1880s. The ground established by the figure of eloquence thus creates a form of unison between speaker and audience, speech and writing, language and spirit, eloquence and action, but it does so because these distinct forms function in powerful opposition to one another. The ideal formulated so eloquently by Emerson does indeed exercise great, wide-ranging influence on antebellum American culture, but its power resides in the dynamism of individual speakers, their belief in the power of speech to lead their audiences toward moral truths and ethical actions, and the evangelical fervor with which they practiced their beliefs.

The six chapters that make up the body of this study follow a rough chronological order, focusing on seven figures of eloquence: Emerson, Thoreau, Margaret Fuller, Elizabeth Peabody, Frederick Douglass, William Gilmore Simms, and Walt Whitman. In discussing the first four figures, I center upon developments in New England transcendentalism and the oratorical culture emanating from Boston and Concord. Emerson's theory of eloquence gains breadth and depth when we see its connections to the linguistic mysticism and Adamic language theories of Boehme and Swedenborg. Thoreau also delves deeply into theories of language, and he resembles Emerson in believing that the poet-orator attempts to speak an essential "language of nature." Even though Thoreau appreciates the power of language to effect cultural reform, however, he repeatedly interrogates its boundaries or limits, both in its representations and in its practical outcomes. Nor is he content to create a purely literary, abstractly aesthetic ground upon which the speaker-writer and listener-reader might meet. Beyond the important sense one gains from reading *Walden* in the light of Thoreau's interests in essential eloquence, the so-called reform papers and late lectures can show how Thoreau creates a cultural space that is the scene of dynamic, reciprocal oppositions. In the next chapter, Margaret Fuller and Elizabeth Peabody take the themes of Adamic language and essential eloquence into the "conversation" classes in order to examine women's place in the culture at large. Such texts as Sarah Josepha Hale's *The Lecturess: or Woman's Sphere* (1839), Fuller's *Woman in the Nineteenth Century* (1845), and Peabody's abortive journal *Aesthetic Papers* (1849) articulate versions of domestic ideology by focusing on the centrality of language to ideas of cultural reform.

The last three chapters move farther out, both spatially and temporally, from the cultural center of New England transcendentalism. Douglass, Simms, and Whitman take us into cultural spaces that are related to but distinct from those created by figures of eloquence such as Emerson, Thoreau, and Fuller. In several particulars, however, I treat these figures in a similar fashion. In all cases, I attempt to relate theory and practice, text and performance, in order to show how the figures of eloquence expand and alter Emerson's vision of the reforming power of language. In all cases, I have found a drama of empowerment and limitation, what I have called earlier a theater of competing ideas and what Whitman called, more felicitously, an "agonistic arena." In all cases, I have found this drama most tellingly played out in lectures, addresses, and orations, rather than in autobiographies, novels, or poems. Finally, even when they fail to realize their dreams of the transforming power of eloquence, the figures of eloquence widen the agonistic arena of language and power.

2

"Ferries and Horses":

Emerson's Theory of Eloquence

A wealth of evidence from sermons, lectures, essays, addresses, journals, and notebooks indicates that throughout Emerson's career language shaped his ideas on a wide variety of subjects. The indexes to the *Journals and Miscellaneous Notebooks*, for example, contain lengthy entries under the headings "Language," "Rhetoric," and "Eloquence," and almost any one of the sixteen volumes of the *Journals* will yield a dozen or more entries relating to linguistic topics.[1] Nor was Emerson's interest merely that of a professional man of letters, for it contributed to his fundamental conceptions of nineteenth-century America as a nation in need of constant reform. My interpretation of Emerson's eloquence takes part in a rereading of his position within antebellum American culture, one that tends to emphasize his role as an engaged, public intellectual.[2] As I

---

1. A good way to appreciate Emerson's nearly lifelong study of language is to consult his "Index Headings and Topics," listed under his name in the indexes to the *Journals and Miscellaneous Notebooks*, ed. William H. Gilman et al., 16 vols. (Cambridge: Harvard University Press, 1960–82). After 1830, the entries "Eloquence," "Language," "Names," and "Rhetoric" yield a host of important passages. In addition, the reader should see the topical notebooks under the titles "Rhetoric," "Theory of Poetry," and "Philosophy," in *The Topical Notebooks of Ralph Waldo Emerson*, vol. 2, ed. Ronald A. Bosco (Columbia: University of Missouri Press, 1993), 142–96, 256–384. The cumulative index to *The Complete Sermons of Ralph Waldo Emerson*, ed. Albert J. von Frank et al., 4 vols. (Columbia: University of Missouri Press, 1989) also has entries on pertinent topics and figures.

2. Recent works that argue this view include Len Gougeon, *Virtue's Hero: Emerson, Antislavery, and Reform* (Athens: University of Georgia Press, 1990); Joel Myerson and Len Gougeon, eds., *Emerson's Antislavery Writings* (New Haven: Yale University Press, 1995); Mary Kupiec Cayton, "The Making of an American Prophet: Emerson, His Audiences, and the Rise of the Culture Industry in Nineteenth-Century America," *American Historical Review* 92 (1987): 597–620; Cayton, *Emerson's Emergence: Self and Society in the Transformation of New England, 1800–1845* (Chapel Hill: University of North Carolina Press, 1989); Peter Carafiol, *The American Ideal: Literary History as a Worldly Activity* (New York: Oxford

argued in the previous chapter, however, we should not confuse Emerson's engagement with the kind of wholesale commitment of a Wendell Phillips or William Lloyd Garrison. Emerson reminds himself to avoid "this thoroughly social & related life," which gives Phillips or Garrison "a *platform*-existence, & no personality" (*JMN* 13:281–82). For Emerson, language is the basis for any other reform—social, political, cultural, or individual—and because language pervades all the spheres of human endeavor, its power can shape every aspect of "related life."

Emerson's pronouncements on language are as pervasive and contradictory as language itself. In his *Wide World 10* journal of 1823, for instance, the young writer makes this self-styled "Dedication":

> When God had made the beasts, & prepared to set over them an intelligent lord, He considered what external faculty he should add to his frame, to be the seal of his superiority. Then He gave him an articulate voice. He gave him an organ exquisitely endowed, which was independent of his grosser parts,—but the minister of his mind & the interpreter of its thoughts. It was designed moreover as a Sceptre of irresistible command, by whose force, the great & wise should still the tumult of the vulgar million, & direct their blind energies to a right operation. (*JMN* 2:104–5)

A salient aspect of the passage is the strong echo of Genesis 2:18–20, the famous verses that narrate Adam's naming of the beasts of the field. Emerson does not name the "intelligent lord," perhaps because he does not wish to limit the "Sceptre of irresistible command" to Adam. Language becomes the "minister of the mind" for all humankind. The young minister Emerson dedicates himself, then, to taking up the "Sceptre" in order to minister to the "vulgar million" by silencing their tumult and directing their energies. The "articulate voice" becomes the emblem of humanity itself, the "seal of his superiority." And most important, this sense of eloquence is directly connected to Emerson's ded-

---

University Press, 1991); David Leverenz, "The Politics of Emerson's Man-Making Words," *PMLA* 101 (1986): 38–56.

For recent discussions of Emerson's theory and practice as a public speaker, see David Robinson, *Apostle of Culture: Emerson as Preacher and Lecturer* (Philadelphia: University of Pennsylvania Press, 1982) and Robinson's "Historical Introduction" to the *Complete Sermons*, 1:1–32. See also Thomas Gustafson, *Representative Words: Politics, Literature, and the American Language, 1776–1865* (Cambridge: Cambridge University Press, 1992), esp. 348–53; Wesley T. Mott, *"The Strains of Eloquence": Emerson and His Sermons* (State Park: Pennsylvania State University Press, 1989); Susan Roberson, *Emerson in his Sermons: A Man-Made Self* (Columbia: University of Missouri Press, 1995).

icating himself to a life of reforming humankind, making it as much like the intelligent lord Adam as possible.

Emerson's dedication to the figure of Adam immediately recalls R. W. B. Lewis's seminal study *The American Adam*, which describes the bardic figure of the self-reliant, unconditionally free and innocent individual that dominates American Renaissance writings.[3] The image of Adam before the Fall is an appropriate emblem for these complex characteristics, all the more because Adam's command of himself and of his world stems, in Emerson's journal entry, from the seal of the articulate voice.

The role of Adam as a figure of eloquence and command is, of course, not original to Emerson. In a variety of reform-minded writings from the sixteenth, seventeenth, and eighteenth centuries, Adam is continually figured in exactly the terms that the young minister uses in his dedication. Indeed, Adam becomes the figure for a multifaceted theory of language that Hans Aarsleff has called the "Adamic doctrine."[4] Focusing on Adam's naming of the animals in Genesis, Adamic theorists posit a language in which word and thing are in perfect correspondence, for Adam is portrayed as seeing into the very essences of things with a near-divine perception. In a sermon by John Locke's contemporary Robert South, for example, Adam is characterized as having come into the world "a philosopher, which sufficiently appeared by his writing the nature of things upon their names; he could view essences in themselves, and read forms without the comment of their respective properties."[5] A more ecstatic version of the same figure appears in John Webster's *Examination of the Academies* (1654), where Adam names the creatures because he "did understand both their internal and external signatures, and that the imposition of their names was adequately agreeing with their natures."[6]

Webster owes his vocabulary and conceptual framework to the German mystic Jacob Boehme, whose work Emerson knew well. In Boehme's masterpiece of linguistics, *Mysterium Magnum*, Adam is figured as the originator of a perfect language: "Now it plainly appears that Adam stood in the divine image, and not in the bestial, for he knew the property of all creatures, and gave names to

---

3. R. W. B. Lewis, *The American Adam* (Chicago: University of Chicago Press, 1955).

4. *From Locke to Saussure*, 25–26, 42–83.

5. Robert South, *Sermons*, vol. 1 (Oxford: Oxford at the Clarendon Press, 1823), 37. See *From Locke to Saussure*, 59.

6. A facsimile of Webster's *Examination* appears in Allen G. Debus, *Science and Education in the Thirteenth Century: The Webster-Ward Debate* (New York: American Elsevier, 1970), 67–192. The third chapter focuses on Adamic language ("the first of Tongues or Languages") and is my source for the quoted passage (111).

all creatures, from their essence, form and property. He understood the Language of Nature, viz. the manifested and formed Word in every one's essence, for thence the name of every creature is arisen."[7] The "Language of Nature" is another name for essential eloquence, and the phrase runs throughout Boehme's many treatises. For example, in the early work *Aurora*, he devotes some five pages to the topic, while in the *Signatura Rerum* he writes almost three hundred densely rhetorical pages on the notion that "the whole outward visible World with all its Being is a Signature, or Figure of the inward spiritual World."[8] Boehme's central point is that the Language of Nature rests upon the correspondence of word to thing, a linguistic correspondence that grounds the mystical correspondence between the "outward visible World" and the "inward spiritual World." Thus one fundamental aspect of Adamic doctrine is a kind of dual correspondence, crystallized in the commanding figure of Adam as namer.

Adamic language theory emerges in Emerson's work most significantly in *Nature*, but the theory appears already in early sermons. In the 1829 sermon on the summer season (Psalms 74:16–17), for instance, the young minister praises the beauty of nature but warns his listeners: "There is more in nature than beauty; there is more to be seen than the outward eye perceives; there is more to be heard than the pleasant rustle of the corn. There is the language of its everlasting analogies, by which it seems to be the prophet and the monitor of the race of man. . . . There is nothing in external nature but is an emblem, a hieroglyphic of something in us. . . . And this day as the fruit is as fresh so is its moral as fresh and significant to us as it was to Adam in the garden."[9] This passage anticipates, of course, the argument of Emerson's first published book. It also takes up the correspondence of word and thing in the phrase "the language of its everlasting analogies." Furthermore, it connects that first correspondence to the second correspondence of "external nature" to "something in us," phrased as an "emblem, a hieroglyphic." Emerson alters the mystical doctrines of a Boehme or a Webster in the last sentence, however, for these correspondences are as "fresh and significant to us" as they were to Adam. That is, the Language of Nature does not necessarily require any arcane, alchemical knowledge or

---

7. *Mysterium Magnum*, trans. John Sparrow (London: M. Simmons for H. Blunden, 1654); rpt. (London: John M. Watkins, 1965), 114.

In *Emerson's Library* (Charlottesville: University Press of Virginia, 1967) Walter Harding gives titles by several writers on language theory, among them Jacob Boehme, Guillaume Oegger, and Emmanuel Swedenborg. For a helpful discussion of the William Low edition of Boehme, which Emerson owned, and of Boehme's influence in England, see Serge Hutin, *Les disciples anglais de Jacob Boehme* (Paris: Editions Denoel, 1960), esp. 151–61.

8. *Signatura Rerum; or, the Signature of All Things* (London: John Maycock for Gyles Calvert, 1651), 77.

9. *Complete Sermons*, 1:299. The editor notes that Emerson preached the sermon three times: 14 June 1829; 19 June 1831; 16 July 1837 (1:296).

divine illumination; for all of us, it requires an inner, moral eye to correspond to the "outward eye" that perceives beauty.

Boehme's doctrine of the Language of Nature implies two types of language. The first is the ordinary language of postlapsarian humankind, the second the language of the prelapsarian Adam. Boehme even extends Adam's linguistic mastery beyond the Fall, but the story of the Tower of Babel (Genesis 11:1–19) narrates the ultimate corruption of Adamic language, its fall into worldly division:

> This tower, on which the tongues were divided, and where the great city, Babel, stood, is a figure of the fallen earthly man who is entered into selfhood, and hath made the formed word of God in him unto an idol. . . .
>
> Hence arise the contrarieties, differences, and opinions, in that we have introduced the unformed word into the form of our own self-made image. Now we contend and strive about these images and conceits; and every one supposeth his own to be best; and when we bring all these images and several semblances again into one language and speech, and mortify them, then the only quickening Word of God, which giveth power and life to all things, is again manifest; and strife ceaseth, and God is all in all.[10]

The multiplicity of contentious, worldly languages would seem to make the retrieval of the one Language of Nature impossible, but for Boehme the retrieval consists of his own divine illumination. The terms "power" and "life" are significant, since the retrieval would restore order to human affairs by reviving the authority of the "one language." Boehme's apocalyptic task is to use the divided, divisive languages of this world in order to reconstruct the "quickening Word of God." The alchemical Language of Nature serves as a metalanguage, a code that functions to unify and render coherent the multiple, strife-ridden languages of humanity. Throughout Boehme's repeated efforts to elucidate the code, the Language of Nature symbolizes the mystic's unifying command over multiplicity. Inherent in that authority is the sense of the dual correspondences of word and thing, world and spirit. For it is only through the correspondence doctrine that the Language of Nature can control and codify the bewildering babble of human tongues.[11]

---

10. *Mysterium Magnum*, 308, 315.

11. For an extensive discussion of Boehme's symbolic code, see Steven A. Konopacki, *The Descent into Words: Jakob Böhme's Transcendental Linguistics* (Ann Arbor: Karoma, 1979); for the Language of Nature

Emerson certainly appreciated both the conceptual framework and the apocalyptic fervor of Boehme's abstruse reflections on language. In the lecture
"Swedenborg, or the Mystic," for example, he explicitly contrasts the tone of
Boehme's writing to that of Swedenborg, although the correspondence doctrine
is essentially the same in both mystical systems: "The warm many-weathered
passionate-peopled world is to [Swedenborg] a grammar of hieroglyphs or an
emblematic free-mason's procession. How different is Jacob Behmen! *he* is
tremulous with emotion, and listens awestruck with the gentlest humanity to
the Teacher whose lessons he conveys, and when he asserts that, 'in some sort,
love is greater than God,' his heart beats so high that the thumping against his
leathern coat is audible across the centuries. 'Tis a great difference. Behmen is
healthily and beautifully wise, notwithstanding the mystical narrowness and
incommunicableness. Swedenborg is disagreeably wise, and with all his accu-
mulated gifts paralyzes and repels."[12] Despite this negative appraisal of
Swedenborg's gifts, Emerson considers them valuable nonetheless. His argument with both Boehme and Swedenborg rests upon the distinction between
a sectarian and a secular interpretation of the correspondence doctrine. Thus
he accuses both writers of having "failed by attaching themselves to the
Christian symbol, instead of to the moral sentiment, which carries innumer-
able christianities, humanities, divinities in its bosom" (*RM* 76). In formulating
the Adamic theory Emerson tends to make theological and ethical demands of
language, but he also represents the moral sentiment as containing a multitude
of possible expressions.

Emanuel Swedenborg and his disciples form a second important influence
on Emerson's language theory. His admiration for Sampson Reed, Theophilus
Parsons, and other writers in *The New Jerusalem Magazine* is well documented
and decisive.[13] One reason for that attitude would appear to be the fact that

as metalanguage, see 162–63. For an alphabetical index of Boehme's metalanguage, see 181–86. The best
introductions to Boehme's complex thought are Hans Aarsleff's article in *The Dictionary of Scientific
Biography* and John Joseph Stoudt, *Sunrise to Eternity: A Study in Jacob Boehme's Life and Thought*
(Philadelphia: University of Pennsylvania Press, 1957). For a more thorough discussion of Boehme's
ideas, see Alexandre Koyré, *La philosophie de Jacob Boehme* (Paris: Vrin, 1929); for an explication of the
correspondence doctrine and the Language of Nature, see esp. 275–78, 393–400, and 456–62. Another
important early discussion of the Language of Nature is Wolfgang Kayser's "Böhme's Natursprachenlehre
und ihre Grundlagen," *Euphorion* 31 (1930): 521–62. For a succinct account of Boehme's theory within
the larger context of linguistic mysticism, see Umberto Eco, *The Search for the Perfect Language* (Oxford:
Blackwell, 1995), 182–85.

12. "Swedenborg, or the Mystic," in *The Collected Works of Ralph Waldo Emerson*, vol. 4: *Representative
Men: Seven Lectures* (Cambridge, Mass.: Belknap Press, 1987), 80. All quotations from this edition will
appear parenthetically cited as *RM* with page numbers.

13. Several pertinent documents by Reed, Parsons, James Marsh, Guillaume Oegger, and Bronson

Swedenborg was both a practical scientist and a mystic: he stands as an example of a mind that can contemplate both the natural and the supernatural with equal aplomb. In "Swedenborg, or the Mystic," Emerson considers the Swedish scientist-mystic as a modern instance of the "introverted mind": "This man, who appeared to his contemporaries a visionary and elixir of moonbeams, no doubt led the most real life of any man then in the world; and now when the royal and ducal Fredericks, Cristierns, and Brunswicks, of that day, have slid into oblivion, he begins to spread himself into the minds of thousands" (*RM* 56).

Not surprisingly, Emerson praises Swedenborg most generously when he treats the "science of all sciences," encapsulated in the doctrine of correspondences:

> Was it strange that a genius so bold should take the last step also, conceive that he might attain the science of all sciences, to unlock the meaning of the world? In the first volume of the "Animal Kingdom," he broaches the subject in a remarkable note.
>
> "In our doctrine of Representations and Correspondences, we shall treat of both these symbolical and typical resemblances and of the astonishing things which occur, I will not say, in the living body only, but throughout nature, and which correspond so entirely to supreme and spiritual things, that one would swear that the physical world was purely symbolical of the spiritual world; insomuch that if we choose to express any natural truth in physical and definite vocal terms, and to convert these terms only into the corresponding spiritual terms, we shall by this means elicit a spiritual truth, or theological dogma, in place of the physical truth or precept: although no mortal would have predicted that anything of the kind could possibly arise by bare literal transposition; inasmuch as the one precept considered separately from the other appears to have absolutely no relation to it. I intend hereafter to communicate a number of examples of such correspondences, together with a vocabulary containing the terms of spiritual things, as well as of the physical things for which they are to be substituted. This symbolism pervades the living body."
>
> The fact thus explicitly stated is implied in all poetry, in allegory, in fable, in the use of emblems, and in the structure of language. (*RM* 65–66)

Alcott appear in Kenneth W. Cameron, *Emerson the Essayist* (Hartford: Transcendental Books, 1945), 1:228–302; 2:12–31, 58–59, 69–75. The best account of Emerson's debt to Reed is Gura, *The Wisdom of Words*, 15–105.

Emerson's comment on the passage he quotes suggests the explicitly linguistic turn he gives to Swedenborg's doctrine of correspondences. Literary language supplies him with most of his examples, but even the "structure of language" itself reveals the correspondence between the physical and spiritual worlds. Indeed, Swedenborg hits upon the linguistic aspect of the correspondence doctrine when he states that "if we choose to express any natural truth in physical and definite vocal terms, and to convert these terms only into the corresponding spiritual terms, we shall by this means elicit a spiritual truth, or theological dogma, in place of the physical truth or precept." In the act of expressing truth, language necessarily reveals the correspondence between the physical and the spiritual, and in Swedenborg's view it also reveals the overwhelming authority of the spiritual over the physical.

If for Swedenborg this "bare literal transposition" uncovers the veiled mastery of the spiritual world over the physical, for Emerson it unveils the primarily figural nature of *both* word and thing. Both are emblematic or hieroglyphic; each is a figure for the other. This figural equivalence of word and thing already appears in the early journals and notebooks. In the 1831 *Blotting Book 3*, for example, Emerson writes, "In good writing words become one with things" (*JMN* 3:271), while in the 1832 notebook *Composition* he records the admonition "Self abandonment to the truth of things makes words things" (*JMN* 4:428).[14]

The early journals show that Emerson repeatedly attaches the literary correspondence of word and thing to the commanding figure of Goethe. In *Journal A* (1834), he writes that "Goethe was a person who hated words that did not stand for things" (*JMN* 4:301), a maxim he repeats in the lecture "Goethe, or the Writer": "He writes in the plainest and lowest tone, omitting a great deal more than he writes, and putting ever a thing for a word" (*RM* 158). The equivalence of word and thing is suggested on the next page of the lecture: "Goethe would have no word that does not cover a thing" (159). In the journal entry on Goethe, words "stand for" things, but in the two sentences from the lecture this one-way representational street becomes a broader avenue. The first sentence reverses the equivalence, since Goethe is "putting ever a thing for a word," while the second seems to hedge the radical equivalence by figuring the word as "covering" the thing.

The ambiguity of the word-thing relationship increases when we read entries from *Journal B* and *Journal C*. In the first entry, from 1835, Emerson discards the interpenetration of word and thing in favor of a more pessimistic view:

14. The term "self-abandonment" echoes Boehme's concept of *Gelassenheit*, a "letting go" of the self described in *De Signatura Rerum* and *Von der wahren Gelassenheit* (1622). See Konopacki, *Descent*, 90–92.

There is every degree of remoteness from the line of things in the line of words. By & by comes a word true & closely embracing the thing. That is not Latin nor English nor any language, but *thought*. The aim of the author is not to tell truth—that he cannot do, but to suggest it. He has only approximated it himself, & hence his cumbrous embarrassed speech: he uses many words, hoping that one, if not another, will bring you as near to the fact as he is.

For language itself is young & unformed. In heaven it will be, as Sampson Reed said, 'one with things.' Now, there are many things that refuse to be recorded,—perhaps the larger half. The unsaid part is the best of every discourse. (*JMN* 5:51)

Here the relationship between the word and the thing becomes one of "every degree of remoteness," and the closest the two come to each other is a linguistic embrace. Even this image fails to satisfy Emerson, who denies language the ability to "tell truth" in any other than an approximate way. Boehme's one "quickening Word of God" becomes a Babel-like multiplicity of "many words." As if to console himself, Emerson paraphrases Sampson Reed's *Observations on the Growth of the Mind*, in which Reed asserts that "there is a language, not of words but of things. When this language shall have been made apparent, that which is human will have answered its end, and being as it were resolved into its original elements, will lose itself in nature."[15] The last part of the journal entry seeks a second form of comfort: just as Goethe omits "a great deal more than he writes," so the "unsaid part is the best of every discourse." The passage balances the idealism of the Adamic theory of language with the realism of the approximate.

The balance is precarious, nor is Emerson's skepticism fleeting. In the 1837 *Journal C*, he returns to the same question: "As Boscovich taught that two particles of matter never touch, so it seems true that nothing can be described as it is. The most accurate picture is only symbols & suggestions of the thing but from the nature of language all remote" (*JMN* 5:353). The quality of remoteness is now a principle of language itself, as bound up in the "nature of language" as the remoteness of particles from one another is bound up in the nature of matter. But, curiously enough, the pessimism of the entry is mitigated by Emerson's poetic act of relating the sphere of language to the sphere of matter. Even in his most pessimistic mood, Emerson forges an analogy between

15. *Observations* is reprinted in Cameron, *Emerson the Essayist* 12:12–31; the quotation leads a paragraph on Adamic language (22).

word and thing, an analogy that eloquently argues against the statement of remoteness.

The journals, sermons, and lectures suggest that Emerson's response to Adamic language theory is a complex mixture of enthusiasm and skepticism. The response is no less complex in *Nature*, where the fourth chapter, "Language," embraces the Adamic theory in order to qualify and alter it. The chapter begins with the famous triad of propositions that assert nature as a "vehicle of thought":

1. Words are signs of natural facts.
2. Particular natural facts are symbols of particular spiritual facts.
3. Nature is the symbol of spirit.[16]

The three propositions present Emerson's version of the dual correspondence theory. The first statement presents the correspondence of word to thing and establishes the linguistic basis of Emerson's epistemology, since "Nature is the vehicle of thought" by virtue of the verbal sign. The second and third propositions present the correspondence of the physical world to the spiritual world, both in particular and in general. Emerson's desire to state the universality of the correspondence doctrine prevents him from constructing a syllogism: instead of a logical conclusion, which would state that "words are therefore signs of particular spiritual facts," the third proposition moves from the multiplicity of the second statement to the absolute unity of nature and spirit. Moreover, this drive toward universal unity causes the word "sign" to be replaced by "symbol," as if the verbal correspondence in the first proposition is no longer necessary for the metaphysical correspondence of the second and third propositions. Language in effect drops out of the equations that Emerson formulates, for he asserts a correspondence beyond the merely verbal.

As Emerson develops the three propositions in the chapter, however, the linguistic basis for the dual correspondence theory remains in control. In addition, his response to Adamic language theory is modified by his use of an entirely opposed tradition, that of Locke and his French follower, Condillac. Both of these assertions are supported in the first section of the chapter, in which the word-thing relationship grounds Emerson's revision of correspondence theory:

16. *The Collected Works of Ralph Waldo Emerson*, vol. 1: *Nature, Addresses, and Lectures*, ed. Robert E. Spiller and Alfred R. Ferguson (Cambridge, Mass.: Belknap Press, 1971), 17. All references to *Nature* are to this edition and are cited parenthetically in my text.

The use of the outer creation is to give us language for the beings and changes of the inward creation. Every word which is used to express a moral or intellectual fact, if traced to its root, is found to be borrowed from some material appearance. *Right* originally means *straight; wrong* means *twisted. Spirit* primarily means *wind; transgression*, the crossing of a *line; supercilious*, the *raising of the eye-brow.* We say the *heart* to express emotion, the *head*, to denote thought; and *thought* and *emotion* are, in their turn, words borrowed from sensible things, and now appropriated to spiritual nature. (*Nature* 18)

The second sentence of this quotation echoes a journal entry from 1824, in which the young Emerson asserts that "metaphysicians are mortified to find how entirely the whole materials of understanding are derived from sense. No man is understood who speculates on mind or character until he borrows the emphatic imagery of Sense. . . . I fear the progress of Metaphys[ical] philosophy may be found to consist in nothing else than the progressive introduction of apposite metaphors" (*JMN* 2:224). The "borrowing" of metaphors from physical objects is associated with a radically sensationalist philosophy, in which "the whole materials of understanding are derived from sense." In the passage from *Nature*, this same figural "borrowing" grounds our conceptions of "the beings and changes of the inward creation."

Much has been made of Emerson's rejection of Lockean sensationalism in favor of the transcendental idealism popularized by Coleridge, Carlyle, Sampson Reed, and others.[17] But while Emerson propounds a form of transcendental idealism, he does not dismiss Locke out of hand. Neither rejecting nor embracing Lockean metaphysics, Emerson uses Locke to add depth and balance to the Adamic language theory. In the passage just quoted, when Emerson gives the series of expressions for "a moral or intellectual fact," he echoes and alters one of the most famous passages from Locke's *Essay Concerning Human Understanding:* "*Spirit*, in its primary signification, is Breath; *Angel*, a Messenger: And I doubt not, but if we trace them to their sources, we should find, in all Languages, the names, which stand for Things that fall not under our Senses, to have had their rise from sensible *Ideas*."[18] This account of figural transference

---

17. Gura, *Wisdom of Words*, 18–24, 83–86. For another view, see Cameron Thompson, "John Locke and New England Transcendentalism," *New England Quarterly* 35 (1962): 435–57; rpt. in Philip F. Gura and Joel Myerson, eds., *Critical Essays on American Transcendentalism* (Boston: G. K. Hall, 1982), 368–86. See also F. T. Thompson, "Emerson's Indebtedness to Coleridge," *Studies in Philology* 23 (1926): 55–76.

18. Edited Peter H. Nidditch (Oxford: Clarendon Press, 1975), 403. Christopher Newfield notes the echo in "Controlling the Voice: Emerson's Early Theory of Language," *ESQ* 38 (1992): 12–13, 26.

may be sensationalist, but it is not more so than Emerson's etymologies. Emerson echoes the *Essay*, however, in order to alter it in two ways. First, the example of "spirit": Emerson traces the origin of the word to the term "wind," rather than to Locke's "Breath"; the alteration emphasizes the role of nature in the etymology, whereas Locke's etymology emphasizes the human, bodily aspect of the metaphysical term. Second, Emerson says that the terms are "borrowed from sensible things," whereas Locke asserts that they "have had their first rise from sensible *Ideas*." Thus Emerson again points toward the role of nature—of things—while Locke interiorizes the connection of word and thing to that of word and idea. In the alterations of the *Essay*, then, Emerson's consideration of figuration tends toward a strict sensationalism, while Locke's original text leans in the direction of nominalism.

Emerson would have appreciated these distinctions. In the essay "Nominalist and Realist," he considers the question of nominal and real essences in arguing that the surest way to truth is to be *both* a nominalist and a realist. Indeed, to be otherwise is to give the lie to nature, since "[she] is *one thing and the other thing*, in the same moment. She will not remain orbed in a thought, but rushes into persons; and when each person, inflamed to a fury of personality, would conquer all things to his poor crotchet, she raises up against him another person, and by many persons incarnates again a sort of whole."[19] Emerson's blending of Adamic correspondence theory and Lockean metaphysics thus acts exactly like nature, for the blending is "*one thing and the other thing*, in the same moment."

This effect of blending dominates the rest of the chapter "Language." So, for example, the remaining sentences of the section "Words are signs of natural facts" blend a rather pure form of Adamicism with the question of the origin of language. As Hans Aarsleff has argued, the question of origin is developed strongly by the Lockean French philosopher Condillac, whose *Essay on the Origin of Human Knowledge* exercised a profound and far-ranging influence on eighteenth-century French and German linguistic philosophy. Emerson does not appear to have read Condillac, relying instead on the views in Victor Cousin's *Cours de Philosophie*.[20] But the question of the origin of language, raised

---

Newfield's interpretation of the "Language" chapter presents an intriguing blend of poststructuralist abstraction and oppositional politics. For a less specific indication of the influence of Locke and his eighteenth-century followers on Emerson's conception of language, see Julie Ellison, *Emerson's Romantic Style* (Princeton University Press: Princeton, 1984), 197.

19. "Nominalist and Realist," in *The Collected Works of Ralph Waldo Emerson*, vol. 3: *Essays: Second Series*, ed. Alfred R. Ferguson et al. (Cambridge, Mass.: Belknap Press, 1983), 139.

20. On the tradition of Condillac, see Aarsleff, *From Locke to Saussure*, 146–224. See Walter Harding,

and developed by the tradition of Condillac, allows Emerson to give a secular-ized account of Adamic language. Focusing on the figural transformation of concrete things into metaphysical terms, Emerson asserts, "Most of the process by which this transformation is made, is hidden from us in the remote time when language was framed; but the same tendency may be daily observed in children. Children and savages use only nouns or names of things, which they continually convert into verbs, and apply to analogous mental acts" (*Nature* 18). Here Emerson posits an aesthetic origin of language, closely akin to the theo-ries of Diderot, Degérando, and Wilhelm von Humboldt.[21] And the image of innocent, uncivilized, and hence unspoiled children and savages approaches the paradisiacal image of Adam as the giver of the "names of things." The primacy of nouns adds to the effect of Adamicism, for it posits language as originally a nomenclature, a vocabulary of essential "natural facts" that are analogous to "mental acts." Emerson's aesthetic vision of language thus mixes the compet-ing traditions of seventeenth-century linguistic mysticism and eighteenth-century inquiries into the origins of language.

In the two sections treating the particular and universal correspondence of the physical and spiritual worlds, we might expect the linguistic correspon-dence of word and thing to drop from sight, but this is far from being the case. Emerson begins by focusing on the *thing* or "natural fact" as inherently figural or symbolic, but his development of the focus, like that of Swedenborg in the passage from the *Animal Kingdom*, depends upon examples of figural language. The second section, for instance, returns to the image of "savages" and to the concept of the origin of language: "As we go back in history, language becomes more picturesque, until its infancy, when it is all poetry; or, all spiritual facts are represented by natural symbols. The same symbols are found to make the orig-inal elements of all languages. It has moreover been observed, that the idioms of all languages approach each other in passages of the greatest eloquence and power. And as this is the first language so is it the last" (*Nature* 19–20). Emerson's aesthetic view of language emerges strongly as a mixture of the Adamic and eighteenth-century linguistic theories. The poetic origin of language grounds

---

Emerson's Library, 70–71, for the editions of Cousin owned by Emerson; for excerpts, see Cameron, *Emerson the Essayist* 1:303–19. Emerson makes an interesting statement on Condillac in the lecture "The Transcendentalist": "Even the materialist Condillac, perhaps the most logical expounder of materialism, was constrained to say, 'Though we should soar into the heavens, though we should sink into the Abyss, we never go out of ourselves; it is always our own thought that we perceive.' What more could an ide-alist say?" (*Nature, Addresses, and Lectures* 202).

21. See Hans Aarsleff's introduction to Wilhelm von Humboldt, *On Language*, trans. Peter Heath, (Cambridge: Cambridge University Press, 1988), xix–xx, xxix–xxx, xlix–lxv.

Emerson's Adamic vision of the unity of all languages in "the greatest eloquence and power." Poetic eloquence and power form the "first language," Adam's naming of the beasts of the field. "And as this is the first language, so is it the last." The decidedly apocalyptic tone of that sentence, enhanced by the telling use of biblical diction and parallel syntax, recalls the prophetic rhetoric of Boehme or Sampson Reed, but Emerson locates the apocalypse in the present. The Language of Nature he seeks is not to be found in Adam's bower or in Reed's Swedenborgian heaven but in "passages of the greatest eloquence and power."

Emerson's own eloquence functions, in the rest of the second section, as a demonstration of the power he calls his readers to discover in themselves and in their own language. Lamenting the "corruption of language" in the modern world, he makes the celebrated assertion "But wise men pierce this rotten diction and fasten words again to visible things; so that picturesque language is at once a commanding certificate that he who employs it, is a man in alliance with truth and God" (20). The figural correspondence of word and thing receives its greatest support in Emerson's use of the dynamic verbs "pierce" and "fasten" and the vivid adjective "rotten." All three words are transferred from concrete "natural facts," and together they give Emerson the "commanding certificate" of Adamic eloquence.

Two related techniques of eloquence, iteration and enumeration, create the Adamic effect of commanding authority when Emerson turns to the example of "the poet, the orator, bred in the woods": "Long hereafter, amidst agitation and terror in national councils,—in the hour of revolution,—these solemn images shall reappear in their morning lustre, as fit symbols and words of the thoughts which the passing events shall awaken. At the call of a noble sentiment, again the woods wave, the pines murmur, the river rolls and shines, and the cattle low upon the mountains, as he saw and heard them in his infancy. And with these forms, the spells of persuasion, the keys of power are put into his hands" (*Nature* 21). The terms "poet" and "orator" are purposely interchangeable, since for Emerson the power of eloquence must serve a practical use. Repeated syntactic formulas create the oratorical effect Emerson is describing, while the catalog of concrete nouns and dynamic verbs "fasten words again to visible things." Finally, the imagery of daybreak figures the dawning of "symbols or words" upon the thoughts of the poet-orator "in the hour of revolution." The essayist's eloquence functions as more than a simple self-description, however, for it hands the "keys of power" to an audience figured as both literary and political. The key to the passage: Emerson fastens cultural reform to the power of eloquence and to an ideal figure of eloquence who guides a community of listeners toward a revolutionary new world.

The third section of "Language" once again promises to dispense with words in order to concentrate on the correspondence of nature to spirit, but once again Emerson grounds his discussion in the word-thing relationship and, more tellingly, in his own search for eloquence. The examples of the universal correspondence take the form of statements of natural laws, proverbs, and dramatic poetry (21–22). Emerson closes the chapter with a cluster of quotations from the Swedenborgian linguist Guillaume Oegger, the Quaker mystic George Fox, and Coleridge.[22] The most extensive quotation is from Oegger's *The True Messiah*, which Emerson read in Elizabeth Palmer Peabody's manuscript translation in 1835. Philip Gura has developed an excellent theological interpretation of Emerson's use of Oegger's Swedenborgian correspondence doctrine.[23] Emerson's notes on *The True Messiah* show that he was just as interested in the text for its language as for its insights into Scripture: "I find good things in this MSS. [*sic*] of Oegger & I am taken with the design of his work. But it seems as if every body was insane on one side & the Bible makes them crazy as Bentham or Spurzheim or politics. The ethical doctrines of these theosophists are true & exalting, but straightway they run upon their Divine Transformation[,] the Death of God &c & become horn mad. To that point they speak reason then they begin to babble. . . . But now & then out breaks the sublimity of truth" (*JMN* 5:60–61). As with Boehme and Swedenborg—and, we might infer, with almost any thinker—Emerson approaches Oegger skeptically, agreeing and disagreeing, perpetually interrogating both the source and his responses.

The most striking aspect of the quotation from Oegger is not the statement of the correspondence doctrine but the language of the statement: "'Material objects,' said a French philosopher, 'are necessarily kinds of *scoriae* of the substantial thoughts of the Creator, which must always preserve an exact relation to their first origin; in other words, visible nature must have a spiritual and moral side'" (*Nature* 22–23). The strange word "scoriae" immediately captures the attention of the reader, as it caught that of the writer. Later, in *Journal B*, Emerson applies the word to a meditation on style: "Language clothes nature as the air clothes the earth, taking the exact form & pressure of every object. Only words that are new fit exactly the thing, those that are old like old scoriae that have been long exposed to the air & sunshine, have lost the sharpness of their mould & fit loosely. But in new objects & new names one is delighted with the plastic nature of man as much as in picture or sculpture" (*JMN* 5:246).

22. The editors of *Nature, Addresses, and Lectures* identify the three sources in their notes (250).
23. Emerson's notes on the manuscript appear in *JMN* 5:66–70; Peabody eventually published the translation as *The True Messiah* in 1842. See Gura, *Wisdom of Words*, 86–89.

Here Emerson is experimenting with the metallurgical imagery of the word, defined as "the slag or dross remaining after the smelting out of a metal from its ore" (*OED*). He applies the image, not to the relationship of material objects to the substantial thoughts of God, but to the relationship of words to things. That application gives the quotation from Oegger a new resonance, for it suggests that Oegger's influence is not so much conceptual as stylistic.

Throughout his long career as a "poet-orator" of the type he describes in *Nature*, Emerson formulates and reformulates figures of eloquence, and these figures insist on the power of language, in its highest form, to reform culture by reforming the spirits of the audience. The figural task is thus as personal and autobiographical as one could wish, but it is equally public and social. In addition, Emerson's wide-ranging scholarship in sometimes arcane language theories takes place within the context of his lecturing and writing career. We should not lose sight of Emerson's own commitment to performing language—to creating himself as a figure of eloquence by shaping his own language into the heightened, elevating "spells of persuasion . . . keys of power."

The resulting viewpoint casts the relationship of lecture and essay in a particularly dynamic, changing light. It also suggests that the poet and orator are synonymous, or nearly so, in Emerson's meditations on Adamic eloquence. In the 1841–42 lecture "The Poet," for example, Emerson returns to the figure of eloquence that he sketched in *Nature*, for he says that poetic genius is to be found "in strange, improbable places,—perhaps, as we said, not so much in metrical forms, as in eloquence" (*ELE* 3:362). He gives two instances of the sudden, surprising presence of poetic genius in eloquence. The first occurs in "Senates" or "the crowd of officials," and "some wild, black-browed bantling, some great boy" recalls, like the poet-orator of *Nature*, the language of authority and command: "In the folds of his brow, in the majesty of his mien, nature shall vindicate her son; and even in that strange and perhaps unworthy place and company, remind you of the lessons taught him in earlier days by the torrent, in the gloom of the pine woods, when he was the companion of crows and jays and foxers, and a hunter of the bear" (*ELE* 3:362). The second occurs in "some lowly Bethel by the seaside," and the figure of eloquence is "a hard-featured, scarred, and wrinkled methodist" (362). The obscure preacher speaks "through a language all glittering and fiery with imagination," and in doing so he "conquers his audience by infusing his soul into them, and speaks by the right of being the person in the assembly who has the most to say, and so makes all other speakers seem puny and cowardly before his face" (362–63). The two figures of poetic genius are, of course, figures of secular and religious eloquence, respectively, but they are alike in exercising "the power of man over men" (363).

That power of command is most significant in the effect it has on the audience: "How willingly every man consents to be nothing in this presence, to share this surprising emanation, and be steeped and ennobled in the new wine of this eloquence" (363). Emerson's sacramental imagery suggests the mysteriously spiritual communion of speaker and audience, one that transforms the event from the obscure or improbable into "this surprising emanation."

Another reason for dwelling on this passage is that Emerson himself returns to it several more times in his career. In notes that probably contributed to his 1847 lecture "Eloquence," Emerson clearly echoes the address from five years earlier: "Every listener gladly consents for the time to be nothing in his presence, & to share this surprising emanation, & be steeped & ennobled in the new wine of this eloquence. He instructs in the power of man over men that a man is a mover,—to the extent of his being, a power, & suggests an efficiency before which our actual life & society is a dormitory."[24] Ultimately, the passage reappears in the 1875 essay "Eloquence," which seems to derive directly from the 1875 lecture of the same title.[25]

In all of these formulations and reformulations, Emerson seeks to create a central figure of eloquence who speaks in a dimly remembered Language of Nature. The orator's language is "new wine" in several senses: in addition to its having a sacramental, transformative function, it both awakens and intoxicates the audience. The most fundamental function of eloquence, then, is to suggest the possibility of new movement, power, and efficiency—in the speaker as well as in each listener—and to embody the possibility in words. As he says in the 1875 lecture, regarding the "Peaceful Professions" of "the Bar, the Senate, Journalism, & the Pulpit":

> Certainly there is no true orator who is not a hero. His attitude in the rostrum, on the platform, requires that he counter-balance his auditory.

24. The quotation is my transcription of the manuscript labeled "Eloquence" in Houghton Library. There are three folders labeled thus, and they bear some relationship to three lectures of that title that Emerson delivered in 1847, 1867, and 1875. But the folders cannot be said to be texts for the three lectures. Many passages from the first folder appear in the 1858 *Atlantic Monthly* essay "Eloquence," which is reprinted in *Society and Solitude* (1870). Much of the third folder appears as the essay "Eloquence" in *Letters and Social Aims* (1875). Quotations from the manuscripts (shelf marks bMSAm 1280.199, 210, 214) are by permission of the Ralph Waldo Emerson Memorial Association and of Houghton Library, Harvard University.

25. The second essay "Eloquence" appears in *Letters and Social Aims*, vol.8 of *The Complete Works of Ralph Waldo Emerson*, ed. Edward Waldo Emerson, 12 vols. (Boston: Houghton Mifflin, 1903–4); the first essay "Eloquence" appears in vol. 7 of the same edition. All quotations from this edition appear cited parenthetically as *W*, with volume and page numbers. The two figures of eloquence appear in *W* 8:113–15.

He is challenger, & must answer all comers. The orator must ever stand
with forward foot in the attitude of advancing. His speech must be just
ahead of the assembly,—ahead of the whole human race, or it is superfluous. His speech is not to be distinguished from action. It is the electricity of action. It is action, as the General's word of command, or chart
of battle is action. I must feel that the speaker compromises himself to
his auditory,—comes for something;—it is a cry on the perilous edge
of the fight,—or let him be silent.[26]

The heroic orator is, as Emerson well knows, an extreme figure, perched both
"ahead of the whole human race" and on the very "edge of the fight."
Moreover, the figure stands at the boundary of speech and action, where one
is indistinguishable from the other. In this incantatory formulation, then, eloquence is the "electricity of action," invisible but nonetheless real.

Emerson's figure of eloquence is, he clearly acknowledges, "a fabulous personage," and the very idea of eloquence becomes "a tantalizing picture."[27] But
Emerson's persistent meditations on language, oratory, and cultural reform suggest that the fabulous, tantalizing figure serves an important function for the
lecturer-writer as well as for the culture. To the imagined scenes of the poet-
orator in *Nature*, the "black-browed bantling" and "wrinkled methodist" in the
lecture "The Poet," and the pugnacious, heroic "challenger" in the lecture
"Eloquence," we can add other, equally tantalizing pictures. One of the most
well known, perhaps, occurs in the 1837 oration "The American Scholar":

He learns that he who has mastered any law in his private thoughts, is
master to that extent of all men whose language he speaks, and of all
into whose language his own can be translated. The poet in utter solitude remembering his spontaneous thoughts and recording them, is
found to have recorded that which men in crowded cities find true for
them also. The orator distrusts at first the fitness of his frank confes-

26. See *W* 8:115–16, for an edited version of the passage. A nearly identical passage appears as sheet
[27] in the second (1867) folder called "Eloquence." The passage does not contain the sentence "It is
the electricity of action," but it ends with a telling contrast: "it is a cry on the perilous edge of battle,
or it is the tooting of a toy trumpet."

27. These lines appear both in *JMN* 9:430, 401 and on the first sheet of the first manuscript folder
of "Eloquence." It is tempting to think that the sentence "I suppose we shall never find in actual history the orator: he is a fabulous personage" would be an appropriate opening for the lecture
"Eloquence." A closely related passage occurs in the 1858 essay, in which Emerson sketches "a large
composite man, such as Nature rarely organizes; so that in our experience we are forced to gather up
the figure in fragments, here one talent and there another" (*W* 7:66).

sions,—his want of knowledge of the persons he addresses,—until he finds that he is the complement of his hearers;—that they drink his words because he fulfills for them their own nature; the deeper he dives into his privatest secretest presentiment,—to his wonder he finds, this is the most acceptable, most public, and universally true.[28]

In all of these passages, the aim of eloquence is to reform conventional language by pointing toward the Adamic Language of Nature. The reform of that most institutionalized of institutions—language itself—will lead, Emerson suggests, to the reform of the theological, educational, and literary institutions that employ language to constitute the culture at large. Thus the reforming instinct begins its work by piercing the rotten, conventional diction of formal education. Emerson's Adamic language theory does more than elucidate particular passages; it clarifies the purposes of his major statements on reform.

Two more aspects of Emerson's theorizing about language and culture deserve special mention. First, each time Emerson produces a figure of eloquence he also creates an audience to which the speaker is a "complement" or "counter-balance." Second, the staging of his "tantalizing pictures" emphasizes the dynamic, active quality of the theoretical or fabulous speaker-audience relationship. In the context of his own career, Emerson persistently reimagines and reinvents an ideal of reciprocity between word and deed, theory and reality, orator and auditors.

The clear inference one draws from these observations is that, for Emerson, eloquence redraws conventional boundaries between contemplation and action. In the 1875 lecture-essay "Eloquence," Emerson defines it as "*the power to translate a truth into language perfectly intelligible to the person to whom you speak*" (*W* 8:126; his italics), and even this formulation blends the elements of *power, language*, and *truth* in the act of "translating." For that reason, perhaps, Emerson calls eloquence a kind of "practical chemistry" (126). In a better and more famous formulation, he distinguishes between the poet and the mystic by appealing to a dynamic theory of language: "All language is vehicular and transitive, and is good, as ferries and horses are, for conveyance, not as farms and houses are, for homestead."[29]

The conversion of truth into perfectly intelligible language assumes, first of all, that some preexisting truth can be translated into some transparent medium.

---

28. *Nature, Addresses, and Lectures*, 63. Henceforth cited as *NAL*.
29. "The Poet," *Collected Works of Ralph Waldo Emerson*, vol. 3: *Essays: Second Series*, 20.

But Emerson does not consistently subscribe to this rather naive model of eloquence. When he imagines the actual scene of public performance, the idea of
eloquence becomes more specific and less innocent. In the lecture-essay published in 1858, for instance, the simple translation of truth becomes instead the
act of persuasion: "The end of eloquence is—is it not?—to alter in a pair of
hours, perhaps in a half hour's discourse, the convictions and habits of years"
(*W* 7:64). As he develops the relationship between orator and audience,
Emerson describes the speaker's "sense of added power and enlarged sympathetic existence" as something the speaker gains from the audience. Power and
sympathy grow together, so that the orator "sees himself the organ of a multitude, and concentrating their valors and powers" (64).

In the manuscript notes for "Eloquence," closely allied to the foregoing passages, Emerson fastens on the idea of eloquence as a dynamic but fleeting
power. In one sentence, for example, he exults, "Brief as it is, what is so excellent of present power as the riding this wild horse of the people!" In another,
he figures the speaker as attempting to grasp the power: "He who attempts to
speak in a public assembly is conscious presently of a certain new and extraordinary power hovering before him, which he cannot seize & use but which
solicits."[30] The power of eloquence is itself a "tantalizing picture," especially in
the second passage, although it is no chimera. The orator becomes, in the first
sentence, a horseman, whose ability to ride the "wild horse of the people" is as
excellent as it is brief. The two manuscript passages combine to represent eloquence as a transitory power, vehicular and transitive, rather than as a fixed,
abstract ideal.

The "new and extraordinary power" calls not for particular skills but for "a
taking sovereign possession of the audience" (65). In that formulation, the orator becomes a figure of Adamic authority, a sovereign creator or, as Emerson
calls him, "an artist who shall play on an assembly of men as a master on the
keys of the piano" (65). In a closely related manuscript passage, Emerson defines
the "possession" as impersonal and spiritual:

> What is eloquence but the call of this soul in one individual to the same
> soul in another? It never troubles the genuine orator what may be the
> composition of his audience; smooth or rugged; good natured or ill
> natured; religious or scoffers; he takes them all as they come,—he pro-

30. The quotations appear in the first "Eloquence" folder, juxtaposed with passages used in the 1858
essay (*W* 7:63–65). The second quotation ends abruptly with the verb "solicits" because it comes at the
end of a sheet.

ceeds in the faith that all differences are superficial, that they all have one fundamental nature which he knows how to address. To address that, is his art; and having this skill to call out his own soul that he may call out theirs, he can make them smooth or rugged, good natured or ill natured, fierce or fearful at his will.

The "genuine orator" is, of course, yet another figure of eloquence, one that here embodies "the call of this soul" or "one fundamental nature." Emerson first records the idea in an October 1836 journal: "There is one Mind common to all individual men" (*JMN* 5:222); the "transparent eyeball" passage in *Nature* can be seen as another important representation of the principle; finally, the idea is fundamental to all of the twelve lectures in the 1836–37 series *The Philosophy of History*, and to the 1837 oration "The American Scholar."[31] In applying the idea to the speaker-audience relationship, Emerson emphasizes the power of the orator to shape the audience according to their deepest nature and to "call out" their universal soul. In this sense, then, the "genuine orator" in effect "composes" the audience "at his will."

In the 1875 lecture "Eloquence," Emerson develops a telling example of the power that "solicits" but never rests easily in one place:

> An incident occurred some time ago, which was so good in its kind, that I may be pardoned for recalling it, though not strictly within the proprieties of the place. Cassius M. Clay & Wendell Phillips were both to speak at New Haven on one day, & almost at the same hour. Mr. Clay, an agricultural address before the State Society half past 6 o'c; Mr P., before the Lyceum, at 7 3/4. Mr Clay really gave Mr P. his audience, by closing his own address before 7 1/2 o'clock, & went himself to attend Mr P.'s lecture, & the whole audience with him. So Mr Phillips opened his discourse with some compliments to Mr Clay, acknowledging the kindness, & all the more, "because," he said, "it was known how widely they differed, & referred to the fact that Mr Clay had said, that, "if a contest should arise between the whites & the negroes, his own part would be taken with the whites." The audience gave three cheers for Mr Clay. "Well," said Mr Phillips, "This, then, we must reckon the roll-call on that side,—the distinguished Senator, & the white

---

31. The best discussion of the idea and its development in the lecture series appears in Robinson, *Apostle of Culture*, 85–111. See also Robert D. Richardson, Jr., *Emerson: The Mind on Fire* (Berkeley and Los Angeles: University of California Press, 1995), 257–65.

population in the States." The audience instantly repeated their cheers. Mr Phillips thought himself in a bad plight for the beginning of a speech, but rescued himself by saying, "Well, gentlemen, now let us see the muster on the other side. Thomas Jefferson says, "that, in this contest, the Almighty has no attribute but must take part with the Slave."— Mr Clay & the Southern gentlemen, on one side, & all the attributes of the Almighty on the other." The audience were utterly silenced, & Mr P. proceeded with his speech.

Emerson tells this story in order to illustrate the speaker's presence of mind, or what he calls "manliness." It serves as a counter to the distressingly humorous tale of Dr. Charles Chauncy, who, surprised to hear that "a little boy had fallen into Frog Pond on the Common and was drowned," prayed for Harvard, for the schools, and finally "implored the Divine Being 'to—to—to bless to them all the boy that was this morning drowned in Frog Pond'" (*W* 8:124). Omitted from the 1875 essay, the story of Phillips's legendary presence of mind also dramatizes how the "genuine orator" can take sovereign possession of an audience. Phillips runs the very real risk of losing control of his audience before he even begins to deliver his address. But he employs incisive wit to construct the opposition between "Mr Clay & the Southern gentlemen, on the one side, & all the attributes of the Almighty on the other," and as a result he silences the unruly audience, enlisting its attention at the same time that he implicitly claims to speak on behalf of the Almighty and the slave. In Emerson's terms, Phillips displays an authentic genius for eloquence because he persuades his audience that they share with him "one fundamental nature."

The principle of a "common mind" or "universal soul" underlying Emerson's theory of eloquence establishes a reciprocal relationship between the orator and the audience. In all of his lectures and essays titled "Eloquence," Emerson figures the reciprocity in terms that temper the potentially egoistic power of the orator. So, for instance, he begins the 1858 essay by asserting that "probably every man is eloquent once in his life" (*W* 7:61), and as he contemplates the universal need to speak, his mind moves from orator to audience and back again:

> And yet, this lust to speak only marks the universal feeling of the energy of the engine, & the curiosity men feel to touch the springs. Of all the musical instruments on which men play, a popular assembly is that which has the greatest compass & variety, &, out of which, by genius & study, the most wonderful effects can be produced. An audience is not a simple addition of the individuals that compose it. Their sympathy

gives them a certain social organism, which fills each member in his own degree, &, most of all, the orator, as a jar in a battery is charged with the whole electricity of the battery. No one can survey the face of an excited assembly without being apprised of new opportunity for painting in fire human thought, & being agitated to agitate. How many orators sit mute there below! They come to get justice done to that ear & intuition, which no Chatham & no Demosthenes has begun to satisfy. It suggests fields & labours not easily achieved. It suggests to us the manifold degrees of power on which we have never drawn. That which we daily exert,—political, social, intellectual, moral, is quite superficial. We talk & work half asleep. We have never yet been searched. Between us & our last energy, lie terrific social, & their sublime solitary exertions.[32]

In imagining the invisible power of eloquence, Emerson uses quasi-scientific or technological figuration. Thus he speaks of "the energy of the engine," "the springs," and, most tellingly, "the whole electricity of the battery." The orator, in this last figure, is "as a jar in a battery," filled with the electrical charge of the entire assembly. When Emerson exclaims, "How many orators sit mute there below," he bespeaks the permanent necessity of speech and the permanent hunger for hearing it. In the lecture itself, moreover, Emerson directly connects this universal reciprocity to broad cultural reform—he uses four adjectives to specify the one broad adjective I use—for the electricity of eloquence suggests "the manifold degrees of power on which we have never drawn." The passage ends with an image of eloquence as a vast, impersonal field of energy, awaking "terrific social, & their sublime solitary exertions."

The lectures and essays on eloquence deliver an active, dynamic sense of language as an electric medium, a constantly changing, transitory power that both solicits and evades the grasp of the speaker. Language does not so much contain the power as embody and transmit it. Emerson's representations imply that language effectively crosses any arbitrary boundary between, say, literature and politics. For his theory of language leads directly to a broadly based, heterogeneous theory of culture. And Emerson propounds and performs both theories in his own career as a lecturer, answering the solicitations of power.

---

32. The quotation is taken from the first manuscript folder "Eloquence" in Houghton Library. The first seven sentences of the passage appear in the 1858 essay (*W* 7:62–63), but the last four do not. See also *JMN* 9:236–37.

3

Henry Thoreau's Tawny Grammar

1

The acuteness of Thoreau's sensitivity to sounds is matched—perhaps surpassed—only by his sense of silence and the power that silence wields. As early as December 1838, the twenty-one-year-old teacher and lecturer drafted "some scraps from an essay on 'Sound and Silence'" (*Journal* 1:60), scraps that would eventually form the concluding movement of *A Week on the Concord and Merrimack Rivers*, published in 1849. During the eleven-year "silence" between the initial draft and the polished publication, Thoreau built the cabin at Walden Pond, kept his journal as a kind of "literary *workbook*" (*Journal* 2:447), drafted the only two books he would publish during his short life, and wrote the lecture that would become known most popularly as "Civil Disobedience."[1] These familiar biographical facts often suggest a renowned retreat to Walden Pond and to the monumental book *Walden*, but the familiarity obscures Thoreau's less renowned commitment to the reform of nineteenth-century American culture.

Thoreau already sees layered complexities of sound and silence, society and solitude, in the "scraps" of 1838, and his vision remains essentially unchanged

---

1. The most succinct account of these years is in Richard J. Schneider, *Henry David Thoreau* (Boston: Twayne, 1987), 1–18. See the two modern biographies: Walter Harding, *The Days of Henry Thoreau* (New York: Knopf, 1965); Robert D. Richardson, Jr., *Henry Thoreau: A Life of the Mind* (Berkeley and Los Angeles: University of California Press, 1986). An important recent discussion of Thoreau's career is by Steven Fink, *Prophet in the Marketplace: Thoreau's Development as a Professional Writer* (Princeton: Princeton University Press, 1992).

Thoreau's *Journal* is being edited by Princeton University Press. At this time, four volumes have appeared: vol. 1: *1837–1844*, ed. John C. Broderick et al. (1971); vol. 2: *1842–1848*, ed. Robert Sattelmeyer (1984); vol. 3: *1848–1851*, ed. Robert Sattelmeyer et al. (1990); vol. 4: *1851–1852*, ed. Leonard N. Neufeldt and Nancy Craig Simmons (1992). Unless otherwise noted, references to the *Journal* are to this edition and are cited parenthetically in my text.

in the published version that forms the concluding five paragraphs of *A Week*: "As the truest society approaches always nearer to solitude, so the most excellent speech finally falls into Silence. Silence is audible to all men, at all times, and in all places. She is when we hear inwardly, sound when we hear outwardly."[2] The relationship between sound and silence is analogous to that between society and solitude, but Thoreau radically redefines the nature of the two terms in each relationship, stating as absolute law the fundamental, silent assumptions that he makes. Thus solitude and silence could be seen as negative terms, defined as the absence of their positive opposites, but Thoreau privileges them as positive presences—indeed, as the respective goals of the "truest society" and the "most excellent speech." In his redefinition, silence becomes universally audible, the one power that unites "all men, at all times, and in all places." The third sentence in the passage suggests the assumptions underlying these paradoxical propositions: the muse or goddess Silence is inner and figural; sound is outer and literal. Thoreau describes the interior realm of solitude and silence with superlatives because it is the source of figuration. The analogical style of the passage suggests that figural language, in its unifying power, is "always nearer" the truth and excellence that society seeks through its many speeches.

My reading of this brief passage is not meant to suggest that Thoreau's writing falls into figuration as inevitably as the "most excellent speech finally falls into Silence." This purely formal rendering would dilute much of the power of his language, for that power resides in relationships *between* sound and silence, society and solitude, exterior and interior. Thoreau's sense of power can be seen in the original scraps, in which he defines silence as "the communing of a conscious soul with itself.—If the soul attend for a moment to its own infinity, then and there is silence" (*Journal* 1:60). This formulation emphasizes the inner power of solitude and silence, and Thoreau's 1844–45 transcription of the scraps in the *Long Book* journal seems, at first glance, to repeat the young writer's one-sided view: "Silence is the communing of a conscious soul with itself—When we attend for a moment to our own infinity—then and there is silence" (*Journal* 2:112). A shift in emphasis takes place in the revisions of "if the soul" to "when we," for Thoreau makes the communion of consciousness both more inevitably temporal and less inevitably solitary than in the first version. Even more important, in the final version of the passage in *A Week*, Thoreau deletes the image

---

2. I quote from the scholarly edition of *A Week on the Concord and Merrimack Rivers*, ed. Carl Hovde (Princeton: Princeton University Press, 1980), 391. The interested reader should consult the Library of America edition of Thoreau's writings (New York: Library of America, 1985) for the "second-edition" text of 1868.

of silent self-communion altogether, preferring to define silence in relation to sounds. Thus silence becomes the "rare mistress" who commands sounds as "her servants, and purveyors," or, in another figure, sounds "are so far akin to Silence, that they are but bubbles on her surface, which straightway burst, an evidence of the strength and prolificness of the undercurrent" (*Week* 391). Both of these figures give silence a position of commanding authority, but both also recognize the mistress's need of purveyors, the undercurrent's need of a surface.

The sequence of the two journal entries and *A Week* suggests a complex silencing of silence, although it would be a mistake to stress this rhetorical strategy as merely self-involved and self-referential. For while it is surely both of these, it is also much more. In his constant refigurings of silence, Thoreau in fact proves the "strength and prolificness" of his words, but in addition he shows the interdependent nature of his chosen oppositions. The self-referential quality of the passage is partly a function of its position at the close of the book— what better way to end *A Week* than to speak of the silence that is about to take the place of words? But Thoreau does not retreat into silence, even though he is willing to represent it as "the universal refuge, the sequel to all dull discourses and all foolish acts" and as "our inviolable asylum, where no indignity can assail, no personality disturb us" (*Week* 392). Instead, he focuses on the substantial power of silence and sounds as they are combined in a figure of eloquence:

> The orator puts off his individuality, and is then most eloquent when most silent. He listens while he speaks, and is a hearer along with his audience. Who has not hearkened to Her infinite din? She is Truth's speaking-trumpet, the sole oracle, the true Delphi and Dodona, which kings and courtiers would do well to consult, nor will they be balked by an ambiguous answer. For through Her all revelations have been made, and just in proportion as men have consulted her oracle within, they have obtained a clear insight, and their age has been marked as an enlightened one. But as often as they have gone gadding abroad to a strange Delphi and her mad priestess, their age has been dark and leaden. Such were garrulous and noisy eras, which no longer yield any sound, but the Grecian or silent and melodious era is ever sounding and resounding in the ears of men. (*Week* 392)

By positioning his ideal orator at the boundary dividing sound and silence, Thoreau creates several paradoxical sources of power. First, the orator stands at the border of society and solitude: by putting off his individuality and becoming "a hearer along with his audience," the orator becomes the Emersonian mouthpiece for the collective mind of the audience. Second, by standing at the border of sound and silence, speaking and listening, the orator achieves true eloquence, which is most closely allied to silence. Third, because the orator "puts off his individuality," eloquence joins inward silence to outward sound, a union suggested by the etymology of the word *eloquence*. Thoreau develops the suggestion by mingling imagery of sound and sight in the rest of the paragraph. Silence is figured as "Truth's speaking-trumpet," the oracular source of divine, infinite revelation. But that oracular source is democratic, in that it is "audible to all men, at all times, and in all places," and it is also interiorized, an "oracle within." The result of consulting the inner oracle, furthermore, is that the orator obtains "clear insight" and the age is "marked as an enlightened one." By shifting the imagery from sound to sight—especially *insight*—Thoreau moves his own language in the direction of silence. And the implication of that move is that the orator's language of boundaries will ultimately border upon the timeless and infinite. Thoreau thus shifts from the image of insight to the "Grecian or silent and melodious era" that "is ever sounding and resounding in the ears of men."

A longer look at Thoreau's literary workbook reveals that in early 1845, as he was drafting a lecture titled "Concord River" that he would deliver on 25 March, he also transcribed the scraps on sound and silence into the *Long Book* and drafted his letter to William Lloyd Garrison's *Liberator*, in which he reviewed Wendell Phillips's lecture at the Concord Lyceum on 11 March.[3] Coming so close to one another in time of composition, the three projects suggest that the abstract, idealized figure of eloquence in "Sound and Silence" is closely related to Phillips. Moreover, the fact that Thoreau was drafting a lecture at the same time suggests that "Sound and Silence" and Phillips provide the young lecturer with models for his own oratory.

The most important quality Thoreau finds in Phillips is a moral stability that recalls the image of Silence as "Truth's speaking-trumpet, the sole oracle":

> We would fain express our appreciation of the wisdom and steadiness, so rare in the reformer—with which he declared that he was not born to abolish slavery, or reform the church—but simply to do the right.

---

3. The collocation of projects appears as follows: "Concord River" lecture (*Journal* 2:103–12); "Sound and Silence" (112–15); "Wendell Phillips Before Concord Lyceum" (120–24). I give a fuller introductory discussion of Phillips and the Concord Lyceum in Chapter 1; see also *Reform Papers*, 60–62, 303–7. For an encyclopedic account of this period, see Linck C. Johnson, *Thoreau's Complex Weave: The Writing of A Week on the Concord and Merrimack Rivers* (Charlottesville: University Press of Virginia, 1986); for the *Long Book* see 266–70.

His positions have the advantage of being not only morally & politically sound and expedient, but philosophically true, and a rare clearness and singleness of perception is coupled with a still rarer felicity of expressive utterance[.] We have heard a few, a very few, good political speakers—Webster & Everett—who afforded us the pleasure of larger intellectual conceptions—strength and acuteness—of soldier like steadiness and resolution—and of a graceful and natural oratory—But in this man there was a sort of moral worth and integrity—which was more graceful than his rhetorick [*sic*] and more discriminating than his intellect which was more stable than their firmness. A something which was not eloquence which was not oratory—or wit or scholarship which was working not for temporary—but for worthy & untrivial ends. (*Journal* 2:122)

Seeking to give a shape to the ineffable quality of Phillips's presence before the lyceum audience, Thoreau continually gestures toward an eloquence that is more than eloquence, a firmness "more stable than [the] firmness" of a Webster or Everett. Thus he insists that the "something" he seeks to capture in words is "not eloquence . . . not oratory," but a moral and philosophical truth. Thoreau's insistence results, I would argue, in a sharper and fuller portrait of Phillips's eloquence, not in a clear sense of truth. But Thoreau does not insist on such absolute choices, in this case, for he concludes the portrait of Phillips by remarking that "we feel ourselves in danger of slandering all mankind by affirming that there is one man who is at once an eloquent speaker and a righteous man" (122). Because Phillips is both eloquent and righteous, the sounds of his words are allied with the silence of his "wisdom and steadiness."

A second quality of the figures of eloquence sketched in "Sound and Silence" and the review of Phillips is their ability to "put off individuality" and give voice to a collective mind shared with the audience. In the *Long Book* draft, Thoreau quotes the reactions of several members of the audience in order to show how they recognize the truth of Phillips's eloquence: "'Well,' says one; 'He put it on to us poor Democrats pretty hard.' 'That's a severe dose' says another, 'Well,' responds the minister it's all true, every word of it'" (123). These responses never appear in the published letter, but they create the postlecture conversation as a colloquial, clear acknowledgment of Phillips's power. The "dose" in the *Long Book* becomes the Latinate "electuary" in Garrison's *Liberator*, and in both cases eloquence acts as a moral medicine. In the last two sentences of the draft, also excluded from the published letter, Thoreau summarizes the relationship between speaker and audience: "But it becomes the many who yield their so easy assent to his positions, and suffer not the sometimes honest prejudice of their neighbors to hinder his free speech to hear him with seriousness & with a spirit at least as prepared and as resolved as his own for the issue. He does not bewilder and mystify his audience with sophistry—as the mere partisan always does—but furnishes a light which all may use to their profit" (124).

The figures of eloquence, speaking to and listening with an ideal audience of hearers, clearly show the relational quality of Thoreau's language, a language that is always figural but never merely "poetic." For Thoreau, the orator must speak a language that is both timely and timeless; hence, in the "Sound and Silence" conclusion to *A Week*, he mingles the nineteenth-century American lyceum and "the true Delphi and Dodona." Likewise, the *Long Book* drafts emphasize the ways in which Thoreau joins abstract, poetic reflections to concrete, cultural reforms, and this unifying vision of the orator's power to act as "Truth's speaking-trumpet" recalls Emerson's pronouncements concerning the orator in *Nature* and "The American Scholar." In the first, as we have seen, Emerson equates the poet and the orator, both of whom must be "bred in the woods" in order to combine the timeless truths of nature with the rush of present events: "Long hereafter, amidst agitation and terror in national councils,—in the hour of revolution,—these solemn images shall reappear in their morning lustre, as fit symbols and words of the thoughts which the passing events shall awaken. At the call of a noble sentiment, again the woods wave, the pines murmur, the river rolls and shines, and the cattle low upon the mountains, as he saw and heard them in his infancy. And with these forms, the spells of persuasion, the keys of power are put into his hands" (*Nature* 21). For Emerson, the orator must speak an Adamic Language of Nature, and if he does so his language will call forth other institutional reforms. In "The American Scholar," the orator exercises this power by realizing "that he who has mastered any law in his private thoughts, is master to that extent of all men whose language he speaks, and of all into whose language his own can be translated" (63).

Thoreau's orator resembles Emerson's poet-orator but also differs from it in important ways. The commanding authority of the Adamic orator is, for example, tempered by the images of false prophets and their false listeners, and the possibility of a "dark and leaden" age is ever present in Thoreau's representation. The more limited sense of linguistic power may account for Thoreau's insistence that Wendell Phillips's eloquence is "not eloquence . . . not oratory." But it appears most sharply in the final paragraphs of *A Week*, in which Thoreau considers the qualities of "a good book" and of his own volume. The ideal book, first of all, "is the plectrum with which our else silent lyres are struck,"

and the young author privileges the "unwritten sequel" of the reader or audience over the "written and comparatively lifeless body of the work." The ideal
book becomes "a mole whereon the waves of Silence may break": this image
of the book as a breakwater or jetty renders the actual words of any text mere
provisionary measures, temporary harbors that resound with the vast waves of
silence.

This sense of the provisionary becomes more intensely personal when
Thoreau applies it to his own volume: "It were vain for me to endeavor to
interrupt the Silence. She cannot be done into English. For six thousand years
men have translated her with what fidelity belonged to each, and still she is little better than a sealed book."[4] Here, the power of silence leads not to the
sounds of the orator's commanding speech but to silence. Thoreau meditates
yet further on the vastness of the untold in relation to the told, so great that
the told will seem, for all authors and readers, "but the bubble on the surface
where he disappeared." Given the relationship of Thoreau's book to his brother's
death, this is a chillingly restrained elegy, both to John and to the survivor's ability to tell anything at all. Thoreau softens the harsh silence somewhat in the
final sentence: "Nevertheless, we will go on, like those Chinese cliff swallows,
feathering our nests with the froth, which may one day be bread of life to such
as dwell by the sea-shore." Characteristically, the sentence borders between hope
and despair, offering its "bread of life" conditionally, but offering it nevertheless. In parallel fashion, the sentence borders between the past and the present,
offering a mixture of oriental and biblical, natural and textual imagery to "such
as dwell by the sea-shore" of today. That "sea-shore" defines, most directly, New
England and America, but it also borders upon the seas of China and Galilee.[5]

In the five-paragraph meditation titled "Sound and Silence" that concludes
A Week, Thoreau engages in an elegant, eloquent play of language, but he never
wavers from his resolute desire to point his own book toward the "unwritten
sequel" of his readers' lives. Despite the power of the orator to obtain clear
insight, the clearest insight Thoreau himself obtains is that of limitation. Thus

4. The text in the *Long Book* transcription and in the first edition of *A Week* reads "interpret," but
Thoreau's revision reads "interrupt" (Library of America, 1081). The gap between the two words speaks
volumes.

5. The phrase "bread of life" alludes to Jesus' speech after the feeding of the five thousand on the
shores of Galilee: "And Jesus said unto them, I am the bread of life: he that cometh to me shall never
hunger; and he that believeth on me shall never thirst" (John 6:35). Also important to this allusion are
the fact that Jesus is a rabbi, or teacher, to the multitude; that he explains or explicates the miracle; that
he opposes literal, physical bread to his figural, supernatural bread; that his explanation offends the Jews,
and also his own disciples; that he tries to be clearer and says that "it is the Spirit that quickeneth; the
flesh profiteth nothing: the words that I speak unto you, they are spirit, and they are life" (John 6:63).

the vast power of silence, which gives ultimate truth and meaning to spoken and written words, is finally "little better than a sealed book." Thoreau's multiple borderings oppose the "sealed book" of silence to the "unwritten sequel" that a good book—"the plectrum with which our else silent lyres are struck"— inscribes as its "most indispensable part." The layering of textual images suggests, first, that the ultimate power of silence is the capacity to silence both spoken and written language, and, second, that this power coexists with the power to make spoken and written words oracular and incantatory in their eloquence. Thoreau's rhetoric of borderings therefore implies a hierarchy of power at the same time that it undermines the very notion of hierarchy.

The conclusion of *A Week* shows that, as a young writer and lecturer, Thoreau was keenly aware of language as a source of power, a force that finds its most important point of application in the "unwritten sequel" of its listeners or readers. But the conclusion also suggests that Thoreau's theory of eloquence, while similar to Emerson's, differs sharply from it in the younger man's sense of the limits of language. Like Emerson, Thoreau believes in a near-mystical Language of Nature, but the power of that language to effect cultural reform is limited, both in its representations and in its practical outcomes.

2

In *Thoreau's Reading*, Robert Sattelmeyer succinctly outlines Thoreau's theory of language as delineated by Michael West and Philip Gura.[6] The problem with this summary is that it underestimates the differences between Thoreau and Emerson, in that Sattelmeyer asserts that Thoreau's mature style, developed in the years between the publications of *A Week* and *Walden*, reflects "his assimilation and extension of the Transcendentalists' language theory as sketched by Emerson in *Nature* and developed in greater detail in 'The Poet'" (Sattelmeyer 77). If the specific influences of such linguistic thinkers as Charles Kraitsir and Richard Trench are to be taken seriously, they show that Thoreau is in fact more up-to-date than Emerson in his theorizings about language. Further, they suggest that Thoreau's theory of language is less optimistic and more relational than

6. Sattelmeyer, *Thoreau's Reading: A Study in Intellectual History* (Princeton, 1988), 76–77; West, "Charles Kraitsir's Influence upon Thoreau's Theory of Language," *ESQ* 19 (1973): 262–74; West, "Scatology and Eschatology: The Heroic Dimensions of Thoreau's Wordplay," *PMLA* 89 (1974): 1043–64; West, "Thoreau and the Language Theories of the French Enlightenment," *ELH* 51 (1984): 747–70; Gura, *Wisdom of Words*, 109–44.

Emerson's, at least as far as the pronouncements of the early lectures and *Nature* are concerned. Finally, Thoreau's mature style, as embodied both in *Walden* and in the later lectures and "papers," can be seen as more than a mere extension of Emerson's theories.

Although many theoretical influences converge in Thoreau's meditations on language, Charles Kraitsir's *Glossology: Being a Treatise on the Nature of Language and on the Language of Nature* is of signal importance because it gives both a summary of the history of linguistic theories and a popularized, somewhat skewed version of Wilhelm von Humboldt's transcendental language theory.[7] The subtitle of Kraitsir's *magnum opus* points to the notion of an Adamic Language of Nature, and *Glossology* therefore appears as an appropriate place to develop a comparison of Emerson's and Thoreau's theories of language.

Kraitsir's affinity with transcendental or "organic" language theorists such as Humboldt is clear from the outset of *Glossology*. In the following passage, for instance, he argues vehemently against the empiricist theory of language as an arbitrary convention:

> Is there a science of language?—Those who think language to be a mere arbitrary contrivance, simply a matter of memory, and only a tool of so-called "practical" ends, deny it. Those, on the contrary, who live, move, and are in Him who—"out of the mouth of babes and sucklings has ordained strength; the work of whose fingers are his heavens" (Ps. viii.2,3; comp. Ps. xix.1,2)—whose "all works are done in truth" (Ps. xxxii.4)—"who covers *himself* with light as with a garment" (Ps. civ.2–32)—think it a blasphemy to except the human mind and its manifestation by speech from the universal harmony of the world (*kosmos*, beauty, comeliness, order; *mundus*, clean, pure, etc.). Should a drop of water be subject to law, but human language not? (10)

In Kraitsir's theoretical and ideological world, the "science of language" can be practiced only by those who believe in the divine origin and inherent aesthetic beauty of language. But Kraitsir's method for displaying these twin beliefs "scientifically" is to give the literal meanings of the Greek and Latin words for *world*, as if these etymologies somehow crystallize the order and beauty of language in the same way that a drop of water crystallizes the order and beauty of

---

7. For a thumbnail sketch of Kraitsir's life and career, see West, "Kraitsir's Influence," 262–64. All quotations from *Glossology* are taken from the first (and only) edition (New York: Putnam, 1852). West argues in "French Enlightenment" that Gura makes too much of Kraitsir's influence.

the physical universe. As Emerson's "Language" chapter in *Nature* shows, more-over, this concern with etymologies is shared by such empiricist theorists as Locke or Horne Tooke. The passage crystallizes the condition of many popu-lar language theorists in the nineteenth century: their vision of language may differ from that of the empiricists, but their methodology does not.

Kraitsir resembles other popularizers of the new science of language in that he distorts the theories of language that arise with the discipline of compar-ative philology. Among the many theorists he quotes or paraphrases, Kraitsir shows unswerving reverence for the work of Wilhelm von Humboldt. When he must support the assertion that "language is a living organism," for exam-ple, he goes directly to Humboldt's famous treatise *The Diversity of Human Language Structure and Its Influence on the Mental Development of Mankind:* "W. v. HUMBOLDT gives several, more or less restricted, definitions of language, the genetic being this: 'Language is the ever recurring labor of the mind, to make the articulate sound an expression of thought.' Ueber die Kawi Sprache, S. lvii. Elsewhere: 'Language is the striving of the power of speech to break forth, according to the mental cast of a people.' S. xxv. He characterizes it as the cen-tre of all the individualities of humanity, of nations and persons" (22). Humboldt's introduction to his work on the Kawi languages contains many of the essential points of transcendental language theory. Most important for Kraitsir is the fact that Humboldt conceives of language as a dynamic activity of the spirit, whether individual or national, an activity that both expresses that spirit and acts upon it. Humboldt gives a concise formulation of this dynamic reciprocity in the third section of the Kawi introduction: "The *bringing-forth of language* is an *inner need* of man, not merely an external necessity for main-taining communal intercourse, but a thing lying in his own nature, indispens-able for the development of his mental powers and the attainment of a world-view, to which man can attain only by bringing his thinking to clarity and precision through communal thinking with others."[8] Humboldt's defini-tion of language employs a dynamic model of development, providing the focus and coherence of a goal for the reciprocal, dynamic relationship between language and mind. The "development of his mental powers" and "the attain-ment of a world-view" present this individualistic, expressive goal, but Humboldt tempers Romantic subjectivity with the image of "communal thinking with others."

8. *On Language: The Diversity of Human Language-Structure and Its Influence on the Mental Development of Mankind*, trans. Peter Heath (Cambridge University Press, 1988), 27. All citations from the "Kawi Introduction," as it is known, refer to this edition and are given parenthetically in my text.

The problem with the dynamic, developmental model of language is that it becomes the vehicle for an ethnocentric interpretation of particular languages and peoples. That problem is inherent both in the model itself and in the connection of the new science of language with ethnology. Nineteenth-century comparatists are given to judging the mental abilities of civilizations, past and present, and their primary evidence for supporting their judgments is nearly always linguistic.[9] Humboldt attempts to avoid a naive ethnocentrism, even though a basic assumption of his theory is that languages reflect the mental capacity of their users. In discussing the so-called stages of languages, for instance, he argues against an evolutionary model that would make Chinese a primitive version of Sanskrit (30–31; cf. 100–108). Humboldt certainly judges *languages* as being more or less perfect, and he does so because his model of linguistic perfection is the Sanskrit language (216), but he does not go so far as to judge the mental development of particular nations. Instead, he uses the simple dynamism of his basic model of language as a means of arguing against the developmental or evolutionary aspects of the model:

> All *becoming* in nature, but especially of the organic and living, escapes our observation. However minutely we may examine the preparatory stages, between the latter and the phenomenon there is always the cleavage that divides the something from the nothing; and this is equally so with the moment of *cessation*. All comprehension of man lies only between the two. In languages, a period of origination, from perfectly accessible historical times, affords us a striking example. We can follow out a multiple series of changes that the *language of the Romans* underwent during its decline and fall, and can add to them the minglings due to invading tribesmen: we get no better explanation thereby of the origin of the living seed which again germinated in various forms into the organism of newly burgeoning languages. An inner principle, newly arisen, rebuilt the collapsing structure, for each in its own fashion, and we, since we always find ourselves situated among its effects only, become aware of its transformations only by the multitude thereof. (43)

Because the "inner principle" of language is noumenal, it both organizes and escapes the dynamic transformations of particular languages. The comparative

---

9. Two excellent analyses of ethnocentrism in Western culture are Edward Said, *Orientalism* (New York: Pantheon, 1978) and Reginald Horsman, *Race and Manifest Destiny: The Origins of American Racial Anglo-Saxonism* (Cambridge: Harvard University Press, 1981). See Aarsleff's discussion in *From Locke to Saussure*, 278–355.

philologist is always working in the aftermath of language and its transformations, reconstructing the principles of change in order to approach, as closely
as possible, the "origin of the living seed." Humboldt thus avoids the developmental aspects of his model by focusing on the "cleavage" between outer phenomena and inner principles, and the absolute distance between the two would
seem to militate against the ethnocentric interpretation of particular languages
and cultures.

When Charles Kraitsir appropriates Humboldt's theory, the distance between
outer phenomena and inner principles quickly closes, and the result is an ethnocentric, evolutionary account of language and spirit. In a section of *Glossology*
called "Elements of Language," for example, Kraitsir attempts to identify the
"natural, organic elements, which constitute the genuine principles of human
speech," for the languages that "contain most of these absolute, original, genetic
and organic principles, in the least disguised form, have a just claim to be considered the best" (145). Not surprisingly, the Indo-European languages show
"the greatest development," and the English language is one of the greatest of
the greats. According to Kraitsir, English is "certainly the most apt medium by
which glossology may be studied" because it contains the most "organic elements" or "germs" (145).

For Kraitsir, germs are the basic units of speech and thought, more basic than
so-called roots, which he says are "already either compounds or results of
germs" (160). Kraitsir follows Humboldt closely in arguing that "speech, issuing from the spirit, reacts also upon it" (25). Indeed, he even appropriates
Humboldt's imagery when he asserts that "thought, like a flash of lightning,
collects—crystallizes the whole power of the mind to one point, and utters
itself by a precise distinct unity of articulate sounds" (25).[10] But Kraitsir differs
from his mentor in an important respect, in that he is more willing to define
the noumenal principles of speech and thought. Thus he proposes, both in the
earlier book *The Significance of the Alphabet* (1846) and in *Glossology*, a triple triad
that purports to explain the connections among nature, language, and spirit:

> We observe three categories in our ideas and in the phenomena of
> nature, yet so that they are also bifid, viz.:

---

10. The sentence echoes Humboldt's pronouncement in Section 9 of the "Kawi Introduction": "Just
as thought, like a lightning-flash or concussion, collects the whole power of ideation into a single point,
and shuts out everything else, so sound rings out with abrupt sharpness and unity" (*On Language* 55).
Note, however, that whereas Humboldt merely points out a parallel between thought and speech, Kraitsir
argues for a strict causal connection between the two "unities."

I. 1) CAUSE, *In;*

II. EFFECT, *Out*, which is again either

    2) "moving, living, or

    3) "standing, dead, dormant.

There are three groups of sounds corresponding to these categories.

I. 1) GUTTURals, symbols of cau-se, ge-t, gai-n, ha-ve, cor (see p. 160), etc.

II. 2) LAB-ials, symbols of move-ment, lif-e, ru-n, flo-w, etc.

    3) DENT-als, symbols of death, st-and, dor-mant, sad, etc. (*Glossology* 161)

Kraitsir's schema is, of course, absurdly reductive. Ideas, phenomena, and sounds have been reduced to a triad apiece, just as the triad of ideas, phenomena, and sounds is supposed to represent the universe. Kraitsir's "theory of germs" is little more than a schematic rendering of etymological essentialism, resembling, in its applications, Horne Tooke's *Diversions of Purley*.[11] In arguing for a fixed correspondence among sounds, ideas, and objects, where a word should sound like what it designates or defines, Kraitsir in fact echoes the linguistic mysticism of a Boehme or Swedenborg, so that his Language of Nature is ultimately a version of the language of Adam, a mastering metalanguage. Thus Kraitsir claims that "*the germs of all languages are the same*" and that "the exposition of the mental and organic (both glossic and acoustic) process, by which language has grown from a centre into rays (radii) or specific tongues (idioms, dialects, patois, jargons, lingos, etc.), has been reserved to this work" (147).

If Charles Kraitsir presents an essentially Adamic language theory, clothed in the garb of comparative philology, Thoreau's response to the pronouncements of *Glossology* resembles that of Emerson to Boehme's *Mysterium Magnum* or Swedenborg's *Animal Kingdom*. The famous "sand foliage" passage in *Walden* clearly shows Kraitsir's influence because it emphasizes liquid and guttural sounds.[12] More important than particular borrowings, however, is what Thoreau makes of Kraitsir's theory. The relationship is complicated, for Thoreau does not follow the rigid scheme of Kraitsir's theory of germs. Instead, he reacts deliberately and reservedly, and he fashions his own ideas about the relationships among ideas, phenomena, and articulate sounds:

11. The best introduction to Horne Tooke is Aarsleff, *The Study of Language in England*, 44–114; see *Glossology*, 151–56, for a long example of Tookean etymologizing.

12. For specific instances, see West, "Kraitsir's Influence," 267–70.

The whole bank, which is from twenty to forty feet high, is sometimes overlaid with a mass of this kind of foliage, or sandy rupture, for a quarter of a mile on one or both sides, the produce of one spring day. What makes this sand foliage remarkable is its springing into existence thus suddenly. When I see on the one side the inert bank,—for the sun acts on one side first,—and on the other this luxuriant foliage, the creation of an hour, I am affected as if in a peculiar sense I stood in the laboratory of the Artist who made the world and me,—had come to where he was still at work, sporting on this bank, and with excess of energy strewing his fresh designs about. I feel as if I were nearer to the vitals of the globe, for this sandy overflow is something such a foliaceous mass as the vitals of the animal body. You find thus in the very sands an anticipation of the vegetable leaf. No wonder that the earth expresses itself outwardly in leaves, it so labors with the idea inwardly. The atoms have already learned this law, and are pregnant by it. The overhanging leaf sees here its prototype. *Internally*, whether in the globe or animal body, it is a moist thick *lobe*, a word especially applicable to the liver and lungs and the *leaves* of fat, (*laibo, labor, lapsus*, to flow or slip downward, a lapsing; *lobos, globus*, lobe, globe; also lap, flap, and many other words;) *externally* a dry thin *leaf*, even as the *f* and v are a pressed and dried *b*. The radicals of lobe are *lb*, the soft mass of the *b* (single lobed, or B, double lobed,) with a liquid *l* behind it pressing it forward. In globe, *glb*, the guttural *g* adds to the meaning the capacity of the throat. The feathers and wings of birds are still drier and thinner leaves. Thus, also, you pass from the lumpish grub in the earth to the airy and fluttering butterfly. The very globe continually transcends and translates itself, and becomes winged in its orbit. Even ice begins with delicate crystal leaves, as if it had flowed into moulds which the fronds of water plants have impressed on the watery mirror. The whole tree itself is but one leaf, and rivers are still vaster leaves whose pulp is intervening earth, and towns and cities are the ova of insects in their axils. (306–7)

Kraitsir's distinction between internal and external germs is clearly at work in the long glossological sentence, marked by the italicized "*internally*" and "*externally*." But Thoreau does not strictly follow the scheme from *Glossology*, although he certainly uses it. For Kraitsir, the labials correspond to outer effects of movement or life; while Thoreau retains the idea of labial sounds indicating life and movement, however, he ranges the sounds on the *internal* side. Thus his examples are *lobe, liver, lungs*, and *leaves* of fat. Thoreau opposes the external "dry thin *leaf*" to the internal "moist thick *lobe*," but within Kraitsir's schema both *leaf* and *lobe* derive from labial germs. Thoreau clearly cuts across the rigid distinction between outer and inner germs.

The passage contains a rather subtle pun that further distinguishes Thoreau's ideas about language from Kraitsir's version of transcendental theory. Thoreau says that "in globe, *glb*, the guttural *g* adds to the meaning the capacity of the throat." Within Kraitsir's glossological schema, the gutturals are the most important of the germs because they are formed by the throat, "the hindmost, internal, hidden, vertical, most complicated, most compact . . . of the organs of speech" (165). At first we might think that Thoreau is being as vague as Kraitsir, for it is impossible to say what the "guttural *g* adds to the meaning." But Thoreau has his philological tongue in his cheek. The word *capacity* means an "ability to do something, a faculty or aptitude" (*American Heritage Dictionary*), and the emphasis on the throat as an organ of speech calls upon that meaning as we read the passage. But *capacity* also means "the ability to receive, hold, or absorb," perhaps the last meaning we might consider in connection with articulated sounds. In relation to the word *globe*, however, this second sense of *capacity* is signally appropriate, forging a figural connection between the world and the word. Thoreau appears, then, to be playing upon the active and passive meanings of *capacity*, confusing the two in much the same way that he confuses Kraitsir's specious distinction between internal and external germs.

Thoreau uses Kraitsir's glossological theory in order to blur the boundaries between assumed opposites. In this way he can, as he says/writes earlier in the passage, come "nearer to the vitals of the globe," for the distinctions between such things as inside and outside, vegetable and mineral, animate and inanimate, and, ultimately, the writer and the world, break down through a consideration of language. Yet Thoreau retains his perspective, seeing clearly that language is the mediating power for making distinctions in the first place. Even in undermining Kraitsir's pedantic, harebrained theory, Thoreau remains faithful to the initial insight that underlies the theory—that "speech, issuing from the spirit, reacts also upon it" (25).

The other major influence on Thoreau in the "sand foliage" passage is certainly Emerson. When Thoreau says he feels as if he were "nearer to the vitals of the globe," he echoes Emerson's assertion that the poet "names the thing because he sees it, or comes one step nearer to it than any other" ("The Poet," 12). More important, Thoreau's focus on the continual, dynamic flux of natural forms recalls Emerson's similar concern for metamorphosis, first announced in the sentence I have just quoted. And Thoreau is like Emerson (and Kraitsir) in giving that dynamic flux an evolutionary, developmental interpretation. "Thus," he says, "you pass from the lumpish grub in the earth to the airy and flutter-ing butterfly. The very globe continually transcends and translates itself, and becomes winged in its orbit."

Thoreau exploits both Emerson and Kraitsir by breaking down the bound-ary between Emerson's visual principle of language and Kraitsir's glossological one. In the sand foliage passage, Thoreau mixes sight and sound to create his own principle of language, a principle that stresses both the limits of words and the need to stretch—even break—those limits. The first part of the passage emphasizes sight: Thoreau first "see[s] on the one side the inert bank," then "on the other this luxuriant foliage." Later he writes that the "Artist" of the world is continually making "fresh designs," another visual image. But as the writer moves *nearer* to the "excess of energy" in the scene, he moves toward sound: the words "globe," "leaf," "leaves," and "labors" appear for the first time, and those words become central in the glossological section of the passage.

No easy boundary marks the end of sight and the beginning of sound. The sentence "The overhanging leaf sees here its prototype," for instance, combines the two sides of the opposition. After that sentence, Thoreau employs a great deal of sound—a luxury of liquid, lobed labials. But there is also an accompa-nying luxury of visual images: the "dry thin leaf" becomes "drier and thinner" in the visual form of "feathers and wings"; the "delicate crystal leaves" appear in the surface of the pond, a "watery mirror." Finally, the last sentence of the paragraph repeats the words "leaf" and "leaves," but the comparison is based on the visual image of rivers as the stems or spines of gigantic leaves.

As in the closing paragraphs of *A Week*, Thoreau persistently crosses bound-aries in order to evoke a principle of dynamic reciprocity. Immediately after the sand foliage paragraph, Thoreau asserts that "it seemed that this one hillside illustrated the principle of all the operations of Nature" (308). As in the clos-ing movement of *A Week*, that principle is the dynamic, shifting character of figuration itself, where the figure, like the sand, "organizes itself," only to be metamorphosed into yet another figure. Hence a figure of sight becomes a fig-ure of sound; a figure of sand becomes a figure of foliage; a figure of a lump-ish grub becomes a figure of a fluttering butterfly. Thoreau's principle of dynamic reciprocity stresses the double aspect of analogy or comparison, where either side of the figural relationship can assume mastery at any time.

Figural reciprocity functions not only on the level of style but also, and per-haps more important, on the level of organization. Four consecutive chapters of *Walden* illustrate this point: "Reading" and "Sounds" are paired, as are "Solitude" and "Visitors"; the two pairs are in turn paired, thus repeating the double opposition that I analyzed in the conclusion of *A Week*. In "Reading," the opposition at first appears to be the rather simple one of spoken and written language, and Thoreau's attitude toward the opposed terms appears to privilege written language over speech:

> Books must be read as deliberately and reservedly as they were written. It is not enough even to be able to speak the language of that nation by which they are written, for there is a memorable interval between the spoken and the written language, the language heard and the language read. The one is commonly transitory, a sound, a tongue, a dialect merely, almost brutish, and we learn it unconsciously, like the brutes, of our mothers. The other is the maturity and experience of that; if that is our mother tongue, this is our father tongue, a reserved and select expression, too significant to be heard by the ear, which we must be born again in order to speak. (101)

Here Thoreau seems to repudiate Kraitsir outright, since his esteem for written language aligns him with Emersonian sight rather than the sounds of speech. Indeed, speech is characterized as being akin to brute nature, whereas written language is given the mastering authority of Adamic naming, the "father tongue." But Thoreau's sense of dynamic reciprocity does not allow for such easy privileging of a term. As the passage continues, he asks for the dynamic *marriage* of the mother and father tongues, nature and spirit, for it is only through that marriage that we can be "born again." The echo of John 3:3 ("Except a man be born again, he cannot see the kingdom of God") mixes sight and sound in much the same way as the "sand foliage" passage: in this case, we will not *see* the kingdom of God but instead will *speak* a new, "reserved and select" language.

Thoreau continually strikes a "reserved and select" note concerning the role of the spoken word in effecting social change. In the following passage of "Reading," for instance, he contrasts the orator and the writer in order to limit the power of mere eloquence:

> However much we may admire the orator's occasional bursts of eloquence, the noblest written words are commonly as far behind or above the fleeting spoken language as the firmament with its stars is behind the clouds. *There* are the stars, and they who can may read them. The astronomers forever comment on and observe them. They are not exhalations like our daily colloquies and vaporous breath. What is called eloquence in the forum is commonly found to be rhetoric in the study. The orator yields to the inspiration of a transient occasion, and speaks to the mob before him, to those who can *hear* him; but the writer,

whose more equable life is his occasion, and who would be distracted by
the event and the crowd which inspire the orator, speaks to the intellect
and heart of mankind, to all in any age who can *understand* him. (102)

The distinction between hearing and understanding points toward a parallel
distinction between physical, transient communication and a spiritualized, permanent communication. Thoreau's privileging of the latter type of communication is clear, as is the way in which the figure of the writer approaches the
universal power of Silence, which "is audible to all men, at all times, and in all
places" (*Week* 391). Indeed, we might conclude that Thoreau explicitly favors
the withdrawn, "reserved and select" life of the writer over the mob-ruled,
vaporous profession of the orator. If so, then Thoreau's favoring of that position
entails a parallel withdrawal from society and its fleeting occasions.

Thoreau appears to delight in provoking such facile conclusions, as if he
wishes to make it difficult for us to read as "deliberately and reservedly" as he
writes. Thus the paragraph I have just quoted contains only one word—"*speaks
to the intellect and heart of mankind*"—that suggests a type of reciprocity
between spoken and written language. In the next paragraph of the chapter,
however, Thoreau is more open with his crossings of boundaries, calling the
written word "the work of art nearest to life itself" because it can "not only be
read but actually breathed from all human lips" (102). Moreover, the chapter
concludes with Thoreau's extended critique of education in American culture.
By calling for "uncommon schools" to replace the "half-starved Lyceum" and
"puny beginning of a library," Thoreau calls for the reform of both speech and
writing (108). The seemingly aloof and reserved writer concludes the chapter
by asserting that "to act collectively is according to the spirit of our institutions" and that "instead of noblemen, let us have noble villages of men" (110).
Reciprocity functions in both cases: speech and writing are reciprocal terms,
as are the villages and the writer. Ultimately, a dynamic reciprocity relates
Thoreau's theory of language to his ideas concerning cultural reform. The
"equable life" of the writer balances opposed terms, and while on occasion this
vision of the writer can seem oppressively elitist, the dynamics of reciprocity
prevent any static hierarchy from reigning for long.

Thoreau's dynamic rhetoric of reciprocity is especially telling in "Visitors,"
for he connects the spatial figure of proximity and distance to the opposition
between speech and silence:

> Individuals, like nations, must have suitable broad and natural bound-
> aries, even a considerable neutral ground, between them. I have found
> it a singular luxury to talk across the pond to a companion on the oppo-

site side. In my house we were so near that we could not begin to hear,—we could not speak low enough to be heard; as when you throw two stones into calm water so near that they break each other's undulations. If we are merely loquacious and loud talkers, then we can afford to stand very near together, cheek by jowl, and feel each other's breath; but if we speak reservedly and thoughtfully, we want to be farther apart, that all animal heat and moisture may have a chance to evaporate. If we would enjoy the most intimate society with that in each of us which is without, or above, being spoken to, we must not only be silent, but commonly so far apart bodily that we cannot possibly hear each other's voice in any case. Referred to this standard, speech is for the convenience of those who are hard of hearing; but there are many fine things which we cannot say if we have to shout. (141)

Characteristically, the passage points toward an absolute standard against which the ordinary event or action is to be judged. In this case, "that in each of us which is without, or above, being spoken to" is the measure of conversation. It nearly goes without saying that the ordinary event or action will always be found wanting, but Thoreau's tendency to make absolute and withering commentaries is matched by his tendency to undercut the absolute quality of the standard. In this passage, for example, absolute silence is undercut by the figure of physical distance, which represents a silence impossible to break: "If we would enjoy the most intimate society with that in each of us which is without, or above, being spoken to, we must not only be silent, but commonly so far apart bodily that we cannot possibly hear each other's voice in any case." The hyperbole of the sentence joins with the paradox of a "most intimate society" based on absolute separation, but the extravagant gestures in fact point toward a "neutral ground," from which we can "speak reservedly and thoughtfully." The echo of "Reading" suggests that the neutral ground is necessary for the reform of both language and culture: only by positioning ourselves on such neutral territory can we combine speech and silence, society and solitude, in a dynamic drama of reciprocity.

The unsurprising conclusion to draw, at this point, is that *Walden* forms exactly that neutral ground. Ostensibly privileging a solitary, silent, distant life and language, Thoreau creates a style that moves in the opposite direction, pointing toward a reformed and reforming social discourse. Of course, *Walden* does not create that new discourse, for that is as unattainable an ideal as absolute silence. But Thoreau's desire for such a mastering speech is clear, perhaps most clear in the "Conclusion":

> I desire to speak somewhere *without* bounds; like a man in a waking
> moment, to men in their waking moments; for I am convinced that I
> cannot exaggerate enough even to lay the foundation of a true expres-
> sion. Who that has heard a strain of music feared then lest he should
> speak extravagantly anymore forever? In view of the future or possible,
> we should live quite laxly and undefined in front, our outlines dim and
> misty on that side; as our shadows reveal an insensible perspiration
> toward the sun. The volatile truth of our words should continually betray
> the inadequacy of the residual statement. Their truth is instantly *trans-
> lated*; its literal monument alone remains. The words which express our
> faith and piety are not definite; yet they are significant and fragrant like
> frankincense to superior natures. (324–25)

The central pun in the passage recalls Thoreau's statement in the sand foliage
paragraph—"the very globe continually transcends and translates itself." In his
pun, truth becomes the translated soul, while the words remain behind as "literal monuments"—gravestones or corpses. "In view of the future or possible,"
then, the individual and corporate spirit would evolve beyond the limiting
bounds of language. Thoreau's dynamic ideal is that the truth should become
so volatile that the words used to express that truth would become merely
"residual" and that the speaker, like a Wendell Phillips, would deliver an eloquence that is "not eloquence . . . not oratory." Once again, however, Thoreau's
insistence creates an extravagant, hyperbolic paradox, for his practice is rather
to make his *words* so volatile that they do not remain within the bounds of conventional literary expectations. Thoreau's words occupy a neutral ground, creating figures of essential eloquence, "like a man in a waking moment" speaking
"to men in their waking moments."

   Although formalist arguments provide certain satisfactions, they do not sat-
isfactorily answer Thoreau's call for an eloquence that would speak "without
bounds," for they effectively mark a textual boundary as the point beyond
which discourse cannot go. If we take Thoreau seriously, the boundary between
the text and its potential audiences cannot remain so hard and fast. An alter-
native reading would interpret the neutral ground as a *cultural* space. The boundary between the literary text and other discursive forms could be more
permeable than formalist interpretations would allow. *Walden*, while it is surely
an aesthetic discourse, is also a social discourse.

3

A cultural space constituted as a scene of reciprocal oppositions would necessarily reform the conceptions of its inhabitants. That is precisely what Thoreau
aims at creating by employing the dynamic rhetoric of reciprocity. In his own
work, this cultural space or neutral ground is most apparent in the *Reform Papers*,
so called because they do not fit any strictly formal category such as essay, lecture, or address. The "papers" create a space between the spoken and the written, and in doing so they create a space between the text and nineteenth-
century American culture. Throughout the papers Thoreau maintains the view
that language can effect reform in any area of culture. This view accords with
the dynamic theories of Emerson, Humboldt, and Kraitsir, and it enables
Thoreau to create a discourse "without bounds."

Two papers prompt an analysis of Thoreau's neutral ground—"Resistance
to Civil Government," first published in Elizabeth Peabody's *Aesthetic Papers* in
1849, and "Reform and Reformers," unpublished lecture material that was first
edited and presented in the 1973 edition of *Reform Papers*.[13] Paired with
Thoreau's lecture-essay, the title of Peabody's volume suggests the kind of broad
definition of *aesthetic* that I have argued is appropriate to *Walden*. In an introduction called "The Word 'Aesthetic,'" Peabody asserts that the term signifies
"neither a theory of the beautiful, nor a philosophy of art, but a component
and indivisible part in all human creations which are not mere works of necessity; in other words, which are based on idea, as distinguished from appetite."[14]
The aesthetic becomes subsumed within a dynamic idealism, one that can touch
on any aspect of "human creations," a synonym for culture.

Thoreau's famous paper occupies a neutral ground in several ways. In the
"extracts . . . inserted since the Lecture was read," for example, Thoreau takes a
writer's advantage of the lecturer:

> No man with a genius for legislation has appeared in America. They are
> rare in the history of the world. There are orators, politicians, and elo-
> quent men, by the thousand; but the speaker has not yet opened his
> mouth to speak, who is capable of settling the much-vexed questions

---

13. My citations refer to the edition of the two papers in *Reform Papers* and appear parenthetically
in my text. The publication history of the two can be read in the same volume, 313–21 and 379–88.
The material of "Reform and Reformers" dates from the same period as the composition of *A Week*
(381); on 10 March 1844 Thoreau delivered a lecture "Reformers" in Boston (Fink, *Prophet*, 127–28).

14. Elizabeth P. Peabody, ed., *Aesthetic Papers* (Boston, 1849), 1. The volume is available in a relatively
old reprint, ed. Joseph Jones (Gainesville: Scholars' Facsimiles and Reprints, 1957).

of the day. We love eloquence for its own sake, and not for any truth which it may utter, or any heroism it may inspire. Our legislators have not yet learned the comparative value of free-trade and of freedom, of union, and of rectitude, to a nation. They have no genius or talent for comparatively humble questions of taxation and finance, commerce and manufactures and agriculture. If we were left solely to the wordy wit of legislators in Congress for our guidance, uncorrected by the seasonable experience and the effectual complaints of the people, America would not long retain her rank among the nations. For eighteen hundred years, though perchance I have no right to say it, the New Testament has been written; yet where is the legislator who has wisdom and practical talent enough to avail himself of the light which it sheds on the science of legislation? (*Reform Papers* 88–89)

This passage launches a general critique of American culture on the eve of the 1848 elections, including such diverse human creations as taxation, "free-trade," and agriculture along with the more pointed triad of "freedom . . . union . . . rectitude." The true "genius for legislation" would transform the "wordy wit of legislators in Congress" into a divine speech, relating human law to Scripture and inspiring its hearers to heroic acts of truth, whether word or deed. Thoreau's jeremiad calls for a reform of American culture, in all of its aspects, by reforming the language of American lawmakers. We can therefore hear an echo of Emerson's peroration to "The Poet": "I look in vain for the poet whom I describe." Thoreau does not seek an Emersonian genius of "tyrannous eye"; rather, he projects the figure of "the legislator who has wisdom and practical talent," for this figure can stand on a neutral ground joining divine and human laws. Both are, nonetheless, figures of eloquence, even though Thoreau's legislator wields decidedly less power than Emerson's poet-orator.[15]

The disdainful tone of "Resistance to Civil Government" also imbues the manuscript fragments published as "Reform and Reformers," which are roughly contemporaneous with the "aesthetic paper."[16] So a sentence such as "Reform keeps many scores of newspapers in its service, but not one man" (75) could just as easily appear in "Reform and Reformers" as in "Resistance

---

15. For an excellent discussion of "Resistance" and the reform "papers" of the 1850s, see Stephen Adams and Donald Ross, Jr., *Revising Mythologies: The Composition of Thoreau's Major Works* (Charlottesville: University Press of Virginia, 1988), 215–39.

16. The paper in Houghton Folder 18B marks the material as contemporaneous with the publication of *A Week*, and sections of 18B also appear in the "Economy" chapter of *Walden* (*Reform Papers*, 380–81).

to Civil Government." In both papers, Thoreau calls for a figure of eloquence to embody the truth he espouses. In the manuscript lecture, for instance, Thoreau asserts that "the Reformer who comes recommending any institution or system to the adoption of men, must not rely solely on logic and argument, or on eloquence and oratory for his success, but see that he represents one pretty perfect institution in himself, the centre and circumference of all others, an erect man" (184). Thoreau expresses disdain for "barren words," as opposed to those that are "cousin to a deed" (185), and his remedy for such barren fluency is similar to that proposed in *A Week*: "If you have nothing to say let me have your silence, for that is good and fertile. Silence is the ambrosial night in the intercourse of men in which their sincerity is recruited and takes deeper root.—There are such vices as frivolity, garrulity, and verbosity, not to mention prophanity, growing out of the abuse of speech which does not belong wholly to antiquity, and none have imparted a more cheerless aspect to society" (190). The agricultural imagery of the passage blends with a deepened moral perspective, for Thoreau calls for sincerity to take "deeper root" in the language of nineteenth-century reformers. Thus the manuscript actually calls for the reform of reformers and, most especially, of their language. Just as silence can make the speaker more sincere—we might say, with *Walden* in mind, more "deliberate and reserved"—so the silence of the audience can cause the speaker to deepen his speech: "It is hard to make those who have talked much, especially preachers and lecturers, deepen their speech, and give it fresh sincerity and significance. It will be a long time before they understand what you mean. They will wonder if you don't value fluency. But the drains flow. Turn your back, and wait till you hear their words ring solid, and they will have cause to thank you!" (193). The humor of the passage depends upon a certain scatological undercurrent, but it makes the serious point that true reform depends upon a true exchange between speaker and listener. Only when the speaker's words correspond to the listener's sense of truth will they "ring solid," and it is for that reason that "it will be a long time before they understand what you mean." The speaker, in other words, must listen, for only through that reciprocal action can the word become cousin to a deeply significant deed.

It is abundantly clear that Thoreau demands a deliberate reform of nineteenth-century American culture by deliberately deepening the discourses of that culture. Equally clear, however, is the near impossibility of meeting the extremity of Thoreau's demand. In the papers of the 1850s, we see the difficulty of Thoreau's ideal eloquence, and we once again see his need for a concrete, flesh-and-blood avatar of the ideal.

Already in early work such as the 1840 essay "The Service," Thoreau associates the figure of the hero with a heightened language: "The brave man is the sole patron of music; he recognizes it for his mother tongue; a more mellifluous and articulate language than words, in comparison with which, speech is recent and temporary. It is his voice. His language must have the same majestic movement and cadence, that philosophy assigns to the heavenly bodies" (*Reform Papers* 9). In the 12 March 1845 "letter" to *The Liberator*, as we have seen, Thoreau praises Wendell Phillips for giving his Concord audience "the pleasure of great intellectual power and acuteness, of soldier-like steadiness, and of a graceful and natural oratory. . . . It is so rare and encouraging to listen to an orator, who is content with another alliance than with the popular party, or even with the sympathising school of the martyrs, who can afford sometimes to be his own auditor if the mob stay away, and hears himself without reproof, that we feel ourselves in danger of slandering all mankind by affirming, that here is one, who is at the same time an eloquent speaker and a righteous man" (61). In the portraits of the brave man and eloquent speaker, Thoreau consistently places the ideal figure and his language in opposition to the "mob" and its "recent and temporary" words.

Four antislavery papers—"Slavery in Massachusetts" (1854) and the three pieces on John Brown (1859–60)—reveal Thoreau's attempts at creating a new cultural discourse that would reform such discursive institutions as the government, the church, and the press. But in directly confronting a crucial social issue of the day, Thoreau creates not a deepening, morally reforming discourse, but silence; not a neutral ground, but a chasm of polarization.

In large measure, the problem with the antislavery papers is their lack of aloofness. It is as if the deliberate, reserved stance of *Walden* cannot accommodate Thoreau's moral outrage, and he therefore abandons the equability and reciprocity that mark the earlier work. In "Slavery in Massachusetts," for example, Thoreau's hyperbolic rhetoric is so forceful and direct that it admits of no humor. The newspaper becomes "a Bible which every man carries in his pocket, which lies on every table and counter, and which the mail, and thousands of missionaries, are continually dispensing. It is, in short, the only book which America has printed, and which America reads" (100). Any potential audience would be hard pressed to respond sympathetically to such rhetorical aggression, especially when the writer says of newspaper readers, "the people who read them are in the condition of the dog that returns to his vomit" (100).

Thoreau's polarizing rhetoric is equally apparent in this account of the judiciary, which he holds responsible for upholding the Fugitive Slave Act:

> Among human beings, the judge whose words seal the fate of a man
> furthest into eternity, is not he who merely pronounces the verdict of
> the law, but he, whoever he may be, who, from a love of truth, and
> unprejudiced by any custom or enactment of men, utters a true opin-
> ion or *sentence* concerning him. He it is that *sentences* him. Whoever has
> discerned truth, has received his commission from a higher source than
> the chiefest justice in the world, who can discern only law. He finds
> himself constituted judge of the judge.—Strange that it should be nec-
> essary to state such simple truths. (98)

Once again Thoreau creates the figure of essential eloquence, a "judge of the
judge" who can speak the truth and thereby "*sentence*" any man eternally.
Thoreau himself assumes that role in the paragraph, since he is stating "simple
truths" concerning the judges of Massachusetts. But this high moral ground
cannot be neutral. Thus Thoreau develops such polarizing disjunctions as country versus city, principle versus expediency, and individual truth versus consti-
tutional law. The rhetoric insistently privileges the first term in each of these
oppositions, and Thoreau does not allow for the kinds of complex, dynamic
reversals of privilege that mark his deepest work. The final image in the paper,
that of the white water lily, points to the most disturbing polarization of all.
Nature and culture are utterly divorced from each other, although Thoreau
implies that cultural reform can bring us closer to the purity of nature: "If
Nature can compound this fragrange still annually, I shall believe her still young
and full of vigor, her integrity and genius unimpaired, and that there is virtue
even in man, too, who is fitted to perceive and love it" (108).

Thoreau's shift in rhetorical strategy is more radical in the three papers on
John Brown, all of which are in fact lectures or addresses. Predictably, Brown
becomes the figure of eloquence, standing in opposition to the institutionalized
words of government and the press. In "A Plea for Captain John Brown," Thoreau
attempts heroically to convert the fanatic into a moderate man of principle:

> A man of rare common sense and directness of speech, as of action; a
> transcendentalist above all, a man of ideas and principles,—that was what
> distinguished him. Not yielding to a whim or transient impulse, but car-
> rying out the purpose of a life. I noticed that he did not overstate any
> thing, but spoke within bounds. I remember, particularly, how, in his
> speech here, he referred to what his family had suffered in Kansas, with-
> out ever giving the least vent to his pent-up fire. It was a volcano with
> an ordinary chimney-flue. Also referring to the deeds of certain Border

Ruffians, he said, rapidly paring away his speech, like an experienced soldier, keeping a reserve of force and meaning, "They had a perfect right to be hung." He was not in the least a rhetorician, was not talking to Buncombe or his constituents any where, had no need to invent any thing, but to tell the simple truth, and communicate his own resolution; therefore he appeared incomparably strong, and eloquence in Congress and elsewhere seemed to me at a discount. It was like the speeches of Cromwell compared with those of an ordinary king. (115)

Here the heroically eloquent but reserved John Brown does not need to exaggerate at all in order to convey the "simple truth" of his principles. In Thoreau's representation, such restraint creates the most effective eloquence: by speaking "within bounds," Brown becomes "a volcano with an ordinary chimney-flue." The restraint, compared to that of "an experienced soldier," is directly contrasted to the wasteful rhetoric of politicians, who talk "to Buncombe" or "constituents" and thereby weaken both their words and their principles.[17] Finally, by comparing Brown's words to "the speeches of Cromwell," Thoreau gives his heroic figure historical depth, implying that Brown stems from a tradition of divinely inspired revolutionaries.

This is the most strategic passage in the "Plea," but in other passages Thoreau loses control of the tone. For instance, he abandons the rhetoric of deliberate restraint by comparing Brown's words to "the manuscript of the New Testament" and contrasting them to "the *cackling* of political conventions" (122). Rather than creating a neutral ground from which to argue for Brown, Thoreau places his hero beyond the reach of his audience: "No, he was not our representative in any sense. He was too fair a specimen of a man to represent the like of us. Who, then, *were* his constituents? If you read his words understandingly you will find out. In his case there is no idle eloquence, no made, nor maiden speech, no compliments to the oppressor. Truth is his inspirer, and earnestness the polisher of his sentences. He could afford to lose his Sharps' rifles, while he retained his faculty of speech, a Sharps' rifle of infinitely surer and longer range" (127). Thoreau's plea to his listeners/readers to read Brown's words "understandingly" recalls the passage in "Reading" in which he contrasts the orator and the writer: "The orator yields to the inspiration of a transient

17. The word "Buncombe" is now usually spelled "bunkum" and is defined as "empty or meaningless talk, especially by a politician; claptrap" (*American Heritage Dictionary*). The word derives from Buncombe County, North Carolina; in 1820, U. S. Congressman Felix Walker made a fatuous speech, calling it "a speech for Buncombe" (*AHD*).

occasion, and speaks to the mob before him, to those who can *hear* him; but the writer, whose more equable life is his occasion, and who would be distracted by the event and the crowd which inspire the orator, speaks to the intellect and heart of mankind, to all in any age who can *understand* him" (*Walden* 102). In both passages, the privileged figure of truth awaits a fit audience, and Thoreau's purpose is clearly to goad the reader into becoming part of that audience. But in the "Plea" this purpose is clouded by moral outrage, and Thoreau attacks his listeners/readers belligerently. The attack is mitigated somewhat by Thoreau's inclusion of himself among "the like of us" who fall so far below John Brown. But the belligerence is palpable, especially in the image of Brown's "faculty of speech" as "a Sharps' rifle of infinitely surer and longer range." The image contrasts the spiritual weapon of language and truth to the merely material weapon used in guerilla raids, but this mechanistic, aggressive figure differs sharply from the figures of eloquence that we have seen in earlier work. Compare Brown to the figure of the orator in *A Week*, for example: the latter "listens while he speaks, and is a hearer along with his audience," but Brown (and, for that matter, Thoreau) is so sure of his truth that he is no longer responding to his audience.

In "Reading," Thoreau creates the dynamic rhetoric of reciprocity by balancing opposed terms, so that the dynamics of reciprocity prevent any static privileging of a set of terms. In the John Brown papers, by contrast, Thoreau is so intent upon counteracting the newspaper accounts and assessments of Brown's raid, arrest, and trial that his language becomes, quite simply, one-sided. Thus, for example, he quotes the journals and Brown in one paragraph, but to a polarizing effect: "'Misguided'! 'Garrulous'! 'Insane'! 'Vindictive'! So ye write in your easy chairs, and thus he wounded responds from the floor of the Armory, clear as a cloudless sky, true as the voice of nature is: 'No man sent me here; it was my own prompting and that of my Maker. I acknowledge no master in human form.'" (137) If Brown's "voice of nature" announces the essential authority of the Adamic speaker, it also isolates the speaker from any human audience. By juxtaposing the strident adjectives of the newspapers to Brown's calm, clear voice of authority, Thoreau wishes to indict the newspapers as being themselves misguided, garrulous, insane, and vindictive. But the deeper effect of the paragraph is more disturbing. It creates two sets of voices—one of culture and one of nature—which cannot speak to one another. The neutral ground that might join the two becomes a chasm dividing them.

The gulf between nature and culture is already apparent in the journal entries that become the material of both the "Plea" and "The Last Days of John Brown." In the long entries from 19 October 1859, when he first heard of

Brown's arrest, to his delivery of the "Plea" in Concord on 30 October Thoreau juxtaposes notes on natural history with reactions, newspaper accounts, and lecture drafts.[18] It is as if Thoreau is unable to perceive any connection between the two realms. In one particularly interesting example, a word seems to prompt Thoreau's mind to cross the gulf:

> It is very cold and blustering to-day. It is the breath of winter, which is encamped not far off to the north.
>
> A great many shrub oak acorns hold on, and are a darker brown than ever.
>
> Insane! A father and seven sons, and several more men besides,—as many, at least, as twelve disciples,—all struck with insanity at once. . . .
> (12:411)

Here "brown" takes the journal-writer from nature to contemporary culture, but the gap between the two remains. That Thoreau himself perceived a danger in such divisions becomes clear in the 22 October entry to the *Journal*: "I do not think it is sane to spend one's whole life talking or writing about this matter, and I have not done so. A man may have other affairs to attend to" (12:430).

Among the "other affairs" Thoreau attended to in his last years is the pair of lectures "Life Without Principle" and "Walking." The latter began with journal entries in January-March 1851, became at least two lectures through 1857, was revised in 1861, and finally appeared in the *Atlantic Monthly* in 1862. The former was first delivered on 26 December 1854, under the title "Getting a Living," and Thoreau delivered it six more times over the following five years, making it his most frequently delivered lecture.[19] Among Thoreau's late works, then, the two lectures usefully summarize the final decade. More important, they show that the problem of nature and culture, which effectively prevents

18. *The Journal of Henry David Thoreau*, ed. Bradford Torrey and Francis H. Allen (Boston: Houghton Mifflin, 1906), 12:400–440.

19. See Adams and Ross, *Revising Mythologies*, 261–62, for a chronology, and 143–55 for a discussion of the stages the lecture/essay "Walking" passed through during its eleven-year development. "Life Without Principle," first published in the October 1863 issue of *Atlantic Monthly*, appears in *Reform Papers*; for the account of its delivery as a lecture, see *Reform Papers*, 369. Quotations from "Walking" refer to the *Atlantic Monthly* text; quotations from "Life Without Principle" refer to the modern edition. For useful background on Thoreau's lecturing, see Walter Harding, "Thoreau on the Lecture Platform," *New England Quarterly* 24 (1951): 365–74; for a thorough scholarly account of Thoreau's lecture manuscripts, see William L. Howarth, "Successor to *Walden*? Thoreau's 'Moonlight—An Intended Course of Lectures,'" *Proof: The Yearbook of American Bibliographical and Textual Studies* 2 (1972): 89–115.

Thoreau from creating a neutral ground of eloquence in the John Brown papers, is capable of being solved by more indirect means. After *Walden*, the two lectures are Thoreau's most effective gestures toward the dynamic neutral ground of eloquence.

Thoreau begins both lectures by expressing his abiding concern for language, his desire to create an eloquence that goes beyond mere words. In "Life Without Principle," the lyceum sets the stage for a drama of self-referentiality: "At a lyceum, not long since, I felt that the lecturer had chosen a theme too foreign to himself, and so failed to interest me as much as he might have done. He described things not in or near to his heart, but toward his extremities and superficies. There was, in this sense, no truly central or centralizing thought in the lecture. I would have had him deal with his privatest experience, as the poet does. The greatest compliment that was ever paid me was when one asked me what *I thought*, and attended to my answer" (*Reform Papers* 155). By placing himself in the audience, Thoreau formulates the ideal auditor's demanding requirement—the "central or centralizing thought." By meeting that demand, the lecturer acts "as the poet does," delivering his "privatest experience" to his listeners. In demanding the "privatest" in a public forum, Thoreau recalls Emerson's tantalizing picture of eloquence in "The American Scholar": "He learns that he who has mastered any law in his private thoughts, is master to that extent of all men whose language he speaks" (*NAL* 63). Thoreau also echoes Emerson in suggesting the power of a "centralizing thought" expressed in public address. The opening of "Life Without Principle" thus suggests the ideal figure of eloquence lurking beneath the actual lecturer's failures.

Thoreau quickly seizes the podium for himself, naming his conditions of speech:

> A man once came a considerable distance to ask me to lecture on Slavery; but on conversing with him, I found that he and his clique expected seven-eighths of the lecture to be theirs, and only one-eighth mine; so I declined. I take it for granted, when I am invited to lecture anywhere,—for I have had a little experience in that business,—that there is a desire to hear what *I think* on some subject, though I may be the greatest fool in the country,—and not that I should say pleasant things merely, or such as the audience will assent to; and I resolve, accordingly, that I will give them a strong dose of myself. (155)

The most intriguing echo, in this passage, occurs in the last clause. Thoreau's "strong dose of myself" recalls the reaction to Wendell Phillips: "'That's a severe dose' says another" (*Journal* 2:123). It also accords with the image of Phillips in the letter to the *Liberator*, in which Thoreau praises the "clear and candid declaration of opinion served like an electuary to whet and clarify the intellect of all parties" (*Reform Papers* 62). In all three texts, Thoreau presents eloquence as a strong, even if distasteful, medicine.

Thoreau's "centralizing thought" is closely allied to one of the main lines of argument in *Walden*: "Let us consider the way in which we spend our lives" (*Reform Papers* 156). Nor would I argue that eloquence is the "real" thought underlying this clear formulation. But it is nonetheless true that one of the central thoughts in "Life Without Principle" is the need to reform a debased social discourse and, thereby, to re-form an effective relationship between speaker and audience. So, for instance, Thoreau good-humoredly notes that some lyceums "have voted to exclude the subject of religion" and that "I have walked into such an arena and done my best to make a clean breast of what religion I have experienced, and the audience never suspected what I was about. The lecture was as harmless as moonshine to them" (168). But the humor does have an edge: Thoreau details the "hollow and ineffectual" quality of "our ordinary conversation" as evidence for the absence of an "inward and private" life (169). Similarly, newspapers are evidence of "the stalest repetition" (170), and the mind is constantly assailed by "the profane and stale revelation of the bar-room and the police court" (172). By contrast, Thoreau seeks to hear "inspiration, that gossip which comes to the ear of the attentive mind from the courts of heaven. . . . The same ear is fitted to receive both communications" (172).

For Thoreau as for Emerson, the reform of social discourse runs parallel to the reform of culture. As "Life Without Principle" proceeds, the tone never becomes strident, but Thoreau clearly delivers a jeremiad on the state of America as "the arena on which the battle of freedom is to be fought; but surely it cannot be freedom in a merely political sense that is meant" (174). Thoreau seeks to free himself and his listeners from the tyranny of debased social discourse, especially as it reveals itself in political parties and newspapers. "The newspapers are the ruling power," he admits, and such horrors as "politics and the daily routine" serve "vital functions of human society" (178). But he ends the lecture with a final "dose of himself." He diagnoses politics as "the gizzard of society" and finds a pervasive "dyspepsia": "Not only individuals, but States, have thus a confirmed dyspepsia, which expresses itself, you can imagine by what sort of eloquence" (179). Naming the illness and deftly alluding to the noxious symptom, Thoreau both humorously and seriously calls for his audience to imagine a different sort of eloquence, one that would express the inner, private state and lead to a community of "*eu*peptics" (179).

"Walking" can be seen as an extension of the "centralizing thought" of "Life Without Principle." When Thoreau says/writes, "I wish to speak a word for Nature, for absolute freedom and wildness, as contrasted with a freedom and culture merely civil" (657), the boundary between nature and culture is no more absolute than that between speech and writing or lecture and essay—such oppositions are placed within the frame of dynamic action evoked, in the title, by the present participle "walking." Thoreau's strategy is to show the active, reciprocal relationship between the opposed terms of his discourse. Moreover, his "wish to make an extreme statement" embodies his desire, expressed in the conclusion of *Walden*, to "speak without bounds."

The connection of cultural reform to Thoreau's ideas about language is implied by the frequency of his references to etymology, names, and grammar. In the second paragraph of the lecture, for instance, Thoreau focuses on the origins of the word *sauntering*, proposing "Sainte Terre" and "sans terre" as allied derivations. The first etymology emphasizes the holy dimension of walking or sauntering, while the second evokes "having no particular home, but equally at home everywhere" (657). The two etymologies, more poetic than scientific, combine to figure Thoreau's "absolute freedom and wildness" as an active quest for a spiritual home. Later in the lecture, Thoreau provides a counterexample, giving a complex of Latin cognates for the word *village* and summarizing his fanciful derivations in two sentences: "This suggests what kind of degeneracy villagers are liable to. They are wayworn by the travel that goes by and over them, without traveling themselves" (660).

Poetic etymologizing is the perfect technique to represent Thoreau's search for an original, primal relationship between culture and nature. For this reason he can wander into a discussion of names, since the apparent digression accords with his search for the wild origins of human culture: "We have a wild savage in us, and a savage name is perchance somewhere recorded as ours. I see that my neighbor, who bears the familiar epithet William, or Edwin, takes it off with his jacket. It does not adhere to him when asleep or in anger, or aroused by any passion or inspiration. I seem to hear pronounced by some of his kin at such a time his original wild name in some jaw-breaking or else melodious tongue" (670).

Thoreau's search for linguistic origins is directly connected to his desire to deepen his contemporary culture, in word and deed. Thus he can lament our ungrateful attitude toward "this vast, savage, howling mother of ours, Nature, lying all around, with such beauty, and such affection for her children, as the leopard," for he prefers "a culture which imports much muck from the meadows, and deepens the soil" (670). A deeper, truer language becomes the means of establishing a deeper, truer relationship between the human and the natural:

"There are other letters for the child to learn than those which Cadmus invented. The Spaniards have a good term to express this wild and dusky knowledge, *Gramatica parda*, tawny grammar, a kind of mother-wit derived from that same leopard to which I referred" (670). "Grammar" and "knowledge" function here as synonyms, figuring the union of language and mind in the union of culture and nature—*gramatica parda*. The deepest form of "mother-wit" is derived, then, from the "vast, savage, howling mother of ours, Nature," and the form it takes is "tawny grammar."

To learn such a grammar means, finally, to speak the language of the leopard, and to speak such a language means to diffuse "what we will call Beautiful Knowledge, a knowledge useful in a higher sense" (671). The higher usefulness would enable a deeper, more fundamental reform of antebellum America, one that would make such institutions of public education as Boston's Society for the Diffusion of Useful Knowledge superfluous. By juxtaposing the "*gramatica parda*" to the Society, Thoreau clearly implies that his Language of Nature would transform the very ideas of knowledge, usefulness, diffusion, and society. It would create a new lyceum—a new eloquence. But even though the passage of contrasts closes with the image of a single man sauntering freely, "go[ing] to grass like a horse and leav[ing] all his harness behind in the stable," Thoreau's tawny grammar functions most fundamentally not as a map or set of directions, but as an eloquent call from another country:

> The walker in familiar fields which stretch around my native town sometimes finds himself in another land than is described in their owner's deeds, as it were in some faraway field on the confines of the actual Concord, where her jurisdiction ceases, and the idea which the word Concord suggests ceases to be suggested. These farms which I have myself surveyed, these bounds which I have set up, appear dimly still as through a mist; but they have no chemistry to fix them; they fade from the surface of the glass, and the picture which the painter painted stands out dimly from beneath. The world with which we are commonly acquainted leaves no trace, and it will have no anniversary. (672)

4

Fuller, Peabody, and the Mother Tongue

1

Writing in November 1837, Bronson Alcott gives a tellingly utopian, communitarian description of the Language of Nature, which he associates with "a rural retreat of simple people." Like Emerson, Alcott asserts that "words are things with them," and like both Emerson and Thoreau, Alcott draws a verbal portrait of an eloquent, Adamic orator:

> He reminds me of Shakespeare. He has retained his epithets. Language appears in its simpler, worthier forms. He deals with its staples. Its great words slip from his tongue. The needs of the soul shine in his speech. His vocabulary is not shorn of woods, winds, waters, sky, toil, humanity. It hath a soul in it. Its images are of God's shaping. It deals in the product of nature, and shames art—save when she, like him, is faithful to the uses and ends of nature. I would rather study simple countryman amidst the scenes of nature, as dictionary of my native tongue, than commune with citizen amidst his conventions, or read with professor in college or hall, the tomes of a library. There is life and meaning in it. It is devoid of pretense. It is mother-tongue.[1]

Alcott's figure of eloquence echoes Emerson's *Nature* (1836), just as it forecasts Thoreau's bookish reaction in *Walden*, where speech is "commonly transitory, a sound, a tongue, a dialect merely, almost brutish, and we learn it unconsciously, like the brutes, of our mothers" (101). More important than these reverberations is Alcott's concern with the *study* of language, for he was one of the most

---

1. Bronson Alcott, *The Journals of Bronson Alcott*, ed. Odell Shepard (Boston: Little, Brown, 1938), 95.

innovative and daring educators in antebellum America. By November 1837, Alcott could well pine for the innocence of a rural retreat: his *Conversations on the Gospels*, published earlier that same year, had raised a storm of conservative protest in Boston and eventually caused his Temple School to close.[2] Alcott could also regret the loss of his two able assistants during the three years he had run the school: first Elizabeth Peabody had left in 1836; then, in the spring of 1837, Margaret Fuller had resigned, pleading ill health.[3] Alcott would manage to keep his extreme version of transcendentalism alive for another fifty years, but the most effective legacy of his "conversations" descends to Fuller, Peabody, and their search for a "mother-tongue."

The cultural position of literary women in antebellum America has been delineated in a host of works in the past twenty years, beginning with Ann Douglas's *The Feminization of American Culture*. Current scholars represent the woman writer as a cultural construction, both from the point of view of the authors themselves and from that of the literary marketplace.[4] Much of the valuable work on antebellum women writers focuses on fiction and domesticity, and to a degree scholars rely most heavily on novelists in order to define paradigms of female authorship for the period. Accounts of women poets are less ample, while scholarship regarding the role of women as public speakers is just beginning to appear.[5]

---

2. For a full account of the Temple School and the scandal surrounding *Conversations*, see Frederick C. Dahlstrand, *Amos Bronson Alcott: An Intellectual Biography* (Rutherford: Fairleigh Dickinson University Press, 1982), 109–43. See also Thomas Wentworth Higginson, *Margaret Fuller Ossoli* (Boston: Houghton, Mifflin, 1884), 75–79.

3. Although Fuller quit because Alcott did not pay her, even while packing her bags to take a new job as a teacher in Hiram Fuller's school at Providence, Rhode Island, Fuller defended Alcott's "elevated aim" and admonished Frederic H. Hedge to refrain from "cutting up" Alcott's *Conversations* for the *Christian Examiner* (*The Letters of Margaret Fuller*, ed. Robert Hudspeth, 6 vols. [Ithaca: Cornell University Press, 1983–94], 1:265–67).

4. The scholarly literature is vast, but the catalog of important works would have to include the following: Ann Douglas, *The Feminization of American Culture* (New York: Alfred A. Knopf, 1977); Mary Kelley, *Private Woman, Public Stage: Literary Domesticity in Nineteenth-Century America* (New York: Oxford University Press, 1984); Barbara Welter, *Dimity Convictions: The American Woman in the Nineteenth Century* (Athens: Ohio University Press, 1976); Jane Tompkins, *Sensational Designs: The Cultural Work of American Fiction, 1790–1860* (New York: Oxford University Press, 1985); Nina Baym, *Woman's Fiction: A Guide to Novels by and About Women in America, 1820–1870*, 2d ed. (Urbana: University of Illinois Press, 1993); Baym, *Feminism and American Literary History* (New Brunswick: Rutgers University Press, 1992); Baym, *American Women Writers and the Work of History, 1790–1860* (New Brunswick: Rutgers University Press, 1995); and Richard H. Brodhead, *Cultures of Letters: Scenes of Reading and Writing in Nineteenth-Century America* (Chicago: University of Chicago Press, 1993).

5. For a concise, informative account of antebellum women novelists and poets, see Nina Baym, "The Rise of the Woman Author," in *The Columbia Literary History of the United States*, ed. Emory Elliott (New York: Columbia University Press, 1989), 289–305. For a recent essay on the subject of women

The subtleties of cultural authority regarding women's position as public speakers emerge sharply in Sarah Josepha Hale's 1839 novella *The Lecturess: or Woman's Sphere.*[6] The central conflict of the story is already clear in the title: woman's sphere is domestic and private; the public forum of lecturing is in no way appropriate for women. Hale drives that simple point home repeatedly, both in the plot and in the narrator's comments on the motives, words, and actions of the central character, Marian Gayland Forrester.

The plot follows three narrative arcs that end in marriage, reconciliation of estranged spouses, and death. In each section of the novella, Marian's role as "lecturess" threatens the sanctity of domesticity and the gendered power relations between the public and the private spheres. Hale raises the stakes by having Marian address the "woman question" as her central subject:

> The lecturess made her appearance in the person of a young and lovely woman. Her manner was slightly embarrassed, but easy and graceful. She commenced her address, by a short appeal to her audience. She knew that she was breaking one of the established rules of society, and setting at defiance, as it were, the long cherished prejudices of the world. She was conscious that she was exposing herself to the animadversions not only of that sex whose interest it is to crush in its germ every feeling of independence and equality in the mind of woman, but also of the large number of her own sex, who, content with the moral slavery that debased them, were willing to smile away their useless lives, the toy and plaything of their masters, in their hours of relaxation; or, bending beneath the chains their own cowardice had helped to bind about them, drag out their existence, the servant and drudge of man. She knew all that she had to encounter; but, strong in the consciousness of right, she would brave it all; and were she but the means of arousing one of her sex from the lethargy in which so many were lulled, she should be content, nor deem her labor in vain. Much more she said to the same effect. Her language was pure and elegant, her voice full and round, but at the same time sweetly toned. (11–12)

---

lecturers, see Caroline Field Levander, "Bawdy Talk: The Politics of Women's Public Speech in *The Lecturess* and *The Bostonians*," *American Literature* 67 (1995): 467–85.

6. For a biographical sketch of Hale, see Nicole Tonkovich Hoffman, "*Legacy* Profile: Sarah Josepha Hale (1788–1874)," *Legacy* 7 (1990): 47–55; *The Lecturess* was published anonymously "by the author of 'My Cousin Mary'" (Boston: Whipple and Damrell, 1839) and is a scant 124 pages in length. All quotations from the novella are taken from this edition and are cited parenthetically in my text.

Hale's copious summary defines Marian not only as an eloquent speaker but as a feminist reformer. As reported by the narrator, Marian's language blends feminism and abolitionism in metaphors that verge on cliché. But if Hale's tone and intention are less than clear in this early passage—if she in fact allows Marian to hold the keys of power—it is not the less clear that she disapproves of Marian's defiance. For while the summary is copious, it is still an indirect reporting of Marian's speech, one that controls the scene by determining how much of the "much more she said to the same effect" will be reported. One might argue, indeed, that the narrator effectively silences Marian, but it seems to me that recognition of the narrator's tight reins raises a much more powerful point.[7]

The second lecture scene strengthens the idea of a narrative silencing of Marian's public voice. As Marian rises to deliver a feminist lecture in Charleston, South Carolina, "instead of the shouts of applause which had always attended her appearance, she was met by hissings and revilings" (54). Again through the indirect report, Marian adds her "disapprobation, in the most decided manner, of slavery" and, "as if to consummate her list of imprudences, and exasperate the people as much as possible, Marian announced her intention of delivering a lecture upon the subject of slavery" (54–55). But she delivers neither the feminist lecture nor the abolitionist address—the audience becomes an "excited mob" and the lecture hall is set on fire. Marian is "overwhelmed with sudden fear, excited to a degree of delirium, heedless of the directions of her friends, and following the instinctive impulse of the moment, she rushed amid the crowd thronging to the doors and windows" (56). Given such madness, in which Marian becomes the mob, Hale rescues her heroine by marrying her off immediately after a convalescence.

The second and third sections follow this same pattern, in which Marian's obstinate pride in her public performances leads her to endanger her marriage and family. In the shape of an unnamed Philadelphia lecturing widow and a nascent "society for the diffusion of knowledge among the blacks in the Southern States" (94), temptation seduces Marian into defying her husband's wishes and pursuing a career as a lecturess. The narrator punctuates these clear movements with warnings, as at the close of the second section: "As a warning, then, to others, must I finish my narrative; go with Marian through the scenes that await her, hoping and trusting that the moral of my tale may prove a blessing to every wife" (92).

7. For a reading of *The Lecturess* as subversive of domestic ideology, see David Reynolds, *Beneath the American Renaissance* (Cambridge: Harvard University Press, 1988), 390–91; for a more persuasive view of Hale's conservative outlook, see Buell, *New England Literary Culture*, 59–60, 437 n. 56.

It will come as no surprise to learn that Marian's scenes lead her to poverty, ruin, and death—and also to a deathbed conversion. In the context of Hale's indirect silencing of Marian's public lectures, moreover, the deathbed speech becomes an emblem of contrite, domestic eloquence. Hale allows Marian to speak directly to her friend Sophia, who will deliver her son and her speech to William Forrester, the estranged husband:

> "And more than all, Sophia, tell him that approaching death taught me how wrong were all my opinions. It taught me that true pride, true independence in a woman, is to fill the place which her God assigns her; to make her husband's happiness her own; and to yield her will to his in all things, conformable to her duty to a higher power. By such conduct will a woman attain her *rights*—the affection of her husband, the respect of her children and the world, and the approval of Heaven. These are the *rights* of woman, and these will ever be hers, if she make truth and virtue her guide." (120–21)

Much more she said to the same effect.

2

Hale's *The Lecturess* shows how women writers, in producing imaginative literature, particularly fiction and poetry, helped to define the domestic sphere as an essentially feminine space. But the work of women writers such as Fuller and Peabody suggests that the boundary between gendered cultural spaces is not hard and fast. By writing for, editing, and publishing a radical intellectual journal such as *The Dial*—as opposed to Hale's respected and respectable editing of the popular *Godey's Lady's Book*—Fuller and Peabody cross boundaries constructed for (and by) women writers within antebellum American culture.[8] Like Hale in *The Lecturess*, however, both Fuller and Peabody make the

---

8. For a subtle reading of Hale's gendered rhetoric in her editing of *Godey's*, see Nicole Tonkovich, "Rhetorical Power in the Victorian Parlor: *Godey's Lady's Book* and the Gendering of Nineteenth-Century Rhetoric," in *Oratorical Culture in Nineteenth-Century America: Transformations in the Theory and Practice of Rhetoric*, ed. Gregory Clark and S. Michael Halloran (Carbondale: Southern Illinois University Press, 1993), 158–83. Tonkovich notes that *Godey's* was one of the most influential and widely circulated literary magazines in the antebellum period, but Hale's vision of cultural and linguistic reform is decidedly conservative.

relationship of culture and language central to the question of women's place in the culture at large. As educated women, Fuller and Peabody specifically address the question of educating women and children, for by reforming education they hope to reform American culture.

Fuller and Peabody were closely associated with each other in several fundamental ways. Both served as Alcott's assistants and "recorders" of conversations held at the Temple School from 1834 to 1837. Both held "conversation parties" of their own with groups of women; Fuller's more famous series of conversations ran from November 1839 to April 1844, many of these held at Peabody's West Street bookshop in Boston. Both pursued literary careers during the 1840s, and both perceived their work of this period as a means of promoting cultural reform.[9]

These similarities mask several equally fundamental differences. In the *Memoirs of Margaret Fuller Ossoli*, Emerson alludes to "some marked difference of temperament" that separated Fuller and Peabody, but that euphemistic formulation gains sharpness in Fuller's letters.[10] Writing to Frederic H. Hedge from Providence on 12 July 1837, for instance, Fuller separates herself from Peabody, then visiting Hedge in Bangor, Maine: "I cannot but laugh when I think of your former way of talking about 'Dr. Channing's women' to hear of Miss P. as domesticated with you—And I too whose youth you misled by your jibes and jeers am now quite under Miss P's wing and in this region of (*entre nous*) as complete Philistency as can exist at Bangor am received as a '*female* whom that truly eminent divine' delighteth to honor. That ever such should be my passport!!"[11] In two letters of April 1842, Fuller warns Emerson that Peabody, the new publisher of *The Dial*, is "variable in her attention" and incapable of writing clear advertising copy: "I never saw anything like her for impossibility of

---

9. Several biographies of Fuller have appeared in the past five years, but no comparable modern biography of Peabody exists. Charles Capper notes the similarities in the two women's careers in *Margaret Fuller: An American Romantic Life*, vol 1: *The Private Years* (New York: Oxford University Press, 1992), 317–18. On Temple School, see 195–200; on the conversations, see 252–306.

For another excellent discussion of Fuller's conversations, see Charles Capper, "Margaret Fuller as Cultural Reformer: The Conversations in Boston," *American Quarterly* 39 (1987): 509–28. For an edition of twelve conversations held in 1839–40, see Nancy Craig Simmons, "Margaret Fuller's Boston Conversations: The 1839–1840 Series," in *Studies in the American Renaissance 1994*, ed. Joel Myerson (Charlottesville: University Press of Virginia, 1994), 195–226.

10. R. W. Emerson, W. H. Channing, and J. F. Clarke, *Memoirs of Margaret Fuller Ossoli* (Boston: Roberts Brothers, 1874), 1: 321. Arthur B. Fuller notes in the preface to this edition that it does not change the first edition (Boston: Phillips, Sampson, 1852). Emerson's notebook for his contribution to the two-volume *Memoirs* appears in *JMN* 11: 455–509.

11. Fuller, *Letters*, 1:292. Hedge's reply of 2 August defends Peabody (293n.). All further citations are to this edition and appear parenthetically in my text.

being clear and accurate in a brief space" (*Letters* 3:58, 60). These letters suggest that Fuller and Peabody were involved in a kind of intellectual rivalry, a
rivalry of which Fuller, in any event, was fully aware.[12]

Fuller was nothing, however, if not honest. In a 26 December 1844 letter to
Peabody, she openly describes Peabody's "tendency to extremes, as to personal
attachments," as well as the "temporary recoil" that results. Whether the description applies to a specific relationship is unclear, although it could easily describe
Peabody's bungled romance with Horace Mann, who married her sister Mary
in 1842, or the attraction Peabody may have felt for Fuller. In any case, Fuller
praises Peabody for being "generous and sympathetic" and cautions her to resist
becoming "infatuated; then the blur, the haste, the tangle would disappear, and
neither I nor any one could refuse to understand you." Ultimately, Fuller perceives Peabody as too foreign to her own personality and goals: "I admit that I
have never done you justice. There is so much in you that is hostile to my
wishes, as to character, and especially as to the character of woman. How could
I be quite candid? Yet where I have looked at you, truly, I have also looked
steadily, and always feel myself in your debt that you cordially pardon all that
must be to you repressing—and unpleasant in me" (*Letters* 3:254). In the phrase
"especially as to the character of woman" Fuller renounces responsibility, in
two ways, for treating Peabody as an intellectual rival. First, she translates her
personal antipathy into a theoretical, abstract concern for "the character of
woman." Second, she represents Peabody's personality as "hostile" to her own
wishes for woman, thus transforming Peabody into the aggressor. In both strategies, her protests notwithstanding, Fuller reveals how easily she can be "repressing—and unpleasant."

But it is perhaps too facile to attribute Fuller's "repressing" attitude toward
Peabody to personal and professional rivalry. A less obvious interpretation of the
passage would focus on the last two words—"in me"—in which Fuller accepts
as internal, personal attributes what she has previously described as relational,
interpersonal problems. I mean to suggest that, however "repressing—and unpleasant" Margaret Fuller may have been toward Elizabeth Peabody, the role of serious intellectual woman in antebellum American culture was decidedly repressing
and unpleasant. Fuller differs most fundamentally from Peabody in her ability to
turn the politics of gender to her own advantage, assuming the dominant role in
the relationship by assuming the culturally defined attributes of authority.

12. For a similar view of the relationship between the two women, see Oscar Cargill, "Nemesis and
Nathaniel Hawthorne," in *Critical Essays on Margaret Fuller*, ed. Joel Myerson (Boston: G. K. Hall, 1980),
179–80.

One dramatic example of this cultural role-playing occurs in Fuller's 26 December 1840 letter to Maria W. Chapman, a leader of the Boston Female Anti-Slavery Society. Mrs. Chapman apparently sent Fuller a note asking her to announce plans (and solicit donations) for the Massachusetts Anti-Slavery Fair, but Fuller chose not to comply with her request: "I received your note but a short time before I went to the conversation party. There was no time for me to think what I should do or even ascertain the objects of the Fair. Had I known them I could not by any slight suggestion have conveyed my view of such movements. And a conversation on the subject would interrupt the course adopted by my class. I therefore, merely requested Miss Peabody to show the papers and your note to me before I began on the subject before us."[13] Since the conversation party was held at Peabody's home-bookshop in West Street, we could read this as simply the reasonable action of a guest toward her hostess. But the roles are less innocuous than this reading pretends. Fuller seizes the role of authority, the leader of the conversation; Peabody functions as a kind of secretary, performing her role in silence.

This type of role-playing reinforces gender stereotypes at the same time that it strains against the limits assigned antebellum women. Given the situation of intellectual women such as Fuller and Peabody, it is hardly surprising to find them involved in contradictory—even compromising—positions. Emerson points out the contradiction and exemplifies its cultural sources in the *Memoirs*:

> She had a feeling that she ought to have been a man, and said of herself, "A man's ambition with a woman's heart, is an evil lot." In some verses which she wrote "To the Moon," occur these lines:—
>
> > "But if I steadfast gaze upon thy face,
> > "A human secret, like my own, I trace;
> > "For, through the woman's smile looks the male eye."
>
> And she found something of true portraiture in a disagreeable novel of Balzac's, "Le Livre Mystique," in which an equivocal figure exerts alternately a masculine and a feminine influence on the characters of the plot. (1:229)

---

13. Fuller, *Letters* 12:197; Hudspeth provides the biographical sketch and background information about Mrs. Chapman and the Fair in his notes (198).

Fuller's division of "man's ambition" and "woman's heart" follows the culturally defined boundary between the realms of public striving and private feeling, a boundary that Hale's *The Lecturess* defines as gender specific. Emerson
adduces two additional texts—Fuller's poem and Balzac's "disagreeable" novel—
as further evidence of the "evil lot" of crossing this boundary. Most important,
however, is the word "evil," for this is Emerson's, not Fuller's. In the notebook
version of the sentence, Emerson quotes Fuller as writing, "A man's ambition
with a woman's heart,—'tis an accursed lot" (*JMN* 11:502). Emerson may have
changed "accursed" to "evil" in order to fit the sentence within his discussion
of Fuller's spiritualist temperament—what he calls the "nocturnal element in
her nature" (*Memoirs* 1:229)—but whatever his intention, his revision erases
Fuller's melodramatic, archaic expression of personal fatedness. Yet more significant is the fact itself of revision: Emerson appropriates Fuller's words and
revises them in order to present his own particular version of Margaret Fuller
Ossoli, and this revisionary representation silences her as effectively as she
silenced Peabody in the West Street bookshop.

The idea that the *Memoirs* belong to Channing, Clarke, and Emerson rather
than to Fuller will startle no one. Nor, for that matter, will the idea that Fuller
herself is thereby appropriated and revised.[14] These are the points from which
any analysis of Fuller's work within the context of antebellum American culture must begin. As my reading of *The Lecturess* suggests, the salient aspects of
this cultural work are linguistic and educational, and we can see them most
clearly in *Woman in the Nineteenth Century* and in Fuller's conversation classes.

From every contemporary report it would be safe to conclude that Margaret
Fuller was a surpassingly eloquent speaker. In praising her abilities in conversation, Emerson notes that "the test of this eloquence was its range. It told on
children, and on old people; on men of the world, and on sainted maids. She
could hold them all by her honeyed tongue" (*Memoirs* 1:215). The source of
such wide-ranging eloquence, for Emerson, is "the broadest good sense" (216),
for "an older philosopher than Anaximenes, namely, language itself, had taught
to distinguish superior or purer sense as *common* sense" (217). Emerson fashions
the Fuller of the *Memoirs* into a figure of eloquence: "Margaret had, with certain limitations, or, must we say, *strictures*, these larger lungs, inhaling this universal element, and could speak to Jew and Greek, free and bond, to each in
his own tongue" (217). Echoing Paul in Galatians 3:28 ("There is neither Jew
nor Greek, there is neither bond nor free, there is neither male nor female: for

---

14. For a succinct account of the *Memoirs* as a literary representation of Fuller, see David Watson,
Margaret Fuller: An American Romantic (New York: Berg, 1988), 91–98.

ye are all one in Christ Jesus"), Emerson confers divine, unifying powers upon Fuller, although at the same instant he places her powers within "*strictures*."

This sense of powers whose potential is never realized becomes stronger when Emerson considers Fuller as a writer. Under the rubric "Woman, or Artist?" he asserts that Fuller's "pen was a non-conductor" (1:294), an assessment that has become a critical commonplace. It would be unfair, however, to accuse Emerson of deforming Fuller in representing her as caught between speech and writing, for that is precisely how Fuller represents herself. In a journal entry from April 1840, for instance, she makes the distinction between her authority in conversation and her lack of it in writing:

> Then a woman of tact and brilliancy, like me, has an undue advantage in conversation with men. They are astonished at our instincts. They do not see where we got our knowledge; and, while they tramp on in their clumsy way, we wheel, and fly, and dart hither and thither, and seize with ready eye all the weak points, like Saladin in the desert. It is quite another thing when we come to write, and, without suggestion from another mind, to declare the positive amount of thought that is in us. Because we seemed to know all, they think we can tell all; and, finding we can tell so little, lose faith in their first opinion of us, *which, nathless, was true.* (*Memoirs* 1:295–96; *JMN* 11:471).

Aside from making punctuation and spelling conform with standard nineteenth-century practice, Emerson does not revise Fuller's text at all. The central problem, as Fuller formulates it, is that writing is univocal and isolating, without the reciprocity, the argumentative give and take, to be found in conversation. Fuller figures her eloquence in martial and sexual terms—herself the "Saladin" to the plodding male crusaders. But without dialogue Saladin has no opponent, and eloquence is tongue-tied.

The problem with the *Memoirs* is that Fuller's journal meditation on the difficulties of writing becomes the principal evidence to support the statement "Her pen was a non-conductor." None of the authors of the *Memoirs* engages in an analysis of Fuller's work, since the volumes are really intended to represent Fuller through her writings. The personal, biographical character of the project is understandable, but it unfortunately has colored much of the critical work on Fuller.[15]

---

15. See Joel Myerson's introduction to *Critical Essays on Margaret Fuller*, vii–xvi. Horace Greeley's introduction to the 1852 edition of *Papers on Literature and Art* provides a good example of the com-

One particularly astute critic, however, did manage to suggest the relationship between speech and writing in Fuller's work. In a series of articles entitled "The Literati of New York City," published in Sarah Hale's *Godey's Lady's Book*, Edgar Allan Poe included the following description of Fuller's style:

> Her literary and her conversational manner are identical. Here is a passage from her "Summer on the Lakes:"—
>
> "The rapids enchanted me far beyond what I expected; they are so swift that they cease to *seem* so—you can think only of their *beauty*. The fountain beyond the Moss islands I discovered for myself, and thought it for some time an *accidental* beauty which it would not do to *leave*, lest I might never see it again. After I found it *permanent*, I returned many times to watch the play of its crest. In the little waterfall beyond, Nature seems, as she often does, to have made a *study* for some larger design. She delights in this—a sketch within a sketch—a dream within a *dream*. Wherever we see it, the lines of the great buttress in the fragment of stone, the hues of the waterfall, copied in the flowers that *star* its bordering mosses, we are *delighted*; for all the lineaments become *fluent*, and we mould the scene in congenial thought with its *genius*."
>
> Now all this is precisely as Miss Fuller would *speak* it. She is perpetually saying just such things in just such words. To get the *conversational* woman in the mind's eye, all that is needed is to imagine her reciting the paragraph just quoted ... speaking in a high key, but musically, deliberately, (not hurriedly or loudly,) with a delicious distinctness of enunciation—speaking, I say, the paragraph in question, and emphasizing the words which I have italicized, not by impulsion of the breath, (as is usual,) but by drawing them out as long as possible, nearly closing her eyes the while.[16]

---

monplace view of Fuller's speech and writing: "One of the most fluent, forcible, and brilliant of talkers, she nevertheless wrote slowly and with remarkable labor; so that, but for the eminence of her conversational powers, it might have been supposed that her years of devotion to foreign languages and literature had impaired her mastery of her mother tongue. Yet this hesitancy in writing, sometimes resulting in obscurity, or even awkwardness of style, affected the manner only, and not the matter, of her essays. I doubt that any woman whose life was mainly devoted to literature has written less for the public eye than Margaret Fuller did; I believe the writings of no other woman were ever so uniformly worthy of study and preservation" (New York: Fowler and Wells, 1852), i–ii.

16. Myerson, *Critical Essays*, 39. The article originally appeared in the August 1846 issue of *Godey's*, and the entire series is reprinted in Edgar Allan Poe, *Essays and Reviews* (New York: Library of America, 1984), 1118–222.

Poe's appreciation of Fuller's writing depends upon his personal knowledge of her speech rhythms and voice, and it thereby crosses the boundary between speech and writing. For Poe, Fuller's pen is by no means a non-conductor; rather, it conducts the "*conversational* woman." And Poe's editorial strategy of italicizing words creates a convincing illusion of speech.

Poe's description of Fuller as conversational alludes, in all likelihood, not only to her reputation as a conversationalist but also to her role as the leader of conversation parties for women in Boston from 1839 to 1844. As Charles Capper's essay shows, the Boston conversations exemplify Fuller's need to establish a forum for expressing her ideas, especially those about the role of women in antebellum American culture. This is clear in her 27 August 1839 letter to Sophia Ripley, which served as a prospectus for the first series of conversations. Fuller describes her ambition as being "to pass in review the departments of thought and knowledge and endeavor to place them in due relation to one another in our minds. To systematize thought and give a precision in which our sex are so deficient, chiefly, I think because they have so few inducements to test and classify what they receive. To ascertain what pursuits are best suited to us in our time and state of society, and how we may make best use of our means for building up the life of thought upon the life of action" (*Letters* 2:87).

Fuller joins her grand ambitions with a specific pedagogical approach. Noting that "the success of the whole depends on conversation being general," she insists that those who join must intend "*if possible*, to take an active part" (88). Fuller presents herself as a discussion leader, one who facilitates and moderates the conversation, but she has a realistic and experienced view of the discussion class: "I should expect communication to be effected by degrees and to do a great deal myself at the first meetings" (88). Moreover, she proposes to put writing in the service of conversation: "When they have not been successful in verbal utterance of their thoughts I have asked for them in writing. At the next meeting I read these aloud and canvassed their adequacy without mentioning the names of the writers. I found this less and less necessary as I proceeded and my companions acquired greater command both of thoughts and language, but for a time it was useful. I hope it may not be necessary now, but if it should great advantages may be derived from even this limited use of the pen" (88). Fuller's vision of the conversation effectively reverses the cultural hierarchy of speech and writing implied by Emerson's statements in the *Memoirs* and openly stated by Thoreau in *Walden*: "a sound, a tongue, a dialect merely, almost brutish, and we learn it unconsciously, like the brutes, of our mothers" (101). For Fuller, conversation is not a debased form of language, subservient to the higher form of writing. Instead, writing serves the purpose of facilitating expression both within the individual and within the group. The pen has a "limited use," leading to a "greater command both of thoughts and language" through the forum of conversation.

Fuller's aims and methods suggest the fundamental importance of language to her vision of cultural reform. The conversation provides a "point of union to well-educated and thinking women" (86), giving them the opportunity to educate themselves in "thoughts and language." Fuller aims at the systematic and analytic examination of "thought and knowledge," and her method combines the invitation to speak with the promise that she will insist on "a precision in which our sex are so deficient." This means that the participants "lay aside the shelter of vague generalities, the cant of coterie criticism and the delicate disdains of *good society*" (87). Thus the reform of culture is predicated upon the reform of language and thought.

The record of the first series of conversations, which may be the work of Elizabeth Peabody herself, shows that language is a central concern in Fuller's philosophy of education. In the initial meeting, for instance, Fuller "enlarged upon the topics which she touched in her letter to Mrs. Ripley. . . . She thought it would be a good plan to take up subjects on which we knew words—& had impressions, & vague irregular notions, & compel ourselves to define those words, to turn these impressions into thoughts, & to systematise these thoughts—" (Simmons 203). During the seventh conversation, Fuller critiques the participants' written definitions of beauty and leads the discussion to a point she has apparently made before:

> She then made some admirable remarks which she has also done before upon the ambiguity & imperfection of language—the absolute inadequacy of the words to express *thoughts*—the absolute necessity of constant definition & mutual explanation—& this the more, the deeper we go into thought & feeling.—But this difficulty of using language should not make us despair—but rather to be more careful to know exactly in what sense words are used—& to explain ourselves. Thus a medium of communication may at last be gained (at least among individuals familiar with one another) which will answer a very good purpose—& enable us to guess with certainty what we may mutually mean. (Simmons 210)

The conversation functions as a kind of laboratory of language, a process in which participants sharpen their skills in thinking, speaking, and listening. This last skill is perhaps least apparent, but the recorder notes three times that communication is a "mutual" and "familiar" process, one that depends upon a complex mental correspondence between speakers and listeners.

The implied goal of the conversation is to improve the verbal and intellectual "self-culture" of the entire group. In the eighth conversation, Fuller reveals the hierarchical theory underlying both her method and her goal:

> The work of Utility speaks of human living, the work of Beauty of divine life. Every work of Beauty is a distinct passage in the universal harmony. I prefer the word harmony to unity, because unity is the "I am," harmony the "being" of the Absolute.
>
> In unity it pauses self enfolded.—in harmony it multiplies & feels itself living. Beauty is thus, or nothing. We need not the word Beauty if not to express one in many. Else would the word Unity suffice to our thought. But these words we use are most of all inadequate to such themes. The best language is that of Nature in which God writes. Next best, the fine arts, especially Music which most of any disarms the senses, & gives Beauty free passage to the soul. Last & worst, this arbitrary language, degraded too by being much used for the low purposes of the prose day. (Simmons 213)

The real goal of defining and refining the words/ideas through the conversations is to escape the limitations and inadequacies of arbitrary language in order to approach the language of the fine arts and, ultimately, the language "of Nature in which God writes." Fuller's method is to transform ordinary, "prose day" conversation into the heightened, intensely analytical and imaginative discourse of a conversation party. Education becomes an aesthetic experience that "gives Beauty free passage to the soul." In other words, harmonious conversation becomes a dynamic, vehicular form of eloquence.

If the conversations in Boston represent Fuller's attempt at establishing a cultural space for "thinking women," they also register her own need for a platform from which to express herself. The letter to Sophia Ripley combines these two needs by posing the "great questions" of all women, "What were we born to do? How shall we do it?" and then answering them with her personal pledge: "I should think the undertaking a noble one, and if my resources should prove sufficient to make me its moving spring, I should be willing to give it a large portion of those coming years which will as I hope be my best" (87). Fuller did, in fact, give the conversations a large portion of the years from 1839 to 1844, and they may have been her best. But she did not exclude the work of writing, for those same years saw the publication of numerous essays and reviews in *The Dial*, the travel narrative *Summer on the Lakes* (1844), as well as translations of *Eckermann's Conversations with Goethe* (1839) and *Correspondence of Fräulein Günderode with Bettina von Arnim* (1842). Finally, the five-year period culminates in the publication of Fuller's most important work, *Woman in the Nineteenth Century* (1845).[17]

In *Woman in the Nineteenth Century*, Fuller employs the strategies of conversation in order to create her closest approximation to a mother tongue. The core of the book is the long essay, "The Great Lawsuit.—Man *versus* Men; Woman *versus* Women," published in the July 1843 issue of *The Dial*. The title of that essay emphasizes the oppositional, argumentative qualities of the cultural problems Fuller addresses. In her introduction to *Woman*, Fuller laments the change of title because "The Great Lawsuit" demands "some thought to see what it means, and might thus prepare the reader to meet me on my own ground."[18] Both of these reasons accord with Fuller's methods in the conversation classes: by eliciting responses from the audience, she hopes to create active listeners/readers and establish a discursive/cultural space joining her audience and herself. Fuller's original title suggests a dynamic model of cultural discourse, whereas the final title implies a static model of description and exposition.

A second element of the conversation is the ability of the "nucleus of conversation" (Simmons 203) to listen to others. In this respect, Fuller's view of eloquence has definite affinities with the ideal orator in Thoreau's *A Week on the Concord and Merrimack Rivers*. In both texts, true eloquence recognizes the limitations of mere words. The following passage could come from either: "We sicken no less at the pomp than the strife of words. We feel that never were lungs so puffed with the wind of declamation, on moral and religious subjects, as now. We are tempted to implore these 'word-heroes,' these word-Catos, word-Christs, to beware of cant above all things; to remember that hypocrisy is the most hopeless as well as the meanest of crimes, and that those must surely be polluted by it, who do not reserve a part of their morality and religion for private use" (*Woman* 254–55). This attack on windy declamation is in fact itself declamatory in style. Fuller employs the syntactic parallelism common to political and religious declamations. The three sentences in this passage begin with the *We*-plus-verb formula, while the last sentence employs parallelisms

17. The standard bibliography of writings by Fuller is Joel Myerson, *Margaret Fuller: A Descriptive Bibliography* (Pittsburgh: University of Pittsburgh Press, 1978). Fuller published five books during her lifetime; the last, *Papers on Literature and Art*, appeared in 1846. Thus there is good reason to consider the years 1839–45 her best; this Keatsian productivity makes Greeley's introduction to the 1852 edition of *Papers* all the more amazing: "I doubt that any woman whose life was mainly devoted to literature has written less for the public eye than Margaret Fuller did" (ii).

18. Margaret Fuller, *Woman in the Nineteenth Century*, in Jeffrey Steele, ed., *The Essential Margaret Fuller* (New Brunswick: Rutgers University Press, 1992), 245. All citations refer to this edition and are cited parenthetically in my text.

repeatedly: "these 'word-heroes,' these word-Catos, word-Christs"; "to beware," "to remember"; "that . . . and that. . . ." Fuller suggests that eloquence should be substantial and sincere; her style implies that this passage, in its clear eloquence, is so.

If Fuller were to continue in a declamatory style, we would probably have to accuse her of cant, if not hypocrisy. But as she develops the attack on "word-heroes," she introduces voices other than her own: "Landor says that he cannot have a great deal of mind who cannot afford to let the larger part of it lie fallow; and what is true of genius is not less so of virtue. The tongue is a valuable member, but should appropriate but a small part of the vital juices that are needful all over the body. We feel that the mind may 'grow black and rancid in the smoke' even 'of altars.' We start up from the harangue to go into our closet and shut the door. There inquires the spirit, 'Is this rhetoric the bloom of healthy blood, or a false pigment artfully laid on?'" (255). By blending allusion and quotation, Fuller adds literary (and perhaps classical or biblical) voices to this stylistic conversation.[19] Moreover, the second sentence ("The tongue is a valuable member," etc.) introduces a voice that joins proverb and pseudoscience, while the final sentence delivers the voice of the spirit, which pronounces the central question of nature and art. Meanwhile, Fuller continues to employ the *We*-plus-verb structure in two sentences, although the second of the two introduces concrete, dramatic action into the passage. Fuller's authorial voice exercises authority over the passage, but it allows many other voices to speak out against the tongue's "harangue." The conversational style seeks to oppose the empty eloquence of "these word-Catos, word-Christs" and prevent Fuller herself from "haranguing too much" (*Letters* 2:88). Finally, the metaphor of conversation may provide a fresh perspective on Fuller's use of allusion and quotation: instead of accusing her of pedantry, we may read the style of *Woman in the Nineteenth Century* as an attempt at creating a regulated play of diverse cultural voices.

A more restricted but dramatic instance of the play of cultural voices involves Fuller's use of dialogue. The two most extended examples of this conversational strategy are, first, the argument between the "irritated trader" of slaves and an unidentified authorial voice (255–56) and, second, the fully developed dialogue between the author and Miranda (261–65). As different as they are from each other, the two dialogues are alike in portraying Fuller as moderate, reasonable, and dispassionate. In the slave trader Fuller creates an extreme figure, one who

---

19. I have not identified the source of "grows black and rancid in the smoke . . . of altars." It does not occur in the *Iliad*, although there are several suggestive passages about animal sacrifices; nor does it occur in book 2 of the *Aeneid*, although similar passages abound there, too.

expresses an authoritarian, repressive paternalism toward his slaves and his wife. He is ultimately an unworthy opponent in argument, since he merely repeats the cliché "I am the head" (256).

Miranda is in some ways just as extreme as the slave trader, although in her case she represents an idealized self-reliance. Fuller begins by introducing Miranda as "a woman, who, if any in the world could, might speak without heat and bitterness of the position of her sex" (261) and then follows this with a brief biographical sketch. Miranda's biography of course parallels Fuller's own. In a journal of 1844, Fuller notes that "last year at this time I wrote of woman, and proudly painted myself as Miranda."[20] But Miranda is not Margaret Fuller, although she may represent a self that Fuller would like to claim as her own. In the dialogue, Fuller asserts that Miranda is "an example, that the restraints upon the sex were insuperable only to those who think them so, or who noisily strive to break them" (262), but Miranda quickly corrects her. "Self-dependence" is her leading characteristic, but while honored in her it "is deprecated as a fault in most women. They are taught to learn their rule from without, not to unfold it from within" (262). Restraints are insuperable to all but the most fortunate, for only the fortunate few are self-dependent enough to realize that the restraints are arbitrary and conventional.

Though arbitrary and conventional, the restraints are no less real. Through Miranda, Fuller presents the voices of men who *said* they wanted "the steel bracelets of strength" on "soft arms of affection" (263). But the male voices soon contradict themselves, seeing females as inevitably weak and inferior, and even Miranda's "intimate friend of the other sex" has told her "that I 'deserved in some star to be a man.'" The reported and quoted male voices point subtly to language as one of the most basic barriers to cultural reform.

Fuller underscores this idea by having Miranda quote Ben Jonson's "On Lucy, Countess of Bedford." Miranda objects to the line "Only a learned and a manly soul," but Fuller chides her for being "too fastidious." In the dialogue, Fuller defends Jonson's word "manly" as "one of the deeper colors," but Miranda notes that the word is always used to evoke "a heroic quality," whereas "womanly" is never used to evoke "persistence and courage." She therefore asks for words "of a larger sense" and revises the poem: "Read, 'A heavenward and instructed soul,' and I should be satisfied. Let it not be said, wherever there is energy or creative genius, 'She has a masculine mind'" (264). Since the epigraph to *Woman* gives the revised line of Jonson's poem (243), Miranda clearly wins the point.

20. Quoted in *Letters* 3:199n. See also Emerson's transcription of the sentence in *JMN* 11:498.

The dialogue between Fuller and Miranda functions in several significant ways. First, it clearly illustrates Fuller's conversational strategies, for Miranda teaches Fuller that language can be a barrier to reform. Second, it represents Fuller as a moderate but malleable thinker, one who can perceive the justness and justice of her interlocutor's argument. Third, the dialogue dramatizes the positive ways in which language can function—ideally, it instructs the soul heavenward. Fourth, it implies that all of these progressive traits are the special province of women, for Miranda functions as the most important figure of Adamic eloquence in Fuller's book. *Woman in the Nineteenth Century* thus employs the techniques of conversation to create a new form of eloquence, one that we could call the language of Eve.[21]

Fuller's meditations upon the relationship of language and culture stress, in both form and content, the power of language to advance or to retard cultural reform. That conclusion does not resolve the many strands of *Woman in the Nineteenth Century* into one tapestry, nor does it provide a totalizing representation of Margaret Fuller's work, but it does indicate that Fuller is remarkably close to Emerson in her view of language and culture. For both, eloquence functions as a means of effecting institutional and individual reform, and the reform of culture acts reciprocally upon language. Given this basic tenet of transcendental language theory, however, the two thinkers move in quite different directions, mainly because of the cultural position each occupies. For Emerson, eloquence takes the form of the secularized sermon—the lecture or address—in which the poet is equally the orator. But for Fuller, as for most women in nineteenth-century America, eloquence develops from the give-and-take of conversation, not from the oracular utterances of a divinely inspired speaker. One striking way of discovering these two modes of eloquence is to note the epigraph to the *Memoirs*. Emerson, Channing, and Clarke print four lines from Jonson's poem, but they print the line "Only a learned and a manly soul." By rejecting the emendation proposed by Miranda and accepted by Fuller, the editors of the *Memoirs* effectively silence both women.

---

21. Fuller attempts to revise the traditional view of Eve in three passages—272, 289–90, and 328. See also Sarah M. Grimké, *Letters on the Equality of the Sexes* (1838), in *The Public Years of Sarah and Angelina Grimké: Selected Writings, 1835–1839*, ed. Larry Ceplair (New York: Columbia University Press, 1989), 204–10. It should also be noted that Fuller mentions Angelina Grimké and Abby Kelley as public figures of eloquence who "subdue the prejudices of their hearers, and excite an interest proportionate to the aversion with which it had been the purpose to regard them" (307). Grimké and Kelley were Quaker abolitionists who first met each other at the Anti-Slavery Convention of American Women in New York City, May 1837. For an informative, informal narrative of Kelley's career, see Dorothy Sterling, *Ahead of Her Time: Abby Kelley and the Politics of Antislavery* (New York: Norton, 1991).

The textual irony of *Woman in the Nineteenth Century* and the *Memoirs* should not be taken too far. It would be wrong to argue that Fuller faced insuperable barriers; indeed, she herself refuses to see the barriers this way. Still, the texts do point to one form of polarization in the cultural discourse of antebellum America. Although the transcendentalists believe in the necessity and power of eloquence, their versions of a Language of Nature differ so sharply from one another as to be, at the extreme, mutually unintelligible. The problem Fuller faces in creating a cultural space for herself and other intellectual women, however, admits of more than one solution. Elizabeth Peabody may have seemed to Fuller to be "hostile" to her wishes for the "character of woman" (*Letters* 3:254), but Peabody's conservative version of transcendentalism eventually leads to fundamental reforms in the education of both men and women.

3

Elizabeth Peabody occupies a privileged position in the study of language theories and in the application of linguistic theories to education. The second edition of *Record of a School* (1836), with her "Explanatory Preface," suggests the connection between language and educational reform, as does the entire book. Peabody translated Guillaume Oegger's *True Messiah* for Emerson and published it in 1842. She published (and ghostwrote) Charles Kraitsir's *Significance of the Alphabet* in 1846. She published the articles "Language" and "The Dorian Measure" in the first issue of her abortive journal, *Aesthetic Papers* (1849). During the heyday of the New England Renaissance, then, Elizabeth Peabody was central to the development and dissemination of current language theories. Most important, she applied her interest in language to the education of children, especially in developing the kindergarten in America.[22]

Peabody connects language and cultural reform from the early stages of her long career. In the "Explanatory Preface" to the *Record of a School*, for example, Peabody notes that the "lessons on language, given in the Record,

---

22. Three biographies of Peabody exist: Ruth M. Baylor, *Elizabeth Palmer Peabody: Kindergarten Pioneer* (Philadelphia: University of Pennsylvania Press, 1965); Gladys Brooks, *Three Wise Virgins* (New York: E. P. Dutton, 1957), 83–153; and Louise Hall Tharp, *The Peabody Sisters of Salem* (Boston: Little, Brown, 1950). Baylor includes a useful bibliography of Peabody's publications, 191–207. The most significant account of Peabody is Philip Gura's "Elizabeth Palmer Peabody and the Philosophy of Language," *ESQ* 23 (1977): 154–63. Gura summarizes the influences on Peabody and places her synthesis of language theories within the framework of Unitarian theology.

have generally been admitted to be most valuable" (vi) and that "spelling and defining words are the most prominent intellectual exercises of the school" (xxviii).[23] Bronson Alcott's emphasis on language in the Temple School develops "spiritual culture" through a characteristic dualism. As Peabody notes in the preface, Alcott's Socratic method leads the students from outward, material things to inward, spiritual realities (vi, xxii). The dualism extends to the type of language that is thus developed, for the scholars "should be led to nature for the picturesque and for poetry, not for the purpose of scientific analysis and deduction. They should look upon its synthesis as sacred" (xxiii). Peabody's view of "spiritual culture" as bound to an aesthetic "synthesis" of nature through language strongly recalls the central arguments of Emerson's *Nature*, which Peabody would eventually review in the February 1838 issue of *U. S. Magazine and Democratic Review*.[24]

Alcott's application of transcendental language theory to the education of children leads his scholars to the Language of Nature, and he employs the outer matter–inner spirit dualism so consistently that it becomes a predictable piety in the conversations of the Temple School. In addition, his version of Socratic method is, as Peabody notes, "very autocratic" (21). While purporting to show the freely developing spirits of children engaged in mind-expanding, contemplative conversations, Peabody's *Record* delivers an image of Alcott as a repressive interlocutor, obsessed with discipline. In the conversation on the word *sign*, for example, Alcott leads his scholars, predictably enough, toward the correspondence theory of language and meaning:

> The word *sign*, gave rise to the following questions and answers. What is a sign? A token. What is a token? Any thing that shows something else. What is the body a sign of? The mind. What is the mind a sign of? Heaven. What is Heaven? Heaven is the sign of goodness, and earth of Heaven. What is goodness a sign of? Happiness. What is happiness a sign of? Goodness. What is goodness a sign of? said Mr. Alcott again. Eternity. What is eternity the sign of? They all said they did not know. Mr. Alcott said that eternity was the sign of God's lifetime, or of God; and that there we must stop—we could go no farther. They all acknowledged it. Mr. Alcott then quoted these lines of poetry:

---

23. All quotations are from *Record of a School: Exemplifying the General Principles of Spiritual Culture*, 2d ed. (Boston: Russell, Shattuck, 1836).

24. My source for this last piece of information is Hudspeth's note in Fuller, *Letters* 1:329n.

> "Significant is all that meets the sense,
> One Mighty alphabet for infant minds."

What is significant? said he. The answer was, all that meets the eyes!
What does it all signify? Something beyond the senses. Mr. Alcott made
this last answer himself. (*Record* 50)

Peabody's disapproval of Alcott's ideas and methods is only tacit here, even
though the dialogue between the tautological scholar and the insistent Alcott
is humorous. A year later, however, she is rebelling against the "common conscience" Alcott promotes through the conversations on the Gospels.[25] By the
time she writes "A Plea for Froebel's Kindergarten" (1869), Peabody has clearly
outgrown Alcott's restrictive reductions.[26]

   In the interim between the *Record* and her wholesale conversion to Froebel's
ideas of kindergarten, Peabody develops versions of transcendental language
theory that parallel those of Emerson and Thoreau. Before 1835, for instance,
she translates Guillaume Oegger's *True Messiah* for Emerson, who records several pages in *Journal B*.[27] In a previous chapter I suggested that Emerson was
interested in Oegger as much for his language as for his ideas, since *The True
Messiah* offers the same dualism between spirit and matter that Emerson found
in Boehme and Swedenborg. Oegger is interesting in connection with Peabody,
however, because the translated subtitle of *The True Messiah* emphasizes the
Language of Nature as a means of reading the Old and New Testaments.

25. The phrase is opposed to the "private conscience," which Peabody favors (*Record* xiv). The issue
of conscience is of course directly related to Alcott's methods of discipline; see Richard Brodhead,
"Sparing the Rod: Discipline and Fiction in Antebellum America," *Representations* 21 (1988): 67–96.
Peabody's sharpest disagreement with Alcott came as a result of his book *Conversations with Children on
the Gospels* (Boston: James Munroe, 1836–37). The two-volume work is available in a reprint edition
(New York: Arno Press, 1972). Peabody's "Recorder's Preface" to the first volume registers her dis-
agreement (iv), as does the "Recorder's Remark" in the second volume (17). See also Peabody's 7 August
1836 letter to Alcott in *Letters of Elizabeth Palmer Peabody*, ed. Bruce A. Ronda (Middletown: Wesleyan
University Press, 1984), 180–83.

26. Originally published as "A Plea for Froebel's Kindergarten as the First Grade of Primary
Education," in *The Identification of the Artisan and Artist* (Boston: Adams, Lee & Shepard, 1869), 42–48,
the essay appears in Elizabeth Peabody, *Last Evening with Allston, and Other Papers* (Boston: D. Lothrop,
1886), 331–42. In the essay, Peabody clearly shows her willingness to include such "outer" elements as
blocks, sticks, curved wires, and drawings in her curriculum.

27. *JMN* 5:66–70 prints the pages of Peabody's manuscript translation that Emerson transcribed into
Journal B, and Emerson discusses Oegger in several other passages in the journal. Peabody eventually
published the translation, *The True Messiah; or The Old and New Testaments, examined according to the Principles
of the Language of Nature* (Boston: Peabody, 1842). Cameron publishes several pertinent passages in *Emerson
the Essayist* (Raleigh, N.C.: Thistle Press, 1945), 2:83–99.

Oegger fits within the tradition of linguistic mysticism that seeks "a perfect language, a language which cannot have been lost but in the lapse of ages, and of which the traces may be found, when Philosophy will direct her researches to that point."[28] Peabody's first recorded work in language theory thus recapitulates the theory Emerson is elaborating in the journals, lectures, and essays of the 1830s. In her 1838 review of *Nature*, Peabody views Emerson himself as a figure of eloquence, exemplifying the authority and power of the poet-orator, and her only complaint is that "our poet grows silent with wonder and worship" instead of expanding upon how "the relation between mind and matter stands in the will of God." For Peabody, language does not involve the accidental or random, just as "there is *no accident in the world*." Words and things are equivalent, and the "true and perfect mind" of the poet perceives their relation to "the will of God."[29]

In the 1840s, however, as Peabody deepens her commitment to the study of language by working with Charles Kraitsir, her ideas move much closer to those of Thoreau. For Thoreau, as for Fuller and the later Emerson, language is subject to severe limitations, and Peabody sees this point most sharply in relation to her own expression. In a letter to Mary Moody Emerson, Peabody remarks that "when occasionally I have ventured out of that magic circle of Silence which seems to be an Eternity enclosing absolute truth, I find clouds arise, and myself lose the vision." She then gives a theoretical explanation for the inadequacies of language: "Since I knew Dr. Kraitsir I have seen a little into the reason why we puzzle ourselves so much and perpetually lose the truths which the great God gives us whereby to live. We have lost the key to language, that great instrument by means of which the finite mind is to compensate itself, for its being fixed to a point in space and compelled to the limitations of the succession we call time. We use words that are no longer symbols but counters."[30] In Kraitsir's theory of the Language of Nature, the "key to language" is the relationship of sound to meaning, a relationship that languages of convention have adulterated. Peabody's letter registers the power of "the great Silence" opposing her, as well as the divided state of current languages, which combine vestiges of the original Language of Nature with latter-day languages of convention. In recognizing a double limitation upon the correspondence between thoughts and words, she sounds remarkably like Thoreau.

---

28. Oegger, quoted in Cameron, *Emerson the Essayist* 2:84.

29. *United States Magazine and Democratic Review* 1 (February 1838): 323, 320.

30. Peabody, *Letters* 264. Peabody concludes the paragraph by saying that she hopes Kraitsir will teach her enough philology and mathematics so that she "may possibly get weaponed to contend with the great Silence adequately" (264).

Charles Kraitsir's importance to Peabody becomes abundantly clear in *The Significance of the Alphabet*, which Peabody edited and published in 1846.[31] The opening paragraph of the book echoes Peabody's letter to Mary Moody Emerson:

> Language is the image of the human mind, the net result of human culture: if it is Babel, it is because men have abandoned themselves to chance, and lost sight of the principles by which language was constructed. But these principles are inherent in their nature, and men cannot lose their nature. All men, however diverse they may become by conflicting passions and interests, have yet the same reason, and the same organs of speech. All men, however distant in place, are yet plunged into a material universe, which makes impressions of an analogous character, upon great masses. (3)

Although language is represented as caught between its original principles and its modern, Babel-like avatars, the paragraph begins and ends with the image of language as a unified, diverse "net result of human culture" that reveals "the same reason, and the same organs of speech." The parallel structure implies a parallel between the mind and speech, suggesting that the Language of Nature can renew the human mind and human culture.

Kraitsir and Peabody develop these connections by focusing on the reform of language-teaching in America, particularly the teaching of Latin and English. Despite the composite, apparently chaotic nature of English, the two theorists adamantly assert the unity of language and thought. Peabody and Kraitsir make three assumptions about language: first, that the basic units of sound are also basic units of meaning; second, that the essential language of humankind is an "organic formation," an Adamic Language of Nature; third, that the apparent Babel of modern languages veils an essential unity of "human thought and feeling," although the unity accommodates the diversity of cultures and languages (*Significance* 19–20).

Kraitsir's version of transcendental language theory provides Peabody with a coherent set of assumptions about the central role that language plays in developing human culture. The significance of *The Significance* is, finally, that it

---

31. In her essay "Language," published in *Aesthetic Papers* (1849), Peabody gives "the history of the book": "It was merely the enlargement by Dr. Kraitsir of some notes taken by a hearer of one or two lectures of a series which he delivered in Boston to an audience of about a score of persons" (223). The "hearer" is, of course, Peabody herself, who in this instance performs the duties of recorder in much the same way she did for Alcott and Fuller.

expresses Peabody's abstract vision of a Language of Nature at the same time that it applies that vision to the practical problems of education in America. The book combines Peabody's two abiding concerns—language and education. This is why the theoretical statements lead so easily to the "vast importance" of studying language: "There is no subject connected with the mind or destiny of man, upon which a profound insight into philology will not throw a broad light" (20). Peabody characteristically combines abstract theory with practical application, although she never appears tempted to deliver public lectures as a means of combining them. Instead, print remains Peabody's medium of choice and the elementary classroom is her abiding point of application. For instance, the glossological table of germs in *The Significance of the Alphabet* (12) becomes the basis for Peabody's *First Nursery Reading Book* (1849).[32] As late as 1863, in *Moral Culture of Infancy, and Kindergarten Guide*, Peabody describes the use of the *First Nursery Reading Book* in a kindergarten and cites Kraitsir as the philological authority for her methods of teaching reading.[33] Kraitsir's influence on Peabody's development of the kindergarten movement is fundamental, although her response to Kraitsir resembles her earlier reaction to Alcott's theories and methods. In applying Kraitsir's theories to the kindergarten, Peabody elaborates and modifies the basic assumptions announced in *The Significance of the Alphabet*.

The processes of modification and elaboration are equally important in Peabody's essays of the 1840s, before she focuses her abundant energies on the kindergarten movement. In the volume of her failed periodical, *Aesthetic Papers*, for example, Peabody employs the language of philology to discuss topics that she explores under the titles "The Word 'Aesthetic'" (1–4), "The Dorian Measure, with a Modern Application" (64–110), and "Language" (214–24). In all three essays her aim is to open new territories of cultural reform, applying the insights of philology to cross boundaries of cultural discourse.

Peabody announces and enacts the strategy of crossing discursive boundaries in her introductory essay, "The Word 'Aesthetic.'" By opposing the restricted

---

32. The *Nursery* version of Kraitsir's table of germs gives concrete, bodily names for the classes of sounds. So, for instance, labials are called "lip letters," gutturals "throat letters," and "lingual dentals" "tongue and throat letters" (*Nursery* 12). The back cover of *Aesthetic Papers*, also published in 1849, advertises the *First Nursery Reading Book, The Significance of the Alphabet*, and the *Lexeology of English*, which will later become Kraitsir's *Glossology*.

33. *Kindergarten Guide* (Boston: T. O. H. P. Burnham, 1863), 75–97. The book is a collaboration between Peabody and her sister, Mary Peabody Mann. The description of the reading lesson occurs in Peabody's introductory essay, "Kindergarten—What Is It?" 18–21. The essay originally appeared in *Atlantic Monthly* 10 (November 1862), 586–93; the lead article in the volume is, by the way, Thoreau's lecture-essay "Wild Apples."

definition of the word, Peabody argues for a new sense of criticism: "The 'aesthetic element,' then, is in our view neither a theory of the beautiful, nor a philosophy of art, but a component and indivisible part in all human creations which are not mere works of necessity; in other words, which are based on idea, as distinguished from appetite" (1). Peabody's aesthetic position lies on the boundaries between the individual and the universal, between the artist and the critic. She resolves these two dualisms by applying the first to the second: art tends, in history, to move from the universal and unconscious expression of national and religious ideals toward the individual artist's expression of his own spirit; criticism, on the other hand, moves from mere reactions of individual taste toward more universally applicable standards. As she succinctly phrases it, "The progress of criticism is the reverse of that of art" (4). Peabody's goal is to create a dynamic, progressive relationship between the poles of her various dualisms. Her discursive strategy crosses boundaries by creating a temporal dialectic: the discussion of a single word and its several definitions becomes a compressed history of art and criticism, ending with a projected future of purified, spiritualized individuality.

In the long second article, the Dorian measure figures the harmony of Dorian civilization, which meets Peabody's demands for the term *aesthetic*. She therefore represents the political, religious, and cultural elements of the Dorians' world as ideally measured: education, in one telling sentence, "was called by the Dorians, *learning music*" (84). Peabody employs the Dorians as an idealized image of aesthetic civilization, so her central question becomes one of correspondence: "But the question for us is, whether, on the new platform upon which Christendom finds itself, now that the spiritual future has descended as it were into human life, there may not be found a harmony corresponding to the Dorian measure;—whether there may not be a social organization which does as much justice to the Christian religion and philosophy, as the Dorian state did to Apollo" (86). The question is for the most part rhetorical, but the second half of the essay outlines the "social organization" that will, according to Peabody, bring nineteenth-century American culture into perfect correspondence with her historical model.

The aspect of culture that Peabody sees as most promising is, not surprisingly, education, "a subject of greater importance than government" for the Dorians (87). Her rhetoric approaches the apocalyptic tone of the jeremiad when she concludes that "a true spirit of culture must do for the national heart what the ever-incoming grace of God does for the individual soul" (98). Peabody's idealism becomes the means of measuring nineteenth-century American culture, and her method for filling in what American culture lacks is to propose "*a system of education* correspondent to our large privileges" (99). The system of education Peabody envisions is hardly systematic or comprehensive. Instead, the Dorian correspondence allows her to make some intriguing proposals about early childhood education. She argues, for example, for physical exercise, dance, and musical training, as well as the traditional training in drawing and geometry (100–106). But her most radical proposals concern reading and writing, which should be taught "in such a manner as to make our own language the 'open Sesame' to all speech" (106).

As she nears the end of her essay, Peabody names glossology as the "true philological art" that will "make the native tongue appreciated in all its deep significance, and prepare the mind for such a comparison of our own with other tongues, as shall immensely facilitate their acquisition" (106). She claims, moreover, that "philology should be studied as the most important of sciences, not only for the sake of knowing the works of art and science that the various languages contain, but because words themselves are growths of nature and works of art, capable of giving the highest delight as such; and because their analysis and history reveal the universe in its symbolic character" (107). Peabody emphasizes the "true study of language" (108) as the key to her projected system of education because language embodies the aesthetic: language crosses all boundaries, since every aspect of culture is bound within words, and a fully renewed culture will therefore find its ultimate measure in language.

Given the structure of Peabody's argument in "The Dorian Measure," we can view her essay "Language" (214–24) as a focused elaboration of her statement that philology is the "most important of sciences." In "The Dorian Measure" Peabody places Charles Kraitsir's theories within the context of cultural arguments; in "Language" she views those theories within the context of "the fact of language, and its want of effectiveness" (214).

Peabody's method of treating the dual nature of language once again depends upon a temporal dialectic, powered by her progressivist vision of the future. She structures the essay by placing Horace Bushnell's "Preliminary Dissertation on Language" in opposition to Kraitsir's *Significance of the Alphabet*.[34] While she approves of Bushnell's observations in several cases, Peabody complains that he does not recognize the necessary connection between sound and sense; hence he defends the arbitrary, conventional origin of language and meaning, focus-

34. Horace Bushnell, *God in Christ. Three Discourses, Delivered at New Haven, Cambridge, and Andover, with a Preliminary Dissertation on Language* (Hartford: Brown & Parsons, 1849). Peabody lists 1837 as the publication date for *Significance*, which is five years before the date of my copy.

35. *Aesthetic Papers* 214–19; cf. *God in Christ*, 14–24, in which Bushnell argues against the "modern ethnologists" who seek a unified origin of language and, in parallel fashion, a unified origin of

ing on the diversity of languages as evidence.[35] Peabody cites *Significance* in order to argue for the universal character of language (216), pronouncing Kraitsir's most important discovery to be "that words are to be considered, not merely or chiefly by their effect on the ear, but *in the process of their formation by the organs of speech*" (220). The dynamic, expressive origin of language becomes the temporal ideal toward which all language-users should strive, and because it is dynamic Peabody sees the proposed origin as natural and essential.

These conclusions lead Peabody to consider how humankind can recapture the Adamic origin of language. Since *Significance* contains the truth about language, she proposes "a sequel of some practical elementary books which may make it possible to apply its principles for the purpose of transforming the present system of language-teaching in schools. It is said the author is superintending the preparation of some. A whole series is necessary, from the *a b c* book to a manual of the Sanscrit" (221). Peabody's disingenuous promotion of her collaboration with Kraitsir represents glossology as a transforming power, a force that will operate on every intellectual level to educate Americans in the Language of Nature.

Peabody's most significant elaboration of Kraitsir's theories appears in the ways in which she translates and expands upon Herder's *The Spirit of Hebrew Poetry* in "Language" (221–23). Although she owned a copy of James Marsh's translation as early as 1833, when she used it as a text in a Boston conversation class, Peabody alters Marsh's translation in several important ways.[36] In introducing Herder, Peabody quotes Marsh's translation exactly, but she inserts an italicized addition of her own: "One of the interlocutors asks,—after having granted, with respect to the Hebrew, 'the symbolism of the radical sounds, or the utterance of the feeling that was prompted, while the object itself was present to the senses; *the sound of the feelings in the very intuition of their causes:*—

---

humankind; Bushnell's version of the origin is to give an "experiment" of two strangers "thrown together" without any language—the two proceed "arbitrarily, or, at least, by causes so occult or remote that we must regard them as arbitrary" (19–20) to name objects and develop a language corresponding to "the Logos in the outward world, answering to the logos or internal reason of the parties" (21). See Gura, *Wisdom of Words*, 15–71, for commentaries on Bushnell and Unitarian theories of language.

36. In a letter of April 1833 to Maria Chase, Peabody proposes to use Herder in a series of conversations with Salem ladies, "on the plan of my Boston class." *The Spirit of Hebrew Poetry* is, she says, "an exquisite book" (*Letters* 107). She reviews the book in *Christian Examiner*, 60 (May 1834): 174–75. In September 1846, Peabody sends a copy of Marsh's translation to Phoebe Gage, calling it "a favorite book of mine" and claiming that Herder's poetic criticism develops "*truth*, on the perception of which is conditioned the apprehension of the more Universal Truth—the prophecy that binds the world's history into a rounded whole" (*Letters* 276). James Marsh, whose translation was published in two volumes (Burlington: Edward Smith, 1833), was responsible for publishing the American edition of Coleridge's *Aids to Reflection*. See Gura, *Wisdom of Words*, 39–51, for a discussion of Marsh.

But how is it with the derivations from these radical terms?" (221) Peabody's insertion emphasizes the intuitive and emotional aspects of sound symbolism because they are closest, she believes, to the "prophecy that binds the world's history into a rounded whole" (*Letters* 267).

Peabody's theoretical emphasis on the intuitive and emotional aspects of language and her practical emphasis on childhood education function within the culturally accepted versions of the feminine that we know as domestic ideology. As Hale's *Lecturess* and Fuller's conversation classes show, domestic ideology distributes and controls power by gendering discursive and cultural space. Peabody knowingly employs the domestic idiom in her translation of Herder: "The root of the mother-word will stand in the centre, and around her the grove of her children. By influence of taste, diligence, sound sense, and the judicious comparison of different dialects, lexicons will be brought to distinguish what is essential from what is accidental in the signification of words, and to trace the gradual process of transition" (222). The compound "mother-word" and the phrase "her children" are Peabody's substitutions for Marsh's more abstract "primitive word" and "its offspring" (Marsh 1:35). Peabody uses the maternal image to represent the "essential" signification of words, while "her children" are the derivations from that central root. By blending horticultural and domestic metaphors, Peabody implies that language is essential and natural, both in form and in meaning. The figuration also gives a nurturing sense of order to the "growth" of language, controlling the emotional and intuitive origins of meaning.

The conjunction of domestic ideology and organic metaphor is most important in Peabody's ideas concerning kindergarten. She introduces the *Kindergarten Guide*, for instance, by asking the question of definition—"Kindergarten—What Is It?"—and her answer strongly echoes the strategies of *Aesthetic Papers:* "*Kindergarten* means a garden of children, and Froebel, the inventor of it, or rather, as he would prefer to express it, *the discoverer of the method of Nature*, meant to symbolize by the name the spirit and plan of treatment. How does the gardener treat his plants? He studies their individual natures, and puts them into such circumstances of soil and atmosphere as enable them to grow, flower, and bring forth fruit,—also to renew their manifestation year after year" (10). Peabody employs the method of Fuller's Boston conversations: examining the word *kindergarten*, she creates an essentialist etymology that applies the organic metaphor of gardening to the problem of educating children. The extended analogy argues for a nurturing approach to education, one that allows the individual child to "grow" in the same way a plant does, although it also allows the gardener/teacher to "prune" redundant growths (11). Peabody's figural strategy naturalizes both language in general and the language of domesticity, for one mother-word reveals the "essential" approach to educating children.

The kindergarten movement becomes, for Peabody, the means of unifying her concerns with language, cultural reform, and education. Circumspect and conservative, Peabody never addresses the public sphere of eloquence by delivering lectures or making orations. So, for instance, in the 1869 essay "A Plea for Froebel's Kindergarten," she confines her plea within the boundaries of domestic ideology. In discussing the training of kindergarten teachers, Peabody begins with grand abstractions encompassing "outward nature" and "human nature," but she uses the "universal motherly instinct" as a means of limiting and controlling the abstractions, bringing them within the grasp of "any fairly cultivated, genial-hearted young woman, of average intellect."[37]

Peabody's conservative strategy entails the continued use of Kraitsir's theory of language in her kindergarten work. As editor and chief writer of the *Kindergarten Messenger*, Peabody asserts that "command of language is the intellectual benefit of the Kindergarten, a benefit that can hardly be too much appreciated."[38] In an essay titled "Command of Language to Be Gained in Kindergarten," Peabody applies Kraitsir's glossological schema to the dynamic, domestic relationship of teacher and child:

> Imagination is baffled in endeavoring to conceive how human communication began; we see how it begins *now* with every individual, by the help of the mother, and those who supply the mother's place. The articulate words are defined to the child by gestures, and expression of face, and modulation of tones; and the play of the organs of speech may be analyzed into symbolization of the moving or dead phenomena, by motions of lips and tongue against the palate and the teeth, while the inward and causal is expressed by the motions of the throat modifying the breath as it comes up from the centre of life and the source of energy.[39]

Peabody's description of the "play of the organs of speech" follows Kraitsir's three-part division of articulatory phonetics/semantics: labial sounds evoke the living phenomena of the outer world; dental sounds signify the dead phenomena of the outer world; guttural sounds express the inner causes of all phe-

---

37. The essay appears in *Last Evening with Allston, and Other Papers*, 340; rpt. edition (New York: AMS Press, 1975).

38. "Language in Children," *Kindergarten Messenger* (June 1875), 129.

39. *Kindergarten Messenger* (November 1873), 8.

nomena (*Glossology* 161). As in the 1869 "Plea," however, Peabody mixes the abstract terms of language theory with a more limited, accessible vocabulary. The imagery of "gestures," "expression of face," and "modulation of tones" suggests the importance of nonverbal—one is tempted to say "preverbal"—communication. Moreover, she cautions her readers to give the children "not scientific process—but the result of science," and she promotes the kindergarten teacher as a model of "elegance of expression" ("Command" 8). Thus the kindergarten teacher becomes a domestic, feminized figure of eloquence.

If, as Nina Baym has persuasively argued, Peabody is important for "the gendering of millenialism," she is no less so for the gendering of nineteenth-century ideas of language and cultural reform.[40] Peabody interprets the Language of Nature within antebellum domestic ideology, but, at the same time, she employs it to create figures of empowered female speakers. Peabody is clearly less radical in her ideas and less artful in her expression than Margaret Fuller, but her version of a mother-tongue is both radical and artful in its implications for the culture at large. By creating a gendered theory of language and providing a specific cultural space for its application, Peabody's own mother-tongue speaks eloquently across the most fundamental boundary dividing word and deed.

40. "The Ann Sisters: Elizabeth Peabody's Millennial Historicism," *ALH* 3 (Spring 1991), 32. The entire article (27–45) is of signal importance to students of Peabody, and it is of equal importance to those concerned with the revaluation of nineteenth-century American literature. Baym argues that we should read Peabody in her own right, on her own terms, and her essay is intended to distinguish Peabody from other (male) writers such as Emerson. From my reading of Peabody's work, I would suggest that she is no more independent of Emerson or Thoreau than they are of her.

5

A Fruitful Nursery of Orators:

Frederick Douglass and the Conditions for Eloquence

1

In the 1846 lecture "Eloquence," Emerson defines the true power of the orator as "strength of character" and notes that "no record at all adequate" to the fame of powerful orators remains:

> Besides, what is best is lost,—the fiery life of the moment. But the conditions for eloquence always exist. It is always dying out of famous places and appearing in corners. Wherever the polarities meet, wherever the fresh moral sentiment, the instinct of freedom and duty, come in direct opposition to fossil conservatism and the thirst of gain, the spark will pass. The resistance to slavery in this country has been a fruitful nursery of orators. The natural connection by which it drew to itself a train of moral reforms, and the slight yet sufficient party organization it offered, reinforced the city with new blood from the woods and mountains.[1]

Emerson characteristically ties the power of eloquence to cultural reform, the meeting of the "polarities" of "fresh moral sentiment" and "fossil conservatism." In the last two sentences of the passage, Emerson offers a concrete, current example of national eloquence and asserts that the antislavery movement instills the "city with new blood from the woods and mountains." He thus explains

---

1. The records show that Emerson delivered his lecture "Eloquence" in Cambridge, Massachusetts, on 16 December 1846 (*JMN* 10:25n.), and the phrase "has been" suggests a prewar delivery. No comparable passage appears in the three manuscript folders of "Eloquence." I quote from the 1870 essay (*W* 7:95).

the political "polarities" by viewing them through his preferred polarity of culture and nature.

In privileging the antislavery movement as the "fruitful nursery of orators," Emerson tells only half of the story. The public debate over slavery in antebellum America does indeed form a fruitful nursery of orators, but those orators appear on both sides of the slavery question. Indeed, the question is too complex to be reduced to polarities, at least in the first two decades of debate. By the time Emerson calls himself an abolitionist "of the most absolute abolition" in 1858, the slavery question has become deeply polarizing.[2] In the 1830s and 1840s, however, America debates the question both in famous places and in corners, and slavery becomes a defining issue for nineteenth-century American culture.

If Emerson's definition of eloquence reflects his own version of the figure of Adamic eloquence, it also reflects the polarized version of social discourse that mastered American culture in the 1850s and brought it to revolution and war. Perhaps most significantly, it oversimplifies the "fiery life of the moment," reducing our understanding of nineteenth-century American culture to a place "where the polarities meet." Unless we reconstruct that fiery life, we must agree that "what is best is lost" and acknowledge that the loss is ours alone.

A salient example of reconstructing cultural discourse is Alison Goodyear Freehling's account of the public debate over abolition and colonization schemes conducted by the 1831–32 session of the Virginia General Assembly. Freehling shows that pragmatic issues such as taxation and legislative representation lie behind the slavery question. The assembly came very close to passing a law calling for the *postnati* emancipation of slaves, and it eventually called for further public debate on emancipation and a bill for the colonization of free blacks on a voluntary basis.[3] The Virginia debate shows that in 1831, on the heels of Nat Turner's insurrection the previous August, the legislature of the

---

2. For a full account of Emerson's relationship to the abolition movement, see Gougeon, *Virtue's Hero*; see also Richardson, *Emerson: The Mind on Fire*, 268–70, 395–99, 496–99. Also valuable is the recent collection of Emerson's *Antislavery Writings*, ed. Joel Myerson and Len Gougeon (New Haven: Yale University Press, 1995).

3. *Drift Toward Dissolution: The Virginia Slavery Debate of 1831–1832* (Baton Rouge: Louisiana State University Press, 1982). The Assembly was divided into three basic groups: conservatives from "Southside" Virginia who proposed to silence debate; moderates who favored colonization of free blacks and gradual, compensated emancipation; abolitionists who proposed uncompensated emancipation of all slaves born after 4 July 1840 and colonization (148). The legislature ultimately passed a special committee report on "insurrectionary movements" and the moderate "Bryce preamble," which "embodied the gradualist emancipation philosophy of the American Colonization Society" (149). For a detailed account of the schemes and voting, see 122–228.

largest slaveholding state in America could engage in a public consideration of the peculiar institution. Second, it shows that nineteenth-century Southern culture is far from being a monolith of "fossil conservatism and the thirst of gain." Third, the debate itself occurs while new laws, passed by the 1830–31 Assembly four months before Turner's rebellion, ban "all assemblages of free blacks for educational purposes" and prohibit whites from teaching slaves to read or write.[4] The Virginia slavery debate thus reveals complex ironies, the most obvious being that white legislators discuss emancipation at the same time that they prohibit blacks from learning about the discussion.

The Virginia slavery debate is important because it reveals the close connection between language and power. In a 19 November 1831 letter, for instance, Governor John Floyd of Virginia writes Governor James Hamilton of South Carolina that "northern incendiaries" are to blame for Nat Turner's insurrection and that "laws governing slaves and free blacks 'became more inactive.' Whites, particularly the 'most respectable . . . females,' taught 'negroes to read and write' so that they 'might read the Scriptures.' Many of these 'pious' ladies became 'tutoresses in Sunday schools and . . . distributors' of northern religious tracts proclaiming the spiritual equality of all men" (Freehling 83). Floyd's letter suggests that Southern culture was in a state of flux in the first half of the nineteenth century, in which "respectable females" could routinely disobey laws prohibiting slave literacy. The legislation of 1830–32 indicates that the government of Virginia sought to exercise a power of silence and denial, so far as black literacy is concerned, in order to protect its own interests—that is, the interests of its white citizens.

The twin power of silence and denial can be seen clearly in Thomas R. Dew's *Review of the Debate in the Virginia Legislature, 1831–'32*, reprinted in the 1852 collection of essays *The Pro-Slavery Argument*.[5] Dew himself practices a rhetoric of silence regarding the question of slave literacy, for he does not directly address the issue. Instead, he argues from the assumption that blacks are inherently inferior to whites: "A race of people, differing from us in color and in habits, and vastly inferior in the scale of civilization, have been increasing and spreading, 'growing with our growth, and strengthening with our strength,'

---

4. The act is dated 7 April 1831 and thus predates Turner's 21 August insurrection by four months. It is recorded in *Acts Passed at a General Assembly of the Commonwealth of Virginia, 1830–1831* (Richmond, 1831), 107–8 (qtd. Freehling 83).

5. Dew was, at the time of publishing his essay, a twenty-nine-year-old professor of political law at William and Mary College. The essay first appeared in the September 1832 *American Quarterly Review* and then in expanded pamphlet form. I quote from the text reprinted in *The Pro-Slavery Argument* (Charleston: Walker, Richards, 1852) 287–490. See Freehling, *Drift*, 202–8, for a summary of Dew's essay.

until they have become intertwined and intertwisted with every fibre of society" (287). The assumption of racial inferiority leads Dew to argue that emancipation would lead not to equality and freedom but to a cruel form of degradation: "Declare the negroes of the South free to-morrow, and vain will be your decree, until you have prepared them for it; you depress, instead of elevating. The law would, in every point of view, be one of the most cruel and inhuman which could possibly be passed. The law would make them freemen, and custom or prejudice, we care not which you call it, would degrade them to the condition of slaves" (435–36). Dew's arguments rest, finally, upon a benevolent paternalism, and we can infer from the *Review* that he would argue that literacy would only make blacks, both free and slave, unhappy.

These same assumptions appear in the other essays of *The Pro-Slavery Argument*. Chancellor William Harper of South Carolina, for instance, argues in his 1837 essay that "Odium has been cast upon our legislation, on account of its forbidding the elements of education to be communicated to slaves. But, in truth, what injury is done to them by this? He who works during the day with his hands, does not read in intervals of leisure for his amusement, or the improvement of his mind—or the exceptions are so very rare, as scarcely to need the being provided for" (36). Since the principal text of slaves is the Bible, Harper meets any possible objections concerning religious training by asserting that "of all methods of religious instruction, however, this, of reading for themselves, would be the most inefficient—their comprehension is defective, and the employment is to them an unusual and laborious one" (37). Finally, literacy would affect slaves in much the same way that Dew contends emancipation would: "If there were any chance of their elevating their rank and condition in society, it might be matter of hardship, that they should be debarred those rudiments of knowledge which open the way to further attainments. But this they know cannot be, and that further attainments would be useless to them" (37).

A third essayist in *The Pro-Slavery Argument*, James Henry Hammond of South Carolina, adds a further dimension to the defense of the slave literacy laws. In two public letters to the British abolitionist Thomas Clarkson, written in 1845, Hammond blames antislavery publications for the South's repressive laws:

> You seem well aware, however, that laws have been recently passed in all these States, making it penal to teach slaves to read. Do you know what occasioned their passage, and renders their stringent enforcement necessary? I can tell you. It was the abolition agitation. If the slave is not allowed to read his bible, the sin rests upon the abolitionists; for they

stand prepared to furnish him with a key to it, which would make it, not a book of hope, and love, and peace, but of despair, hatred and blood; which would convert the reader, not into a christian, but a demon. To preserve him from such a horrid destiny, it is a sacred duty which we owe to our slaves, not less than to ourselves, to interpose the most decisive means. If the Catholics deem it wrong to trust the bible to the hands of ignorance, shall we be excommunicated because we will not give it, and with it the corrupt and fatal commentaries of the abolitionists, to our slaves? Allow our slaves to read your writings, stimulating them to cut our throats! Can you believe us to be such unspeakable fools? (124)

Although Hammond, like Harper, focuses on the Bible as a forbidden text, his ire is aroused by the "corrupt and fatal commentaries of the abolitionists." The laws forbidding slave literacy are, in fact, directly connected to the "incendiary" literature of the antislavery movement.

The fourth essayist in *The Pro-Slavery Argument*, William Gilmore Simms, makes explicit the connection between literacy laws and abolitionist literature. "The Morals of Slavery" is cast as a response to Harriet Martineau's *Retrospect of Western Travel* (1838), although the English reformer's *Society in America* (1837) appears to be Simms's real target. Simms is the most rhetorically sophisticated writer in the proslavery volume, blending the nationalism of the "Young America" movement with a defense of slavery. Martineau emerges as a reformer who is deaf—literally and figuratively—to the "true" conditions of slavery and Southern society. For example, Simms quotes Martineau as asserting that "the abolitionists sent no incendiary tracts among the slaves" and that "slaves cannot read" (199), and he offers the following rebuttal:

Thousands of negro slaves do read, as any body may see who has ever visited the cities of the South; but, the slaveholders allege—though the abolitionists may deny—that, lest the slave should labor under this disability, and for the better conveying the lesson to the thousands that do read, gross *cuts* are employed in these abolition newspapers, and are even stamped upon manufactured cottons, of the kind usually furnished for negro consumption, and insinuated, here and there, at decent intervals, among the bales designed for the Southern market. (199–200)

Simms's defense of the "morals of slavery" is aggressively ironic, effectively accusing antislavery propagandists of subterfuge and oversimplification. His message is clear: abolitionist tactics are far from "decent," and the South has every right to protect itself from words and woodcuts "insinuated" into its marketplace. By undercutting Martineau's assertions, Simms attacks the right of any outsider to apply "New-England morals" to Southern institutions.

One of the most incendiary texts to enter the South in the 1830s is *Walker's Appeal, in Four Articles, Together with a Preamble, to the Colored Citizens of the World*. Walker, a free black living in Boston, mailed thirty copies of the pamphlet to Thomas Lewis, a free black in Richmond, and the mayor of Richmond confiscated twenty of the pamphlets as well as Walker's letter to Lewis. The mayor then forwarded a pamphlet and the letter to Governor William B. Giles, who sent a confidential communiqué to the Virginia House of Delegates in early January 1830. The legislature took no immediate action, but when William Lloyd Garrison began publishing *The Liberator* in 1831, the General Assembly passed the 7 April 1831 act against slave literacy and educational assemblages of free blacks.[6]

Walker's second article, "Our Wretchedness in Consequence of Ignorance," addresses the combined topics of literacy, religion, and racism: "Men of colour, who are also of sense, for you particularly is my appeal designed. Our more ignorant brethren are not able to penetrate its value. I call upon you therefore to cast your eyes upon the wretchedness of your brethren and to do your utmost to enlighten them—*go to work and enlighten your brethren!*—let the Lord see you doing what you can to rescue them and yourselves from degradation" (*Appeal* 40). For Walker, "sense" is synonymous with the ability to read and write effectively, and that ability is a prerequisite to true freedom. He therefore appeals to "men of colour" to become literate and to disseminate education and religion among their "brethren." Walker appeals to his audience in the incendiary rhetoric of the jeremiad, and his exclamatory style borders upon the heightened tone of speech: "An ignorant father, who knows no more than what nature has taught him, together with what little he acquires by the senses of hearing and seeing, finding his son able to write a neat hand, sets it down for granted that he has as good learning as any body; the young, ignorant gump,

---

6. Freehling, *Drift*, 82–83. The *Appeal* first appeared in September 1829, and by 1830 it was in its third printing. The reaction to the work was immediate and extreme, including a reward of one thousand dollars for Walker's death, ten thousand dollars if he were delivered alive to the South. For an extended study of the pamphlet's effects, see Clement Eaton, "A Dangerous Pamphlet in the Old South," *Journal of Southern History* 2 (August 1936): 1–12; Eaton also discusses the laws passed by Georgia, North Carolina, Mississippi, and Louisiana in *Freedom of Thought in the Old South* (Durham: Duke University Press, 1940), 121–26. I quote from *Walker's Appeal in Four Articles* (New York: Arno Press and the New York Times, 1969), which reprints the second edition (1830).

hearing his father or mother, who perhaps may be ten times more ignorant, in point of literature, than himself, extolling his learning, struts about in the full assurance, that his attainments in literature are sufficient to take him through the world, when, in fact, he has scarcely any learning at all!!!!" (43). The command of language—grammar, reading, and writing—proves humanity, and it also enables those in command to acquire knowledge. The unstated assumption is that the dissemination of skills in language will lead to emancipation. Walker's emphasis on the education of "our children" recalls the work of Fuller and Peabody, and he is particularly close to Peabody in joining "education and religion."[7]

Walker is especially prescient in his view of language as the means of empowerment. Although he reserves his severest indignation for "the Americans" and their "powerful obstacle," he sharply criticizes blacks for a facile complacency. Literacy entails more than being able "to scribble tolerably well," for that is merely the appearance of education: "Most of the coloured people, when they speak of the education of one among us who can write a neat hand, and who perhaps knows nothing but to scribble and puff pretty fair on a small scrap of paper, immaterial whether his words are grammatical, or spelt correctly, or not; if it only looks beautiful, they say he has as good an education as any white man—he can write as well as any white man" (43). The "powerful obstacle" of literacy laws is no more oppressive than the empty facade of literacy; it is merely a more blatant expression of an ultimately insidious and disabling power. Aimed primarily at exposing the hypocrisy of "white Americans," whom he calls "this *charitable* people," Walker's jeremiad portrays an "almost universal ignorance" (46) among blacks, both free and slave, and although Walker reserves his most vitriolic rhetoric for the South, he exposes the powerful structures of limitation on both sides of Mason and Dixon's line.

Those structures are clearly visible in William Lloyd Garrison's notice of Walker's *Appeal* in the first issue of *The Liberator*. Garrison notes that the North Carolina legislature has "lately been sitting behind closed doors, in consequence of a message from the Governor relative to the . . . pamphlet" and calls the

---

7. The conjunction of the abolitionist and feminist movements in nineteenth-century America is well known. Leaders of women's rights and antislavery include Susan B. Anthony, Elizabeth Cady Stanton, Lucretia Mott, Lucy Stone, and the Grimké sisters. See Ellen DuBois, *Feminism and Suffrage: The Emergence of an Independent Woman's Rights Movement in America* (Ithaca: Cornell University Press, 1978), 82–93. For a recent analysis of the conjunction in terms of representations of the body, see Karen Sanchez-Eppler, "Bodily Bonds: The Intersecting Rhetorics of Feminism and Abolition," in *The Culture of Sentiment: Race, Gender, and Sentimentality in Nineteenth-Century America*, ed. Shirley Samuels (New York: Oxford University Press, 1992) 92–114. See also Sanchez-Eppler, *Touching Liberty: Abolition, Feminism, and the Politics of the Body* (Berkeley and Los Angeles: University of California Press, 1993).

Appeal a "promoter of insurrection" and "one of the most remarkable productions of the age." But he also states that he has "already publicly deprecated its spirit."[8] Similarly, letters from the anonymous "V." concerning the *Appeal*, appearing in *The Liberator* on 14 May 1831 and 28 May 1831, mix approval and disapproval. In the first letter, V. praises Walker's spirit and style, but at the same time the pseudonymous writer expresses sympathy for the slaveholding South: "I fear, very much fear, that the retribution predicted in the book in question is at hand. It is a hard case for the South to be sure" (Nelson 18). Regarding the literacy laws, V. comments, "The law makers of some of the slave states have done wisely (in some points of view) in making it highly penal to teach a slave to read. If things are to remain as they are, it is sound policy: that is, supposing it practicable to enforce such laws. Yet I think they will only put off, not prevent the catastrophe" (13–14). V. writes without irony or invective, placing his review of the *Appeal* within the context of a rational, neutral discourse. In this respect, V. effectively rewrites Walker's *Appeal*, sanitizing its indignant call for immediate emancipation and secularizing its tone of Old Testament prophecy: "The tears of the innocent and the groans of the oppressed cry to Heaven for vengeance, and though I do not look for the arrival of any relief through supernatural agency, I am persuaded that a great change must take place before the lapse of another century" (24). By rewording Walker, V. makes an appeal to the spirit of liberal humanism, but his gradualist language silences the *Appeal* more effectively than Southern legislatures were able to do.

2

The drama of limitation takes place throughout the discourses of both proponents and opponents of slavery, assuming many forms and arguments, but it is especially dramatic in the career of Frederick Douglass, without doubt the most eloquent and effective black orator of the nineteenth century. In an exemplary way, Douglass embodies the struggle for empowerment through language. Moreover, in his speeches as well as in his antebellum autobiographies, Douglass enacts the drama of empowerment by directly addressing the twin issues of lan-

---

8. *The Liberator* 1 (1 January 1831), quoted in Truman Nelson, ed. *Documents of Upheaval: Selections from William Lloyd Garrison's The Liberator, 1831–1865* (New York: Hill and Wang, 1966), 5. Garrison had deprecated the spirit of the pamphlet in Benjamin Lundy's *Genius of Universal Emancipation* for April 1830 (Nelson 4).

guage and power. In his first recorded speech, delivered in Lynn, Massachusetts, in October 1841, Douglass notes that "a large portion of the slaves *know* that they have a right to their liberty.—It is often talked about and read of, for some of us know how to read, although all our knowledge is gained in secret."[9] Nor does Douglass allow his Northern audience to remain comfortably indignant: "My friends, we are not taught from books; there is a law against teaching us, although I have heard some folks say we could not learn if we had a chance. The northern people say so, but the south do not believe it, or they would not have laws with heavy penalties to prevent it" (5). Like Walker, Douglass attacks "northern prejudice" (5) as well as Southern legislatures.

The broadening of abolition to include abolishing all racial barriers, north and south, is a marked tendency in Douglass's antebellum speeches and lectures. Speaking on the topic "American Prejudice Against Color" in Cork, Ireland, Douglass asserts that "the inferiority of the slave" is "the burden of all their defence of the institution of slavery" (*FDP* 1:59) and then focuses on literacy laws to prove his point:

> Mr. President, I shall give you a few specimens of these laws. In South Carolina in 1770, this law was passed. "Whereas the teaching of slaves to write is sometimes connected with inconvenience, be it enacted that every person who shall teach a slave to write, for every such offence shall forfeit the penalty of £100." Mark, we are an inferior race, morally and intellectually. Hence 'tis right to enslave us. The same hypocrites make laws to prevent our improvement. In Georgia in 1770 similar laws were passed; and in Virginia. South Carolina, in 1800, passed the following—that the assemblage of slaves and Mulattos for the purpose of instruction may be dissolved. In Louisiana the penalty of teaching a black in a Sunday school is, for the first offence 500 dollars fine, for the second death. This is in America, a Christian country, a democratic, a republican country, the land of the free, the home of the brave—the nation that waged the seven years warfare to get rid of a three-penny tea tax, and pledged itself to the declaration that all men are born free and equal, making it at the same time a penalty punishable with death for the second offense to teach a slave his letters.[10]

9. *The Frederick Douglass Papers. Series One: Speeches, Debates, and Interviews*, 5 vols., ed. John W. Blassingame (New Haven: Yale University Press, 1979–92), 1:4. All references to Douglass's speeches are taken from this edition and appear cited parenthetically in my text as *FDP*.

10. *FDP* 1:61; the address was delivered on 23 October 1845. As the editors note, Douglass's source for the literacy laws is George M. Stroud, *A Sketch of the Laws Relating to Slavery in the Several States of*

The focus on literacy laws serves at least two purposes. First, it brands as hypocritical the paradox of repressive laws within the "land of the free." Second, it exposes the legal construction of racial inferiority. Douglass employs ironic juxtaposition and palpably specious logic in giving "a few specimens of these laws," and he points to the ironies of history by alluding to the Revolutionary War and the Declaration of Independence, ironies that would be particularly compelling to a British audience.

As in the 1841 speech in Lynn, however, Douglass does not restrict his rhetorical attack to Southern slaveholders. Instead, he turns from the legal to the personal, narrating the near-riot that occurred aboard the *Cambria* when he addressed the passengers. According to Douglass, several listeners objected to his speech, and a certain J. Hazzard from New Haven, Connecticut, called him a liar:

> Well, said I, ladies and gentlemen, since what I have said has been pronounced lies, I will read not what *I* have written but what the southern legislators themselves have written—I mean the law. I proceeded to read—this raised a general clamour, for they did not wish the laws exposed. They hated facts, they knew that the people of these countries who were on the deck would draw their own references from them.
>
> Here a general hurry ensued—"Down with the nigger," said one—"he shan't speak" said another. I sat with my arms folded, feeling no way anxious for my fate. I never saw a more barefaced attempt to put down the freedom of speech than upon this occasion.[11]

By juxtaposing the treatment he received aboard the *Cambria* with that he has just experienced in Cork, Douglass in effect congratulates his Irish listeners for

---

the United States of America (Philadelphia, 1827), 88–89. Another compendium of the period is William Goodell, *The American Slave Code* (New York: American & Foreign Anti-Slavery Society, 1853); see esp. 319–25.

11. *FDP* 1:64. The editors identify Hazzard, who had lived for many years in Georgia, from the article in the New York *Herald*, 1 December 1845. Earlier in the Cork speech, Douglass refers to the editor of the *Herald*, James Gordon Bennett, as "one of the greatest slave haters in the world" (62). In the 1855 *My Bondage and My Freedom* (rpt. Chicago: Johnson, 1970), Douglass says that the "New Orleans and Georgia passengers were pleased to regard my lecture as an insult offered to them, and swore I should not speak" (285), but in the same chapter, writing to Garrison in a 1 January 1846 letter, he dissolves the boundary between North and South: "In the southern part of the United States, I was a slave, thought of and spoken of as property; in the language of the LAW, *'held, taken, reputed, and adjudged to be a chattel in the hands of my owners and possessors, and their executors, administrators, and assigns, to all intents, constructions, and purposes whatsoever.'* (Brev. Digest, 224). In the northern states, a fugitive slave, liable to be hunted at any moment, like a felon, and to be hurled into the terrible jaws of slavery—doomed by an inveterate prejudice against color to insult and outrage on every hand" (287–88).

their humanity at the same time that he condemns his American compatriots for their hypocrisy. Like Emerson, Douglass points to a place in which "the polarities meet," although in this case the polarities represent a pervasive American prejudice against color, one which crosses the sectional line between North and South.

Douglass personalizes the connection between language and power in recounting his own battle for literacy, and in several famous instances he focuses especially on the roles of his Baltimore owners, Hugh and Sophia Auld. In *Narrative of the Life of Frederick Douglass, An American Slave* (1845), the account is spare, filling one long paragraph:

> Very soon after I went to live with Mr. and Mrs. Auld, she very kindly commenced to teach me the A,B,C. After I had learned this, she assisted me in learning to spell words of three or four letters. Just at this point of my progress, Mr. Auld found out what was going on, and at once forbade Mrs. Auld to instruct me further, telling her, among other things, that it was unlawful, as well as unsafe, to teach a slave to read. To use his own words, further, he said, "If you give a nigger an inch, he will take an ell. A nigger should know nothing but to obey his master—to do as he is told to do. Learning would *spoil* the best nigger in the world. Now," said he, "if you teach that nigger (speaking of myself) how to read, there would be no keeping him. It would forever unfit him to be a slave. He would at once become unmanageable, and of no value to his master. As to himself, it could do him no good, but a great deal of harm. It would make him discontented and unhappy." These words sank deep into my heart, stirred up sentiments within that lay slumbering, and called into existence an entirely new train of thought. It was a new and special revelation, explaining dark and mysterious things, with which my youthful understanding had struggled, but struggled in vain. I now understood what had been to me a most perplexing difficulty—to wit, the white man's power to enslave the black man. It was a grand achievement, and I prized it highly. From that moment, I understood the pathway from slavery to freedom. It was just what I wanted, and I got it at a time when I the least expected it. Whilst I was saddened by the thought of losing the aid of my kind mistress, I was gladdened by the invaluable instruction which, by the merest accident, I had gained from my master. Though conscious of the difficulty of learning without a teacher, I set out with high hope, and a fixed purpose, at whatever cost of trouble, to learn how to read. The very decided manner with which

he spoke, and strove to impress his wife with the evil consequences of giving me instruction, served to convince me that he was deeply sensible of the truths he was uttering. It gave me the best assurance that I might rely with the utmost confidence on the results which, he said, would flow from teaching me to read. What he most dreaded, that I most desired. What he most loved, that I most hated. That which to him was a great evil, to be carefully shunned, was to me a great good, to be diligently sought; and the argument which he so warmly urged, against my learning to read, only served to inspire me with a desire and determination to learn. In learning to read, I owe almost as much to the bitter opposition of my master, as to the kindly aid of my mistress. I acknowledge the benefit of both.[12]

The three characters in this scene of instruction provide the three-part structure of the paragraph. Sophia Auld's role as a teacher covers only two sentences—one devoted to letters, the other to simple words. Hugh Auld takes her place, first instructing his spouse in literacy laws and their logic ("it was unlawful, as well as unsafe, to teach a slave to read") and then, "to use his own words," instructing the young slave himself. In his imitation of Auld's speech, Douglass repeats the word *nigger* four times and rings changes upon the theme of racial inferiority. But the master's authoritative voice is silenced by the ironic effect his words have upon the slave. Douglass devotes more than half the paragraph to the lessons he has learned, not from Sophia but from Hugh Auld. The master's words cause "a new and special revelation" in Douglass, who "from that moment" understands "the white man's power to enslave the black man" as well as "the pathway from slavery to freedom." Reading is that pathway because it "would *spoil* the best nigger in the world" and "unfit him to be a slave." The difficult secret of the "white man's power" resides in denying the black man the right to read.

The three-part structure of this scene presents three versions of power in three versions of language. Sophia Auld is silent, a mere accessory ("she assisted me in learning"), and her power is severely limited. Hugh Auld represents "the white man's power" in its most naked form, a power that seeks to silence both the wife and the slave. Douglass, finally, fashions a rhetoric of resistance by constructing a series of antitheses between his master and himself. The antitheses create an Emersonian meeting of polarities, but in the last two sentences of the revelation Douglass synthesizes "the bitter opposition of my master" and "the

12. *Narrative*, ed. Benjamin Quarles (Cambridge, Mass.: Belknap Press, 1960), 58–59.

kindly aid of my mistress." The closing sentence ("I acknowledge the benefit of both") is the most powerful of the entire passage, for it replaces the paternalistic language of the master with the simple, inclusive rhetoric of a polite individual. Having made the "grand achievement" he "prized" so "highly," Douglass can afford to pay tribute to his former owners, since the tribute in fact establishes both the power of language and the power to which language leads.

In subsequent retellings, Douglass revised the episode to suit his audience or occasion. On 6 January 1846, when the Belfast Anti-Slavery Society presented him with an "elegantly bound" and "beautifully gilt" Bible, Douglass used the gift as an emblem:

> The happy incidents of this morning, have called into remembrance some of my early struggles after knowledge, and the difficulties that then lay in the way of its attainment. I remember the first time I ever heard the Bible read, and I tell you the truth when I tell you, that from that time I trace my first desire to learn to read. I was over seven years old; my master had gone out one Sunday night, the children had gone to bed, I had crawled under the centre table and had fallen asleep, when my mistress commenced to read the Bible aloud, so loud that she waked me—she waked me to sleep no more! I have found, since I learned to read, that the chapter which she then read was the 1st chapter of Job. I remember my sympathy for the good old man; and my great anxiety to know more about him led me to ask my mistress—who was at this time a kind lady—to teach me to read. She commenced, and would have, but for the opposition of her husband, taught me to read. She ceased to instruct me, but my desire to read continued, and, instead of decreasing, increased; and, by the aid of little boys, obtained at different times, I finally succeeded in learning to read. (Applause.) (*FDP* 1:127)

By specifying the Bible as the source of his "first desire to learn to read," Douglass wraps the revised scene of instruction in a divine aura, one whose sanctimonious tone is—mercifully—mixed with humor ("so loud that she waked me—she waked me to sleep no more"). More interesting, however, is his specific reference to the first chapter of Job. As Douglass notes, the chapter is mainly devoted to Job's calamities, and Job clearly figures the faithful man's perseverance, parallel to Douglass's own. But the first chapter also contains the dialogue in which Satan asks God, "Hast not thou made a hedge about him, and about his house, and about all that he hath on every side? thou hast blessed the work of his hands, and his substance is increased in the land. But put forth thine hand now, and touch all that he hath, and he will curse thee to thy face" (Job 1:10–11). God's reply ("Behold, all that he hath is in thy power; only upon himself put not forth thine hand") marks the difference between possessions and the self, between outer things and inner faith. By referring to the chapter, Douglass represents himself as, like Job, an essentially free and faithful self, a self who can lose everything and still say "blessed be the name of the Lord" (Job 1:21).

Douglass's self-representations in the *Narrative* and the Belfast speech raise a less obvious but equally important point. In both versions, Douglass focuses on himself as a "self-made man," a theme that he developed, in the 1850s, into his most popular lecture.[13] But this ideal of self-construction, while necessary for Douglass himself and central to American mythology, underplays the role of Sophia and Hugh Auld in the scene of instruction. In the 1845 *Narrative*, the origin of Douglass's literacy is in fact complex, involving a kind white mistress, an authoritarian white master, and a young slave awakening to consciousness. In the Belfast speech, on the other hand, the Bible becomes the single, divinely inspired source of the revelation, and Douglass represents himself as a single, divinely inspired speaker. The two versions thus represent the origin of language and self in two different ways. It is as if Douglass were saying, along with the four messengers in the first chapter of Job, "and I only am escaped alone to tell thee" (14–19). But like Melville, who would take that statement as his text five years later in *Moby-Dick*, Douglass presents the isolated, self-constructing speaker along with more complex and communal constructions of self and language.[14]

In *My Bondage and My Freedom* (1855), Douglass combines the two versions, retaining the basic structure of the paragraph in the 1845 *Narrative*. He begins with a sentence that summarizes the scene from the Belfast speech: "The frequent hearing of my mistress reading the bible—for she often read aloud when

---

13. See William S. McFeely, *Frederick Douglass* (New York: Norton, 1991), 197 and 298. The earliest surviving published text of the lecture, delivered 4 January 1860 in Halifax, England, appears in *FDP* 3:289–300. Earlier versions are "Self-Help," delivered 8 May 1849 in New York City (*FDP* 2:167–70), and "Work and Self-Elevation," delivered 14 April 1854 in Cincinnati (*FDP* 2:475–79). See also Rafia Zafar, "Franklinian Douglass: The Afro-American as Representative Man," in *Frederick Douglass: New Literary and Historical Essays*, ed. Eric J. Sundquist (New York: Cambridge University Press, 1990), 99–117, and Waldo E. Martin, *The Mind of Frederick Douglass* (Chapel Hill: University of North Carolina Press, 1985), 253–78.

14. The sentence is Ishmael's self-descriptive epigraph for the epilogue to the 1851 novel (New York: Norton, 1967), 470. For a recent, incisive interpretation of Ishmael's role in the novel, one that is more complicated and just than my sketch, see Carolyn Porter, "Call Me Ishmael, or How to Make Double-Talk Speak," in *New Essays on Moby-Dick*, ed. Richard H. Brodhead (New York: Cambridge University Press, 1986), 73–108.

her husband was absent—soon awakened my curiosity in respect to this *mystery* of reading, and roused in me the desire to learn" (113). The phrasing recalls the Belfast version ("she waked me to sleep no more!"), but Douglass's style is abstract and impersonal. Sophia Auld becomes even less powerful here than in the earlier version, for now it is "the frequent hearing" that awakens the slave's "curiosity," not the mistress herself. As the paragraph continues, Sophia Auld's kindness is likewise restricted: "the duty which she felt it to teach me, at least to read *the bible*." Douglass figures his former mistress as a pious but unwitting teacher.

Similarly, Douglass restricts Hugh Auld's role and amplifies his own. The master's authoritarian views are delivered in a series of fragments, divided by semicolons, rather than as a single speech, and Douglass adds this sentence: "If you learn him how to read, he'll want to know how to write; and, this accomplished, he'll be running away with himself" (114). Auld's colloquialism ("learn him") lowers the master's position of authority, while the rest of the sentence specifies the "pathway from slavery to freedom"—reading leads to writing, and writing leads to running away. When Douglass calls this "Master Hugh's oracular exposition of the true philosophy of training a human chattel" and "the first decidedly anti-slavery lecture to which it had been my lot to listen" (114), he creates not only an ironic distance between the speech and its effect on the listening slave but also a stylistic distinction between his former master's command of language and his own more formal narrative voice.

Other revisions foreground the ironies of the "new and special revelation" and emphasize the slave boy's role as a self-constructing individual. So, for example, Douglass characterizes Auld's words as "iron sentences—cold and harsh" rather than simply as "words." In a similar revision, he says that Auld's speech "stirred up not only my feelings into a sort of rebellion, but awakened within me a slumbering train of vital thought" rather than "stirred up sentiments within that lay slumbering, and called into existence an entirely new train of thought." These changes make the slave boy into an already rebellious self, one whose "train of vital thought" is by no means "called into existence" or "entirely new," even if it is slumbering. Similarly, to the 1855 account Douglass adds the internal speech "'Very well,' thought I, 'knowledge unfits a child to be a slave,'" in order to stress his awakened consciousness, and he adds the analysis "Wise as Mr. Auld was, he evidently underrated my comprehension, and had little idea of the use to which I was capable of putting the impressive lesson he was giving to his wife" (114–15), in order to distinguish his own enlightened state from the blind prejudice of his master.

Douglass's rewritings of himself function within the larger context of his career as an antislavery lecturer and writer. As an agent for the American

Anti-Slavery Society, which published the 1845 *Narrative*, Douglass portrays the scene of instruction as a mixture of slaveholders' kindness and cruelty, but he keeps his narrative within the bounds set by abolitionist purposes. Thus he prefaces the scene by describing Sophia Auld's transformation from motherly to devilish: "But alas! this kind heart had but a short time to remain such. The fatal poison of irresponsible power was already in her hands, and soon commenced its infernal work. That cheerful eye, under the influence of slavery, soon became red with rage; that voice, made all of sweet accord, changed to one of harsh and horrid discord; and that angelic face gave place to that of a demon" (*Narrative* 57–58). Purpose and audience also account for the fact that the *Narrative* halts on 11 August 1841, when Douglass delivered his first public speech as an abolitionist. As critics have noted, the 1845 text exemplifies the slave narrative, and it therefore functions to serve the aims of the abolitionist movement.[15]

By 1855, however, with the publication of *My Bondage and My Freedom*, Douglass succeeds in rewriting himself within an American culture that is becoming truly biracial. The speeches in Britain during 1845–47 take place while Douglass is planning to make himself into an independent black editor, a move that would cause consternation among the "Boston Clique" of abolitionists.[16] It is hardly surprising, then, to find Douglass revising his origins as a literate self in order to emphasize his own Job-like self-creation. Nor should it be any more surprising to read speeches that attack "American Prejudice Against Color." Douglass's experiences as an abolitionist orator, fighting prejudice both in hostile crowds and among his white colleagues, make his self-revisions both necessary and persuasive.

In *My Bondage and My Freedom*, Douglass recounts the process of self-revising as a function of how he gains power over his own language:

15. See James Olney, "'I Was Born': Slave Narratives, Their Status as Autobiography and as Literature," in *The Slave's Narrative*, ed. Charles T. Davis and Henry Louis Gates, Jr. (New York: Oxford University Press, 1985), 148–75, and, in the same volume, Robert Burns Stepto, "I Rose and Found My Voice: Narration, Authentication, and Authorial Control in Four Slave Narratives" (225–41), and Houston A. Baker, Jr., "Autobiographical Acts and the Voice of the Southern Slave" (242–61).

For Douglass's background as a local preacher in the American Methodist Episcopal Zion Church, see William L. Andrews, "Frederick Douglass, Preacher," *American Literature* 54 (1982): 592–97.

16. For a succinct account of the break between Douglass and the American Anti-Slavery Society, see Lawrence J. Friedman, *Gregarious Saints: Self and Community in American Abolitionism, 1830–1870* (New York: Cambridge University Press, 1982), 187–95. The best comparison of the two autobiographies is by William L. Andrews, *To Tell a Free Story: The First Century of Afro-American Autobiography, 1760–1865* (Urbana: University of Illinois Press, 1986), 214–39.

During the first three or four months, my speeches were almost exclusively made up of narrations of my own personal experience as a slave. "Let us have the facts," said the people. So also said Friend George Foster, who always wished to pin me down to my simple narrative. "Give us the facts," said Collins, "we will take care of the philosophy." Just here arose some embarrassment. It was impossible for me to repeat the same old story month after month, and to keep up my interest in it. It was new to the people, it is true, but it was an old story to me; and to go through with it night after night, was a task altogether too mechanical for my nature. "Tell your story, Frederick," would whisper my then revered friend, William Lloyd Garrison, as I stepped upon the platform. I could not always obey, for I was now reading and thinking. New views of the subject were presented to my mind. It did not entirely satisfy me to *narrate* wrongs; I felt like *denouncing* them. I could not always curb my moral indignation for the perpetrators of slaveholding villainy, long enough for a circumstantial statement of the facts which I felt almost everybody must know. Besides, I was growing, and needed room. "People won't believe you ever was a slave, Frederick, if you keep on this way," said Friend Foster. "Be yourself," said Collins, "and tell your story." It was said to me, "Better have a *little* of the plantation manner of speech than not; 'tis not best that you seem too learned." These excellent friends were actuated by the best of motives, and were not altogether wrong in their advice; and still I must speak just the word that seemed to *me* the word to be spoken *by* me. (281–82)

This episode echoes the scene of instruction in several ways. Most obviously, the white voices sound eerily like that of Hugh Auld, telling Douglass to restrict himself, to keep his place and "have a *little* of the plantation manner of speech." But the white men's advice is, after all, only a benevolent version of restrictive power, especially galling to one who sees the connection between language and power as clearly as Douglass. When he says, "I was growing, and needed room," Douglass speaks of his own power as a speaker and thinker, the same space-seeking power he exercises in rewriting the scene of instruction in *My Bondage and My Freedom*. In narrating his resistance to "excellent friends," Douglass opposes his own natural growth to the mechanical repetition of his story and reappropriates the language of self-creation and self-empowerment: "still I must speak just the word that seemed to *me* the word to be spoken *by* me." To speak, for Douglass, means to be.

Douglass's style in this passage is, to use a favorite term of contemporary reports, "chaste," for he employs none of the ghoulish hyperbole of the 1845

Narrative. That shift in style, like the lofty irony of the narrative voice in general, registers the "growing" that Douglass does between 1845 and 1855. He adapts his rhetoric to address the same problem he faces in the scene of instruction, but here the "white man's power" wears a benevolent mask. Whether north or south of Mason and Dixon's line, that power seeks to control Douglass's language and, by extension, to confine the growth of the individual self. By addressing his "excellent" friends' restrictions in the "chaste" language of deliberation, Douglass presents himself as having "grown" beyond the cultural space occupied by the fugitive slave of the 1845 *Narrative.*

Douglass faces, then, a problem that is peculiar to himself and yet applicable to all the writers/speakers I have discussed. Emerson attempts to create a language of authority by occupying a secular pulpit on the lyceum circuit and on commencement days. More ambivalently, Thoreau creates a "neutral ground" that positions him between silence and sound, the world and the text. Fuller and Peabody likewise attempt, with varying success, to clear a cultural space in which women can speak and write, and Peabody succeeds in much the same way as Douglass: she "genders" the theory of essential eloquence, whereas Douglass "racializes" it. Douglass's eloquence thus fits within the cultural context set, in part, by linguistic essentialism, but it also remains specific both to himself and to his cultural situation.

3

In the last two paragraphs of *My Bondage and My Freedom*, Douglass addresses the multiple layers of his cultural situation. He begins by noting the changes in his position brought about by the independence of his newspaper, the *North Star.* "Since I have been editing and publishing a journal devoted to the cause of liberty and progress, I have had my mind more directed to the condition and circumstances of the free colored people than when I was the agent of an abolition society" (314). Imbued with the rhetoric of reform, the sentence applies to Douglass's own "condition and circumstances" as a "free colored" editor and writer. Behind the mask of dispassionate statement lies an intense battle for independence from Garrisonian abolitionists, who actively discouraged Douglass from starting the *North Star* and made his resignation as an agent of the American Anti-Slavery Society a precondition of editing the journal.[17] Douglass

---

17. The break with the Society was acrimonious, although Douglass's account in *My Bondage and*

is also largely silent about his allegiance to Gerrit Smith and the Liberty Party, a fealty that enabled him to publish the newspaper and renounce the Garrisonian doctrine of apolitical "moral suasion."[18] Only in the last sentence of *My Bondage and My Freedom* does he allude to political power as a means to freedom: "Believing that one of the best means of emancipating the slaves of the south is to improve and elevate the character of the free colored people of the north I shall labor in the future, as I have labored in the past, to promote the moral, social, religious, and intellectual elevation of the free colored people; never forgetting my own humble origin, nor refusing, while Heaven lends me ability, to use my voice, my pen, or my vote, to advocate the great and primary work of the universal and unconditional emancipation of my entire race" (314). The phrase "or my vote" is almost lost in the paragraph-long close to the 1855 book, especially since Douglass does not mention the political "elevation" of free blacks. More important, it would seem, are "my voice, my pen," which steer voters and nonvoters alike toward "universal and unconditional emancipation."

My reading of this passage suggests that Douglass pursues the goal of emancipation, in the broadest sense, through moral suasion and political commitment. He does not approach the problem of emancipation in a narrow or doctrinaire fashion; any measure that will elevate the condition of blacks—free or slave, North or South—should be taken. In addition, the series "my voice, my pen, or my vote" personalizes the project of elevation, making Douglass's labors both his own and universal. Like other figures of eloquence in antebellum America, Douglass conceives of himself as a voice of moral authority, but that voice crosses boundaries that other figures do not approach. Douglass speaks for American blacks in a white culture, and speech is often the measure of emancipation. In the 1849 address "Self-Help," for example, Douglass asserts that "the time was coming when the colored man would occupy the same platform with the white man" and that "colored people are now beginning to exercise their gifts. They are now in a position to be heard" (*FDP* 2:169–70).

Douglass's entire career is an effort to place himself "in a position to be heard," and nowhere is the effort clearer than in "The Claims of the Negro Ethnologically Considered," an address he delivered to the literary societies of Western Reserve College during commencement week in 1854. The occasion

---

My Freedom is characteristically calm and dispassionate (305–6); compare McFeely's account, *Frederick Douglass*, 146–53.

18. See John R. McKivigan, "The Frederick Douglass-Gerrit Smith Friendship and Political Abolitionism in the 1850s," in Sundquist, *New Literary and Historical Essays*, 205–32. The best account of Douglass's shift toward political abolitionism is Martin, *The Mind of Frederick Douglass*, 32–54.

is itself significant, for it was the first time a black person was the keynote speaker at a major American university commencement. Douglass uses the occasion to mount an academic attack on the "American School" of ethnology, which had been arguing for a decade or more that science proved the natural inferiority of the black race.[19]

Ethnology was a new discipline in the nineteenth century, embracing craniology, archeology, Egyptology, and philology, as well as other sciences and pseudosciences. The most important figure in the American School, Samuel George Morton, made comparative studies of skulls and published two influential books—*Crania Americana* in 1839 and *Crania Aegyptiaca* in 1844. Other figures include the Harvard naturalist Louis Agassiz, the popularizer of Egyptology George R. Gliddon, the Southern physician Josiah C. Nott, and the archeologist Ephraim George Squier. Douglass mentions all of these men by name except Squier, calling attention to their "profound discoveries in ethnological science" (*FDP* 2:503). Although Douglass's statement may not be without irony, it accords with the general reputation of the American School, which even influenced American foreign policy: in 1844 Gliddon and Morton presented their books to Secretary of State John C. Calhoun, who used them to argue against abolition in his correspondence with Great Britain and France.[20]

The American School argued that the races of humankind form what Douglass terms "a sort of sliding scale, making one extreme brother to the ourang-ou-tang, and the other to angels, and all the rest intermediates" (502). This heterodox claim went hand in hand with the argument that there was no single origin of the human races; rather, there were several separate species within the genus *homo sapiens*, and they had separate origins and readily discernible differences in abilities. In the popular compilation *Types of Mankind*, for instance, Nott and Gliddon present the "grand problem" of ethnology as "that which

19. For the circumstances of the address, see *FDP* 2:498–99; an extensive analysis of Douglass's arguments can be found in Martin, 225–50. My own interest in the address focuses on the role of philology in the debate over humankind's origins.

20. The best account of the "American School" is William Stanton, *The Leopard's Spots: Scientific Attitudes Toward Race in America, 1815–59* (Chicago: University of Chicago Press, 1960). For the relationship of Morton and Gliddon to Calhoun, see Stanton, 61–65, and Josiah C. Nott and George R. Gliddon, *Types of Mankind* (Philadelphia: Lippincott, Grambo, 1854), 50–52. For an excellent discussion of how scientific racialism was disseminated in the journals of the day, see Reginald Horsman, *Race and Manifest Destiny: The Origins of American Racial Anglo-Saxonism* (Cambridge: Harvard University Press, 1981), 139–57. Nott, the only Southerner among the American School ethnologists, was particularly favored by Southern journals: William Gilmore Simms published several of Nott's articles in the *Southern Quarterly Review* in the 1850s, as did *De Bow's Review*.

involves the *common origin* of races" (50), and they repeatedly assert the inherent inferiority of the Negro race and the inherent superiority of the Caucasian race:

> In the broad field and long duration of Negro life, not a single civilization, spontaneous or borrowed, has existed, to adorn its gloomy past. (52)

> Those groups of races heretofore comprehended under the generic term Caucasian, have in all ages been the rulers; and it requires no prophet's eye to see that they are destined eventually to conquer and hold every foot of the globe where climate does not interpose an impenetrable barrier. No philanthropy, no legislation, no missionary labors, can change this law: it is written in man's nature by the hand of his Creator. (79)

These two statements suggest the implications of the American School's polygenetic theories. The Negro race is innately inferior to the Caucasian, incapable of civilization and equality, which are distinctly Caucasian attributes. Nott and Gliddon directly connect the theory of polygenesis to nineteenth-century American culture: "While, on the one hand, every true philanthropist must admit that no race has the right to enslave or oppress the weaker, it must be conceded, on the other, that all changes in existing institutions should be guided, not by fanaticism and groundless hypotheses, but by experience, sound judgment, and real charity" (52).

Not surprisingly, Douglass reacts sharply to the assertions of Nott and Gliddon: "Perhaps, of all the attempts ever made to disprove the unity of the human family, and to brand the negro with natural inferiority, the most compendious and barefaced is the book, entitled *Types of Mankind*, by Nott and Glidden [*sic*]. One would be well employed in a series of Lectures directed to an exposure of the unsoundness, if not the wickedness of this work" ("Claims" 519). Most hostile reviews of *Types of Mankind* condemned the "wickedness of this work" because it questioned the Mosaic account of creation, but few pointed to any "unsoundness" in the science.[21] Douglass places himself in the very center of a cultural controversy, but his arguments in "Claims of the Negro" run counter to prevailing nineteenth-century assumptions of racial inferiority.

21. See Stanton, *Leopard's Spots*, 163–73, for an account of the reviews, which appeared in both Northern and Southern journals. The scientist who objected most strenuously to *Types* was John Bachman, who reviewed the book in *Charleston Medical Journal* 9 (1854): 627–59 and followed with a review of Agassiz's contribution a year later, 10 (1855): 482–534. Nott replied to Bachman in both cases in the same journal (9:862–64; 10:753–67).

Douglass points out the "novelty of my position" (500) in his opening remarks, distinguishing the occasion from the "usual course," which is "to call to the platform men of age and distinction, eminent for eloquence, mental ability, and scholarly attainments—men whose high culture, severe training, great experience, large observation, and peculiar aptitude for teaching qualify them to instruct even the already well instructed" (499). But the title of the address suggests that this opening apologia is more than merely conventional. By presenting claims *of* rather than *for* the Negro, Douglass figures himself as "the Negro" of the title, the representative of and for his race. The commencement exercises become an opportunity for Douglass to dramatize his novel position and to "instruct even the already well instructed."

"The Claims of the Negro" exploits this opportunity by focusing on language, both as a subject of argument and as a performance. The argument is divided into two parts—a brief prelude, in which Douglass claims that "the negro is a MAN" (502), and a long, multisectioned treatment of ethnological theories, in which Douglass claims that the black race, as part of the human family, deserves the human rights "supported, maintained and defended for *all* the human family" (524). In both parts, Douglass uses language as evidence. In the prelude, for instance, he answers the assertion that the Negro is not a man by appealing to "common sense": "His speech, his reason, his power to acquire and to retain knowledge, his heaven-erected face, his habitudes, his hopes, his fears, his aspirations, his prophecies, plant between him and the brute creation, a distinction as eternal as it is palpable" (502). The catalog moves from speech to prophecies, creating an image of the Negro as an Adamic figure, marked by quasi-divine attributes. Douglass answers negative essentialism with positive essentialism, and language functions as the crux of the essentialist argument.

The ethnological argument concerning the unity of the "human family" is, as Douglass says, "beset with difficulties" (503), and the principal problem is the relationship between nineteenth-century American blacks and whites. In a section called "The Bearings of the Question," Douglass clearly states the essentialist assumptions of proslavery arguments:

> Ignorance and depravity, and the inability to rise from degradation to civilization and respectability, are the most usual allegations against the oppressed. The evils most fostered by slavery and oppression are precisely those which slaveholders and oppressors would transfer from their system to the inherent character of their victims. Thus the very crimes of slavery become slavery's best defence. By making the enslaved a character fit only for slavery, they excuse themselves for refusing to make

the slave a freeman. A wholesale method of accomplishing this result is to overthrow the instinctive consciousness of the common brotherhood of man. For, let it be once granted that the human race are of multitudinous origin, naturally different in their moral, physical, and intellectual capacities, and at once you make plausible a demand for classes, grades and conditions, for different methods of culture, different moral, political, and religious institutions, and a chance is left for slavery, as a necessary institution. (507)

Here Douglass opens the debate to a cultural interpretation of race relations, an interpretation that would analyze the construction of the Negro as a separate, distinct object of ethnological study. Such an approach would, in addition, uncover cultural assumptions that allow ethnologists to place the Negro within an imaginative geography, and it would analyze the strategies by which ethnologists codify—and thus master—the discipline, its object, and its audience. The project, in short, would be to analyze what Josiah Nott called "Niggerology" in much the same way that Edward Said has analyzed Orientalism.[22]

In the section called "Ethnological Unfairness Towards the Negro," Douglass takes a step in Said's direction, quoting and analyzing the language of Morton's *Crania Americana*: "'Although the Nubians occasionally present their national characters unmixed, they generally show traces of their social intercourse with the Arabs, and *even* with the negroes.' The repetition of the adverb here 'even,' is important, as showing the spirit in which our great American Ethnologist pursues his work" (509). But Douglass is not Said; in a characteristic antebellum fashion, his critique pits one essentialism against another. He therefore argues for "a near relationship between the present enslaved and degraded negroes, and the ancient highly civilized and wonderfully endowed Egyptians" (517). In Said's terms, Douglass revises the imaginative geography of ethnology by creating his own imaginative geography.

Language functions as a major element of Douglass's imaginative mapping:

Language is held to be very important, by the best ethnologists, in tracing out the remotest affinities of nations, tribes, classes and families. The

---

22. My description of the project is an incomplete summary of the process that Said analyzes in "Imaginative Geography and Its Representations: Orientalizing the Oriental," in his *Orientalism* (New York: Pantheon, 1978), 49–73; for Said 's analysis of ethnology and oriental philology, see 123–48.

Nott uses the term "niggerology" in a letter to Squier, 7 September 1848; quoted in Stanton, *Leopard's Spots*, 118.

color of the skin has sometimes been less enduring than the speech of a people. I speak by authority, and follow in the footsteps of some of the most learned writers on the natural and ethnological history of man, when I affirm that one of the most direct and conclusive proofs of the general affinity of Northern African nations with those of West, East and South Africa, is found in the general similarity of their language. The philologist easily discovers, and is able to point out something like the original source of the multiplied tongues now in use in that yet mysterious quarter of the globe. (517)

Although he follows this passage with citations from Robert Gordon Latham's *Man and His Migrations*, Douglass is purposely general in presenting philological evidence. The parallel between "the general similarity of their language" and "the general affinity of . . . African nations" implies "something like the original source" of all African languages and nations. The unstated conclusion is the same as Douglass's initial claim: "a strong affinity and a direct relationship may be claimed by the negro race, to THAT GRANDEST OF ALL THE NATIONS OF ANTIQUITY, THE BUILDERS OF THE PYRAMIDS" (517).[23]

Douglass creates yet another myth of origins in the section "The African Race But One People":

Having shown that the people of Africa are, probably, one people; that each tribe bears an intimate relation to other tribes and nations in that quarter of the globe, and that the Egyptians may have flung off the different tribes seen there at different times, as implied by the evident relations of their language, and by other similarities; it can hardly be deemed unreasonable to suppose, that the African branch of the human species—from the once highly civilized Egyptian to the barbarians on the banks of the Niger— may claim brotherhood with the great family of Noah, spreading over the more Northern and Eastern parts of the globe. (519–20)

The affinity of languages becomes the ground for Douglass's reimagined Africa, in which the "Egyptians may have flung off the different tribes seen there at different times." Thus Douglass represents Egypt as "something like the origi-

23. The American Ethnologists relied upon physical evidence rather than philological evidence because they believed physical characteristics were permanent whereas languages were influenced by external factors such as conquest and trade, which brought unrelated peoples into contact with one another. In 1847, for instance, Morton pronounced philology "a broken reed" (Stanton, *Leopard's Spots*, 98).

nal source" of all African languages and nations. Because of its admitted grand-ness, Egypt grants all of Africa admission into the family of humankind, so that the "African branch" can make its claim to "brotherhood with the great fam-ily of Noah." Douglass's myth of origins turns the representations of the American School of ethnology on their head, staking a claim to Adamic geneal-ogy that is, at the very least, equal to the claims of "the great family of Noah."

This reading of "Claims of the Negro" already suggests the importance of Douglass's rhetoric in combating the claims of the American School. The per-formance is itself novel in the canon of Douglass's speeches, for, as he said in his final autobiography, "Written orations had not been in my line." But Douglass is wrong, I believe, in calling "Claims" a "very deficient production."[24] He exploits the language of ethnology in order to revise the imaginative geog-raphy of the Negro, and his oration emerges, finally, as another attempt at self-creation. Through quotation and paraphrase, Douglass appropriates an academic style of argumentation and embeds it within his performance. Even the use of capitalized headings for six sections of the oration can be seen as an act of appropriation, since the hallmark of ethnological method is classification. Douglass adopts the style of ethnology in order to subvert the claims of the American School of ethnology. But the performance goes beyond that initial subversion. By positioning himself between opposing camps of ethnologists—monogenists versus polygenists—Douglass assumes the role of the Negro and effectively revises the claims of both camps.[25]

Douglass's appropriations and revisions of ethnological discourse create a cultural space for the Negro, taken as both himself and his race. The strategy recalls the description of writing in the 1845 *Narrative*: "I used to spend the time in writing in the spaces left in Master Thomas's copy-book, copying what he had written. I continued to do this until I could write a hand very similar to that of Master Thomas. Thus, after a long, tedious effort for years, I finally succeeded in learning how to write" (71). In "Claims of the Negro," Douglass in effect speaks/writes "in the spaces" left by white ethnologists, and his style is "very similar" to theirs. But the style, like the argument and its conclusions, rewrites the master's hand.

24. *The Life and Times of Frederick Douglass* (Hartford, Conn.: Park, 1881; rpt. Secaucus, N.J.: Citadel Press, 1983), 413.

25. John Bachman, the most vociferous opponent of polygenism, ended his review of *Types of Mankind* by defending "the institutions of South Carolina" and asserting that the Negro was inherently inferior to the Caucasian (Stanton, *Leopard's Spots*, 172). Philologists, who tended to argue for the unity of humankind, were nevertheless prone to ethnocentric judgments of racial/linguistic superiority and inferiority; see Horsman, *Race and Manifest Destiny*, 32–37.

The claims of the American School of ethnology continued to occupy Douglass's attention throughout his long career, although he never addressed them as directly as he had in "Claims of the Negro." In "Advice to Black Youth," he names Nott, Gliddon, and Agassiz as part of the "crusade" to represent blacks as "an inferior people intellectually and morally," while in "The Trials and Triumphs of Self-Made Men" he notes that the black man "would be read out of the human family by the Notts, Gliddens, Mortons, and other American ethnological writers."[26] Douglass repeatedly reads the black man back into the human family, and as late as 1887 he writes that he has "long been interested in ethnology, especially of the North African races. I have wanted the evidence of greatness, under a colored skin to meet and beat back the charge of natural, original and permanent inferiority of the colored races of men. Could I have seen forty years ago what I have now seen, I should have been much better fortified to meet the Notts and the Gliddens . . . in their arguments against the negro as a part of the great African race."[27]

Douglass's abiding interest in ethnology suggests the pervasive racialism of nineteenth-century American thought, and in that respect Douglass does not differ greatly from the American School ethnologists. Douglass is like the "Notts" in connecting ethnology to the legal and social institutions of antebellum America. The literacy laws of the antebellum South and the subtler restrictions placed on Douglass as an abolitionist orator hinge, ultimately, upon the definition of "the Negro." That definition, whether positive or negative, is always essentialist, and as such it necessarily leads to a polarization of social discourse.[28] Douglass can rightfully lay claim to a special authority because he speaks, in antebellum America, as a fugitive slave and then as a free black. In Emerson's terms, he brings "new blood" and a new voice to a crucial debate in antebellum American culture, and in doing so he fashions himself as a figure of eloquence. But his words and ideas function, in the final analysis, within "conditions for eloquence" controlled as much by white America, in the North and in the South, as by himself.

26. *FDP* 3:4, 296; the first address was delivered on 1 February 1855 in New York City, the second on 4 January 1860 in Halifax, England.

27. The text appears in a letter published in the *Christian Recorder* of 10 February 1887; Douglass wrote from Paris, on his way to visit Egypt. For an account of the journey, see McFeely, *Frederick Douglass*, 324–33; I quote the letter as cited by McFeely, 329.

28. For a concise and persuasive account of polarization in antebellum social discourse, see Carolyn Porter, "Social Discourse and Nonfictional Prose," *Columbia Literary History of the United States*, ed. Emory Elliott (New York: Columbia University Press, 1988), 345–63.

6

William Gilmore Simms and the Necessity Of Speech

1

On 4 July 1844, William Gilmore Simms delivered the obligatory Independence Day oration to the town of Aiken, South Carolina. Simms was under no obligation himself, although he was an unofficial candidate for the state House of Representatives, to which he was elected the following October. More important than his political ambition is Simms's position as the leading man of letters in the antebellum South. In his speech, *The Sources of American Independence*, Simms becomes a figure of cultural authority, defining the spiritual history and future prospects of his audience, and he begins to create this role by focusing on the relationship between speaker and audience: "The advocate has great reason to rejoice, my friends, who, in addition to the merits of a noble cause, can lay claim to a perfectly sympathizing audience—who feels that he has only to unfold his own sentiments to embody theirs, and who, in the utterance of his own emotions possesses himself of all the avenues to their confidence." Simms calls the central figure in his opening portrait "the advocate," and in speaking he creates a second image, this time of an ordinary speaker who finds it "so easy a matter to play the orator on the great day of our nation." These two figures further multiply into "many eloquent voices that fill the land." From ordinary—perhaps even contrived—occasions, however, Simms imagines a "perfectly sympathizing audience," one that joins a series of opposites in a nationwide "necessity of speech." As he ends his exordium, Simms catalogs the parts that make up the ideal necessity of speech, and the "exulting" whole expresses "that universal sentiment of country" in endlessly multiplied Fourth of July speeches.[1]

---

1. *The Sources of American Independence* (Aiken, S.C.: Published by Council, 1844), 5; all references

Simms's opening gesture toward an ideal figure of eloquence, "strong and striving in the necessity of speech," recalls similar figures created by Emerson, Thoreau, Fuller, Peabody, Alcott, and Douglass. The figure balances audience and speaker—"the ear of faith and the tongue of eloquence"—through the medium of language. The cadence of syntactic parallelism and antithesis itself balances between spoken and written language. Simms thus creates a totalizing image of American culture, defined through a verbal drama of reciprocity, and in doing so he joins "many eloquent voices" in defining antebellum America as a culture of eloquence.

The exordium recalls other figures of eloquence, but the echoes of Emerson are particularly strong. Like Emerson, Simms presents the ideal of eloquence as a distant, even unattainable goal. In addition, he figures his own situation as hopelessly belated, for the present speaker follows "the fiery accents of Patrick Henry,—the energetic volume of John Rutledge,—the copious thought and stern propriety of Daniel Webster,—the classic freedom and Ciceronian fullness of Hugh Legaré" (6). The rhetorical effect of this double distancing threatens to reduce the speaker to silence, but Simms recuperates his authority by investing it in the subject of the oration:

> I am not among those who imagine that its freshness is exhausted, and that the soil, which has been so frequently and deeply furrowed, no longer possesses fertility. I am very sure, indeed, that such is not the case—very sure that there are tracts yet uncleared—virgin recesses, in which new paths may be explored, and new prospects unveiled to the eager eyes of patriotic inquiry. The true difficulty in the way of our orator seems rather in the variety than in the exhaustion of his material. . . . He feels it less easy to write an oration than a history. (7)

The imagery in this passage makes the subject of American independence into an eroticized frontier, one that may threaten "our orator" with its overwhelming plenitude and fertility but that remains to be explored and settled. The imagery further suggests that the orator should fill a masculine, mastering role, clearing "tracts yet uncleared" and unveiling "new prospects . . . to the eager eyes of patriotic inquiry." Finally, it transfigures the obligations of the orator into a vast field of future words and deeds. Like Emerson, Simms transforms

---

are to this edition and are cited parenthetically in my text. John Caldwell Guilds narrates Simms's electoral campaign and political career in his definitive biography, *Simms: A Literary Life* (Fayetteville: University of Arkansas Press, 1992), 114–17.

his sense of limitation and belatedness into a performance of dynamic verbal power.

Simms resembles Emerson in other significant ways. The orator that Simms describes resembles the prophetic genius Emerson figures in the early lectures, in *Nature*, and in later addresses and essays. In the 1838 lecture "Genius," for instance, Emerson contrasts the "slovenly and tiresome" speaker to "the chosen man," who becomes "the poet and master of the crowd" (*ELE* 3:83). We also recall the poet-orator of *Nature*, "bred in the woods," who makes memories into "fit symbols and words of the thoughts which the passing events shall awaken. . . . And with these forms, the spells of persuasion, the keys of power are put into his hands" (*NAL* 21). In *Sources of American Independence*, Simms interprets the colonial history of America as guided by just such prophetic spirits. For Simms as for Emerson, the principal source of American independence is "highest intellectual strength," found in particular "master spirits" (14) and synonymous with the authors of the Declaration of Independence and the Constitution. In a later passage, Simms further defines these Revolutionary War leaders as "men . . . of deep thought and searching eloquence; of equal nerve and purity; of great powers of endurance; unflinching in resolution, and of the most exquisite capacities for conduct" (16). While they are not exclusively orators or prophets, eloquence is nonetheless the fundamental sign that the leaders of American liberty could "grapple, on equal terms, with the highest intellectual strength of the oppressor" (14).

The figures of eloquence created by both Simms and Emerson strongly recall the "double service" of the antebellum Whig orator, who "must not only defend the people's true interests but show the people themselves where those interests lay" (Howe 27). The doubleness extends yet farther. Through eloquence, the prophetic genius exercises a quasi-sacred form of stewardship on the audience. Drew Faust argues that the roles of prophet and steward present "seemingly inconsistent images of the worldly position of the intellectual," but Simms mingles the two roles in the figure of "Moses among the Israelites," in which the audience becomes a chosen people who are being conducted "in safety to the Land of Promise."[2]

A second major resemblance pertains to Simms's theory of language. Although Simms never develops so elaborate a theory of language as those of the New England transcendentalists, his popular literary lecture, "Poetry and

2. *Sources*, 14. For a particularly telling account of Simms's concept of Romantic genius within the social context of the antebellum South, see Drew Gilpin Faust, *A Sacred Circle: The Dilemma of the Intellectual in the Old South, 1840–1860* (Baltimore: Johns Hopkins University Press, 1977), 15–60; for Faust's discussion of the roles of steward and isolated prophet, see 53–55.

the Practical," contains sentences that sound positively Emersonian. In an 1851 version of the lecture, for example, Simms presents an Adamic theory of poetic language:

> By some, it has been held that poetry was the earliest mode of speech, common to the race, during the world's innocence & childhood. It may have been so. No doubt that, when the Deity was wont to descend visibly upon the earth, and when his angels walked among its holy avenues, in which nothing but good was to be beheld, there must have been, in the possession of man, a language not wholly unworthy of Divine Senses. In his innocence,—with all his faculties fresh, keen, quick & intensely appreciative, with peace in his heart, and Beauty forever in his sight,—his sentiments must have been of a superior excellence, and necessarily craved a corresponding superiority in the language through which they were made known. In some degree the race still possesses the endowment. Man is the only animal still in possession of the gift of speech. Still, measurably, does he speak in music. How happily may the voice be tutored to the rarest compass—how exquisitely modulated to the most subdued, & subduing, tones of sweetness![3]

Simms imagines a prelapsarian form of language, one that perfectly realizes every possibility of expression. He may even be directly alluding to Emerson's famous formulation in *Nature*: "Because of this radical correspondence between visible things and human thoughts, savages, who have only what is necessary, converse in figures. As we go back in history, language becomes more picturesque, until its infancy, when it is all poetry" (*NAL* 19). Or he may have in mind Emerson's 1844 revision of the idea in "The Poet," where Emerson defines language as "fossil poetry" but does not find a divine origin beneath the strata (*Essays: Second Series* 13). Unlike Emerson, however, Simms does not cast doubt upon the divine origin of language, and he ends the passage by focusing on the "gift of speech" in its present state, comparing language to music in an idealized image of the "subdued, & subduing" human voice.

---

3. Five manuscript versions of lectures titled "Poetry and the Practical" are housed in the Charles Carroll Simms Collection of the South Caroliniana Library. At this writing, there is no published version of the lecture; I quote from my transcription of the fifth manuscript, which is dated 4 January 1851.

Simms delivered the lecture, singly and in a series of three evenings, repeatedly in the 1850s. See *The Letters of William Gilmore Simms*, ed. Mary C. Simms Oliphant, Alfred Taylor Odell, and T. C. Duncan Eaves, 5 vols. (Columbia: University of South Carolina Press, 1952–56), 3:73n., 86n., 272n., 301n.

This version of Adamic language theory especially resembles transcendental theories when Simms considers the role of the poet in making language. Like Emerson in "The Poet," he asserts an aesthetic origin of the English language: "He is the first maker of Language. You owe it to him that you speak the noble English tongue this day—as noble a tongue as ever marshalled the Hosts of Eloquence, or found the adequate voice for inspiration." If the poet is the "first maker of Language," both for Simms and for Emerson, he is also, for Simms, the preserver of the "native language" or "Saxon speech." Simms creates a stark power struggle between English poets, on the one hand, and the combined "powers of the State," on the other. The poet is figured as the sole "power in society" who resists the tyranny of "the Sovereign, the Princes, the nobles," the "courts of Law," the "man of learning," and "the Church." Simms's initial aestheticism results in a practical, decidedly political function for poets and poetic language, for the preservation of "Saxon speech" implicitly combats the subjugation of the people by the "powers of the State."[4]

Simms conducts a similar argument in the second part of *Sources of American Independence.* The relationship between speaker and audience suggests a parallel one between the "master spirit" and the people. In *Sources,* however, Simms focuses on "the gradual progress of English liberty" (7), retelling English history as an abstract narrative of spiritual and ethnological development. The conflict between Saxon and Norman becomes a source of American independence, for the Saxon parallels the colonial American in being subjugated, a "conquered people" (8). In reinterpreting Anglo-American history as a struggle, Simms largely ignores "the necessity of speech" with which he begins the oration. Instead, he moves to "the necessities of the race," defining America as a fundamental requirement of "gradual progress": "America was the appointed battlefield for European liberty. Here was the old fight of the Saxon with his Norman tyrant, to be renewed, and set at rest forever!" (10). Simms reads the history of the American Revolution as a retelling of the "old spirit of the Anglo-Saxon, warring with his Norman tyrant" (13), and he therefore attempts to portray political and economic events as "pretexts only" (16). The Revolution becomes "a revolt of the native mind of the country" (17).

---

4. This passage appears in the third lecture of a three-lecture series, probably the text for the series delivered in Charleston, May–June 1854; see Simms, *Letters* 3:300–301. Simms published a book of apothegms, *Egeria: or, Voices of Thought and Counsel, for the Woods and Wayside* (Philadelphia: E. H. Butler, 1853), which contains apposite remarks on such topics as "Genius," "The Poet," "The Race," and "National Prosperity," but "Poetry and the Practical" contains his most developed statements about language.

In this spiritual and ethnological reading of history, Simms once again recalls Emerson, who delivered a series of ten lectures under the title "English Literature" in 1835 (*ELE* 1:203–385) and another series of twelve lectures, "The Philosophy of History," in 1836–37 (*ELE* 2:1–188). Throughout these performances, as in the 1856 book *English Traits*, Emerson fearlessly generalizes upon the "national genius," "national character," and "race." In the chapter "Race," for instance, Emerson asserts that "in race, it is not the broad shoulders, or litheness, or stature that give advantage, but a symmetry that reaches as far as to the wit. Then the miracle and renown begin. . . . The hearing ear is always found close to the speaking tongue; and no genius can long or often utter any thing which is not invited and gladly entertained by men around him."[5] Emerson does more than simply celebrate the efficacy of the eloquent genius in transmitting spiritual power to an audience; he spiritualizes the concept of race and imagines eloquence as the means by which exceptional individuals create an entire people.

If Simms and Emerson share interests in eloquence, ethnology, and cultural history, they diverge sharply from each other in their views of the large-scale social, economic, and political conflicts marking antebellum America. In *Sources of American Independence*, Simms's revisionary history of the "revolt of the native mind" leads him to deny any linguistic or cultural inheritance that he might share with Emerson. He might almost be speaking of Emerson himself when he says, "What unity of feeling was there between the Bay of Massachusetts and the settlements on Ashley River? As little then as now! Nay, there was positive diversity, if not dislike, between them" (19). With these words, Simms announces sectionalism, the theme that structures the last third of his Independence Day oration. Thus he tells the history of the "national mind" yet a third time, and in this final retelling the South inherits the "old spirit of the Anglo-Saxon" (13). In clipped rhythms and ironic phrasing, Simms forges a strong sense of reciprocity between speaker and audience, but that union defines itself through its refusal to accept the judgments of "the modern Puritans" of New England. It comes as no surprise, then, to hear Simms call, "In this cause, against this danger, the people of the South must unite in season" (25). The command bespeaks both "the necessities of the race" and "the necessity of speech."

That imperative call for unity leads Simms back to the sources of independence and to the figures of eloquence with which he began the oration:

---

5. *Essays and Lectures* (New York: Library of America, 1983), 791–92. This sanguine vision of genius contrasts with Simms's view of genius as a neglected, dishonored prophet who "always plants his standard far in advance of his people. . . . Succeeding generations at length reach the spot where his mantle has fallen. This is the history of social progress" (*SQR* 7 [1845]: 316). See Faust's discussion in *A Sacred Circle*, 45–60.

And why should there not be gatherings of the people,—and great orators—in this, as in the temporary cause of local parties, and presidential
elections? How unworthy are such inferior objects when the glorious
rights which have rendered past struggles sacred, are escaping from our
grasp. Let us labor to instill this lesson—to inculcate this duty—to bring
our kindred States together in the common cause. To the statesman who,
armed only with the sufficient spear of truth, shall make a political
progress among us—who shall devote his genius and his life to this con-
summation,—whose eloquence shall bind conflicting parties,—who
shall compel the deference of sordid politicians,—and teach, with the
eloquence of a perfect faith, the single principle, "the South, and the
South all together,"—and shall succeed in rallying our united powers in
the great domestic issues which are before us,—there shall be an eminence of fame superior to that of President or Sovereign—a fame worthy of that of Washington, as proud, as peaceful, as enduring. (27)

Instead of moving from a single "advocate" to "many eloquent voices," as he
did in the exordium, Simms takes us from many "gatherings of the people" and
"great orators" to the single "statesman who, armed only with the sufficient
spear of truth, shall make a political progress among us." Although it is tempting to see this as a figure for Simms himself, especially in his role as cultural
spokesman/statesman, the repeated first-person plural places Simms among the
expectant audience, awaiting the arrival of the statesman. That statesman is, of
course, a quintessentially eloquent speaker, a figure who transcends contemporary issues, although Simms does treat such topics as the annexation of Texas
and Oregon in some detail. In the idealizing parallelisms that close the passage,
he creates a figure who is no longer diminished or belated, a figure who instead
approaches Washington as an equal, the progenitor of a new country. Thus
Sources of American Independence narrates three parallel histories, all of which tell
the same story of cultural necessity. In revising and retelling, moreover, Simms
creates further parallels—eloquence, "perfect faith," and Southern unity are
clearly synonymous.

In the last paragraph of *Sources*, Simms addresses his "brethren of the South"
and warns them that "we are in a transition state, and must prepare for changes"
(30). The apocalyptic tone of the peroration builds to a subtle crescendo, holding the audience in a fragile union with the North:

A few more shocks—one ruder blow—the phrenzy of an audacious, or
the malignity of a hostile spirit,—and the noble temple of our confederacy, built by the mighty Architects of the Revolution, is thrown down

in irretrievable ruin. When that time shall arrive, my countrymen,—
when the sound shall go forth, of fate, and a bitter lamenting through
the land,—let it be our boast that our hands have not prepared this
overthrow,—that we are not guilty of this ruin. The guilt and the
shame of a catastrophe, which shall mock and mortify the whole
world's hope of Liberty, must not rest on the fair fame and the conscience of the South. (31)

The repeated word *shall* combines with the echo of the Book of Jeremiah,
which foretells the doom of Jerusalem at the hands of "a people . . . from the
north country" (6:22) and "most bitter lamentation: for the spoiler shall suddenly come upon us" (6:26). The prophetic aura of the jeremiad mingles, however, with a certain reluctance, as if Simms hesitated to recommend a particular
course of action for the South. Filiopietism and prophecy keep the audience
in a "transition state," one that calls for listeners and readers to "prepare for
changes" but that does not say exactly how they are to do so.

2

Reluctantly prophetic and frighteningly accurate in *Sources of American
Independence*, Simms quite knowingly takes on the role of cultural spokesman
for the South. During the two decades leading to the Civil War, Simms aspires
to act as both the steward and the advocate of the South, "strong and striving
in the necessity of speech," and he puts his strivings into an impressive variety
of forms. By the time Simms took the podium at Aiken in 1844, he had published some fifteen novels and half a dozen volumes of poetry; he had written
two schoolbooks on the history and geography of South Carolina; he had published dozens of reviews and articles in periodicals, North and South; and he
had established himself as a careful, competent editor of Southern literary journals and a zealous promoter of Southern writing.[6]

Simms's career as a public speaker is somewhat harder to trace, although we
know that it had begun already in 1828, when he delivered an oration before
the Palmetto Society of Charleston. His letters show that periodically in the

---

6. For a discussion of Simms's career as an editor, especially his editing of the *Magnolia* (1842–43),
Southern and Western Monthly Magazine and Review (1845), and *Southern Quarterly Review* (1849–54), see
Guilds, *Simms*, 130–61; for a chronological list of books published by Simms, see Guilds, 359–65.

1830s and 1840s he delivered public addresses, either to political groups on civic occasions or to literary societies at Southern colleges or cities. The oration at Aiken is one of three published as pamphlets in the 1840s: on 13 December 1842, he delivered an oration to the Erosophic Society of the University of Alabama, published in 1843 as *The Social Principle: The True Source of National Permanence*; on 10 November 1847, he addressed the literary societies of Oglethorpe University in Milledgeville, Georgia, and the oration was published later that year as *Self-Development*.[7] In *The Social Principle* and in *Self-Development*, Simms once again looks at what he calls "that strange philosophical romance, the progress of society" (*Social Principle* 7). In both of these orations, Simms locates true progress or reform within the family and individual, rather than in political institutions, and in both he represents literature and art as the highest achievements of the American "race." In all three orations, Simms blends a faith in cultural progress with a disdain for materialism and a respect for traditional hierarchies. The result of combining these three positions is a fundamental nostalgia for a golden age, much like the position of the orator at the opening of *Sources of American Independence*. As Simms puts it in *Self-Development*, "The task before the race, is the restoration of its standards to the beautiful ideal of its original" (13). Nor does conservatism imply that Simms is simply antiprogressivist. "True Conservatism," he writes in *Egeria*, "is rather the bold spirit which leaps into the car of progress, and, seizing upon the reins, directs its movements with a firm hand, and an eye that sees the proper goal for which the race should aim" (15–16).

Simms develops a lucid view of oratory and cultural reform in a review article titled "Popular Discourses and Orations," published in the October 1851 issue of his *Southern Quarterly Review*. The article notices seven publications, including *The Death and Funeral Ceremonies of John Caldwell Calhoun*, political speeches in Congress and on the stump in South Carolina, an address inaugurating the Teacher's Association of South Carolina, an address before the South Carolina Institute, and two academic addresses delivered at the College of Charleston.[8] The miscellaneous character of the "quarterly treasures of

---

7. For information about the early orations and the three published addresses from the 1840s, see Simms, *Letters* 1:lxxxiv–lxxxvi, 123, 180, 191–92, 287–88, 332–33; 2:352, 367, 371–72, 473. Simms lists Burges & James of Charleston as the publishers of the three pamphlets, and they do appear as the printers on the verso of the title page for all three; see the editors' note, *Letters* 2:470.

8. *SQR* 4 (October 1851): 317–51; for Simms's authorship of the unsigned review, see *Letters* 3:144n. Founded in 1848, the South Carolina Institute was similar to the mechanics' institutes of the Northeast; see Drew Gilpin Faust, *James Henry Hammond and the Old South* (Baton Rouge: Louisiana State University Press, 1982), 275.

popular eloquence" is itself significant because it suggests the variety of directions in which eloquence can attempt to guide the "car of progress." Simms
first offers a wry apology for gathering the "gems which have fallen from our
inspired lips, our prophets, statesmen and priestly minds . . . in one sacred place,"
but then he becomes serious: "Lectures, orations and addresses, in the South,
are required to assert a higher rank than they are apt to do in other regions.
They, in fact, constitute a great portion of the literature proper of our section.
. . . This is the only open medium by which the leading minds of the South
may approach their people,—and this, in consequence of certain facts in our
condition, operating as barriers and embarrassments, which, for the present, are
not likely to be quickly overcome" (319). Simms does not so much praise popular eloquence as criticize the cultural conditions of the South, the "barriers
and embarrassments" that limit the cultural productiveness of the section. He
assumes a magisterial position of cultural authority, but he does so by employing a rhetoric of diminishment and limitation.

The same rhetorical stance creates a tone of apologetic defiance, guiding Simms
to a number of characteristic assertions. He claims, for instance, that "there is
no such thing as a professional literature in the South" and that "it is rare that
you find an individual, addressing himself to it as an occupation—the essential
object of his care—the essential necessity of his genius" (319). By formulating
the rule to which he is himself the rare exception, Simms transcends the limiting conditions he describes.

The same drama of limitation and transcendence is played out in the "transition" from oral performance to "printed speech" (320). Because the audience
of the actual performance is a "popular assembly," the speaker must limit himself, but the necessary limitation posed by a popular audience imposes a "beset-
ting infirmity" in print. Thus "the author owes it to the reader, that his speech,
if printed, should be purged of its commonplace, and made fit for the higher
judgment which he entreats upon it" (321). Simms's cultural diagnosis depends
on his position as editor, critic, and writer, which he places above the position
of the orator; likewise, he appeals to the "higher judgment" of the reader, who
is not so limited as the popular audience. Indeed, he adds that "the very great
good nature of a Southern audience exercises a very detrimental influence upon
the literature of its public men" (321).

Simms ends the review with a pair of recommendations. First, he asserts that
"the value of habitual exercise in composition, even to the orator, is hardly to
be exaggerated," for the "habitual writer" learns to "rise into real excellence,
and assert a classical dignity which will rather grow than diminish in public
esteem, with the progress of years" (322). Second, he reminds his readers that
"the want of *wholeness* and finish in our popular discourses, however, must not

make us heedless of the real merits which they occasionally display" (323). Simms recommends improvement by both speaker/writer and listener/reader, and as a result he can forecast the continuing "growth" of the national mind and its expressions: "These are fruits, found on a luxuriant tree, which needs pruning only, to make it at once productive in high degree, and as precious in the quality of its fruits as productive in quantity. We must not, because of its bad cultivation, neglect[,] and want of training, combined with unnecessary foliage, and overrun with weeds and vines, abandon it to indifference or contempt. We should rather labour at the elevation and improvement of a form of literature, which is the most natural to our present condition" (323). The horticultural metaphor combines nature and culture, growth and guidance, and it exemplifies the complex balance of conservatism and progressivism that Simms strikes as a cultural spokesman. In the series of imperatives, moreover, Simms recalls the rhetorical stance of *Sources of American Independence*, although his brief review complicates the earlier call for Southern unity by adding the specific requirements of a professional editor and author. The complication could in fact be seen as Simms's effort to give "*wholeness* and finish" to his own critical writing.

Simms's attitude toward popular eloquence grows in complexity at the same time that he grows in popularity as a speaker. In April 1852, for instance, he writes to John Pendleton Kennedy, outlining the editorial position of the *Southern Quarterly Review* on a host of social and political issues. He concludes the long letter by turning to broadly literary concerns, retracing the argument in "Popular Discourses and Orations" but adding the evil of party politics to the earlier list of "barriers and embarrassments." He then directs that point specifically at Kennedy himself, contrasting his own dedication to literature and "private distribution" to Kennedy's role as a public servant, who "fritter[s] away [his] mind in occasionalities for the pleasant public." Then Simms gives his most pointed advice: "Beware these Lectures & addresses. I have refused no less than seven in the last nine months. You are used only as a convenience by people who do not care a straw about you. The performance costs a world of trouble & frequently research. You have to force yourself into an artificial fervor,—there is no enthusiasm & can be none,—and when you have done your best, what remains?"[9] The extended warning against "Lectures & addresses" applies as much to Simms, however, as to Kennedy. In addition to repeating many of the criticisms from the 1851 review article, Simms heaps scorn upon the empty,

9. Simms, *Letters* 3:175. A native of Baltimore, Kennedy is best known as the author of *Swallow Barn* (1832) and *Horse-Shoe Robinson* (1835), but he was more active, after 1838, in national politics than in literature. In July 1852, he became Millard Fillmore's Secretary of the Navy. See Charles Bohner, *John Pendleton Kennedy: Gentleman from Baltimore* (Baltimore: Johns Hopkins University Press, 1961), 199–210.

emotionless performance and the temporary effect it may have upon an audience. In writing to Kennedy, then, Simms portrays himself as wholly estranged from political and popular endeavors, especially those relating to "Lectures & addresses."[10]

Simms's success in lecturing between 1853 and 1856 suggests a very different portrait. In February 1854, for instance, he delivered four lectures in Washington, D.C.: two titled "Poetry and the Practical" at the Smithsonian Institution, and two titled "The Moral Character of Hamlet" at the Young Men's Christian Association. While in Washington, Simms wrote to three literary friends in an attempt to extend his lecture tour to the North: John Pendleton Kennedy in Baltimore, Henry Carey Baird in Philadelphia, and Evert Augustus Duyckinck in New York City (*Letters* 3:275–87). Although none of his correspondents was able to act as his lecturing agent, during the month of March Simms lectured twice in Richmond, once in Petersburg, and twice in Savannah. The reception of the lectures led a group of Charleston citizens to invite Simms to lecture in his home state, and he delivered the three lectures "Poetry and the Practical" to enthusiastic audiences on the evenings of 31 May, 2 June, and 8 June 1854.[11]

The image that emerges from this narrative is that of a novice professional. Simms does not have a literary agent for his lecturing forays; instead, he appeals to friends or simply waits to "get a *call* . . . with a moderate quid" (*Letters* 3:278). The disadvantage of the approach is also clear. Without a professional connection to the various parts of the lecturing system in the North, Simms is forced to confine his successes to the principal and secondary cities of the upper South.

Simms's handling of two requests to publish public addresses delivered in 1855 reveals his continuing interest in developing a supplementary career as a public lecturer. On 23 February, Simms delivered "On the Choice of a Profession" to the Crestomathic Society at the College of Charleston; on 22 August, Simms gave the inaugural address at the Spartanburg Female Academy (*Letters* 3:365–68, 390 n. 166). In both cases, the sponsoring institution requested Simms's permission to publish the oration. Simms declined to publish the first

Bohner discusses the relationship between Kennedy and Simms and views it as cooling after Simms's letter (224–27). But see Simms, *Letters* 4:549–51, for a friendly meeting between the two men in postwar Charleston.

10. The subject and success of *Norman Maurice*, a blank verse tragedy subtitled *The Man of the People*, casts some doubt on Simms's ingenuousness. See Guilds, *Simms*, 198–201, and Simms, *Letters* 3:145–46, 153–54.

11. For documents and commentary relating to the tour in Virginia and Georgia, see Simms, *Letters* 3:285–93. For the invitation to lecture in Charleston and copious extracts from the Charleston *Mercury* and *Courier*, see *Letters* 3:300–302, especially note 92.

address, pleading that "the composition of it was so hurried (and my leisure just now is too limited to suffer its revision), that I should do no credit to your judgment, or my own reputation, by putting it in print" (370). But he complied with the second request, noting that the oration "was written at your instance, and if you think its publication can be of any service to your Institution, or to the public, I have no right, and can have no reason for refusal" (393).

The difference between the two responses lies in the use to which Simms can put the particular address. In the reply to Spartanburg Female College, Simms acknowledges that the address was written especially for the occasion at which it was delivered. It is therefore no longer useful for Simms himself, and with revisions it can meet the criteria for publication Simms describes in the review of "Popular Discourses and Orations." But even though the reply to the Crestomathic Society argues that "On the Choice of a Profession" is simply unworthy of publication, we should also note that Simms used the lecture repeatedly for the rest of his career. So, for example, he used the text several times during "Lecturing expeditions" he made in South Carolina and Georgia in February, March, and April 1856, evidently employing it alongside "Poetry and the Practical" as a standard.[12] The evidence suggests, then, that Simms retained the text of "Choice of a Profession" so that he could continue to use it before "live" audiences.

In a number of ways Simms's role as a public speaker and cultural spokesman reaches a crucial point of development in 1856. First, his earlier sense of the limitations inherent in popular eloquence gives way to a much more enthusiastic view. In a 30 December 1855 letter to Duyckinck, for example, Simms congratulates his friend on the recent completion of the *Encyclopedia of American Literature* and then offers a suggestion: "You should now, having got through one labour, meditate upon another. American Oratory—a field particularly American—has never had any justice done to it. Two vols. of Biography, with samples, of the size and in the plan of your Encyclopedia would, I fancy, be a good speculation. It would enable you to do a good deal towards the development of Southern literature" (3:412). Simms clearly echoes his 1851 review article, envisioning oratory as "particularly American" and as an important part of "the development of Southern literature." But he also believes oratory should have "justice done to it" and

---

12. See Simms, *Letters* 3:422–25. The Cheraw *Gazette* and Sumter *Watchman* both praise Simms's lectures and describe their subjects as "the choice of professions" and "the Ideal and Real" (422n.). The latter title suggests the same dichotomy as "Poetry and the Practical," and I have found no evidence of a lecture distinct from it.

that it deserves the kind of monumental treatment the Duyckinck brothers accorded other types of American writing.

This more expansive view of the possibilities inherent in oratory extends, of course, to Simms's own career. As early as April 1856, he was once again contemplating a lecture tour of the North, and he therefore wrote to Duyckinck asking for help: "I am thinking seriously of preparing a couple or more of lectures suitable for the North, and appropriating a portion of my next winter to the work of lecturing in some of your Northern regions. If you can promote this object let me beg you to have the matter in mind, and act upon it whenever an opportunity shall offer" (3:425). In a letter written the next day, Simms gave the Boston publisher James T. Fields a more specific plan for a "rambling Lecturing campaign in the North": "I design one or two Lectures touching the scenery, the society, habits manners, of the South, especially for your people & to establish better relations between North & South" (429). A month later, in a letter to the editor and historian Benson John Lossing in Poughkeepsie, New York, Simms expanded yet further on his ambitions:

> If you can give me any hints in regard to this Lecturing business, which is new to me *as a business*, I shall be most grateful. . . . The Lecturing business seems to promise me that respite from the desk which I so much require, while affording me as liberal an income as I could possibly acquire at the desk. . . . I should like to start from N.Y. and take the Northern Capitals & States—to so arrange, as to follow no crossing routes, but to make one scene, the step towards another—even as we do in the manufacture of a novel. Now, in your precincts, where the business is regularly understood, you might teach me every thing touching the several points in this order,—the expense the modes & degree of compensation,—and especially, what subjects would be most likely to please the Northern ear, from Southern lips. (3:435)

Simms presents himself as a novice intent upon learning the "Lecturing business . . . *as a business.*" But beyond his practical questions concerning the scheduling, expenses, and compensations he can expect from a lecture tour of the North, Simms is most concerned to hear "what subjects would be most likely to please the Northern ear, from Southern lips." For Simms, the lecturing business entails pleasing an unfamiliar audience, and his request for advice implies that he sees a great distance between the Northern ear and Southern lips. That impression is confirmed by a 27 June letter from Simms to Lossing, in which he thanks his Northern friend for judicious counsels and then requests more: "You will perhaps be able to say if any of the subjects which I now name to you will be likely to prove of interest to the Northern audience. They are those of Lectures which I have been using popularly in the South" (3:436–37).[13]

3

The story of Simms's failure to please the Northern ear, told and interpreted several times in the recent past, bears retelling because of the light it sheds on the relationship between literary culture and sectional politics in the antebellum period.[14] With J. S. Redfield acting as his agent in New York City, Simms prepared a winter lecture tour of the North and a "campaign South" for the following spring (3:443). But events in the territory of Kansas and on the floor of the United States Senate conspired to alter Simms's plans and doom his "campaign North" to failure.

The ultimate cause of these events, in all likelihood, was the Kansas-Nebraska Act of 1854. As James McPherson puts it, "this law may have been the most important single event pushing the nation toward civil war."[15] It opened the newly formed Kansas Territory to the doctrine of popular sovereignty, which ensured that over the next two years a bloody conflict, verging upon civil war, was waged between slaveholders and free-soilers. In addition, it galvanized the antislavery forces in the North and eventually led to the founding of the Republican Party. In the spring of 1856, as Simms was planning his lecture expedition to the North, the conflict in Kansas was mirrored in Congress by competing bills for admission of the territory as a state. On 21 May, the free-

13. In addition to "Poetry and the Practical" and "Choice of a Profession," Simms lists "The Moral Character of Hamlet" and "Ante-Colonial History of the South" as possible topics, for a total of eight lectures (3:437). Simms gave two lectures on the last topic in Augusta, Georgia, on the evenings of 4 and 5 April 1856 (3:424n.).

14. The best account is by Miriam J. Shillingsburg, "Simms's Failed Lecture Tour of 1856: The Mind of the North," in *"Long Years of Neglect": The Work and Reputation of William Gilmore Simms*, ed. John Caldwell Guilds (Fayetteville: University of Arkansas Press, 1988), 183–201. Shillingsburg's earlier treatment should also be consulted: "The Southron as American: William Gilmore Simms," in *Studies in the American Renaissance 1980*, ed. Joel Myerson (Boston: Twayne, 1980), 409–23. John Hope Franklin has written two other significant versions of the story; see his *A Southern Odyssey: Travelers in the Antebellum North* (Baton Rouge: Louisiana State University Press, 1976), 231–43, which recasts an earlier treatment of the material in "The North, the South, and the American Revolution," *Journal of American History* 62 (June 1975): 5–23.

15. *Battle Cry of Freedom: The Civil War Era* (New York: Ballantine, 1989), 121.

soil town of Lawrence was sacked by proslavery raiders, many of them Missourians.[16]

By the time news of the attack reached Washington, a greater outrage had occurred. On 19 and 20 May, Charles Sumner, the junior senator from Massachusetts, delivered his famous speech "The Crime Against Kansas." The performance lasted five hours, but the most noteworthy parts were gratuitous digressions. On both days of the speech, Sumner attacked Senator Andrew P. Butler of South Carolina, who had been an important figure behind passage of the Kansas-Nebraska Act of 1854. Butler was not the only colleague Sumner attacked, but he was clearly singled out for special scorn. Most venomous, perhaps, was the figure of Butler as "chivalrous knight" to the "mistress to whom he has made his vows, and who, though ugly to others, is always lovely to him,—though polluted in the sight of the world, is chaste in his sight: I mean the harlot Slavery." But Sumner even alluded to Butler's labial paralysis, charging him with speaking "with incoherent phrase" and discharging "the loose expectoration of his speech, now upon [Kansas's] representative, and then upon her people." In addition, Sumner accused Butler of false pride in his native state, since, he said, "He cannot, surely, forget [South Carolina's] shameful imbecility from Slavery, confessed throughout the Revolution, followed by its more shameful assumptions for Slavery since." Two days after finishing the speech, Sumner was attacked on the floor of the Senate by Butler's kinsman, Congressman Preston S. Brooks, who beat Sumner over the head and shoulders with a gutta-percha cane.[17]

Simms's request for advice regarding "what subjects would be most likely to please the Northern ear, from Southern lips" becomes deeply ironic when we note that he wrote the letter to Ben Lossing on 22 May 1856, but the irony deepens further when we see him striving to remain detached from the sectional uproar of the summer and fall of 1856. In a 7 September letter to James H. Hammond, for instance, Simms complains that "Butler and Evans [the two Senators from South Carolina] are flooding me with the attacks of the Northern Press on South Carolina. Butler says, 'I have no time to answer them.

16. McPherson, 145–49. For a full account of the events I sketch here, see McPherson, 3–233, but esp. 145–69.

17. "The Crime Against Kansas," in *The Works of Charles Sumner* (Boston: Lee and Shepard, 1871) 4:144, 240–41. The entire document, with appendix, covers more than two hundred pages (125–342). All quotations are taken from this edition and are cited parenthetically in my text. The best account of the speech, the caning, and Sumner's long convalescence appears in David Donald, *Charles Sumner and the Coming of the Civil War* (New York: Alfred A. Knopf, 1960), 278–347. See also William E. Gienapp, "The Crime Against Sumner: The Caning of Charles Sumner and the Rise of the Republican Party," *Civil War History* 25 (1975): 218–45.

It is the business of the Historian.' But his blunderings have provoked them, & he is one of the victims in all the attacks. In brief he wants me to take up the cudgels and fight his battles" (3:446). Simms sees two ironies in the situation. The first is rather bitter, since he finds himself called upon to defend Senator Butler for his "blunderings" without any hope of reward. The second, however, is almost jolly. Juxtaposing the ungrateful, weak Butler with Lorenzo Sabine, whose attacks on South Carolina's role in the Revolutionary War had sparked Simms's pen in 1848 and 1853, Simms shares a rather delighted sense of irony with Hammond: "I have just got a long letter from Lorenzo Sabine, apologetic & complimentary, who invites me to visit him!" (447). For Simms in the fall of 1856, friends and enemies trade places in surprising ways. Thus he writes to Sabine the very next day, "Sumner properly owes his cudgelling to you! He followed in your tracks, and relied upon your Introductory essay."[18]

Given Simms's clear sense of multiple ironies in the situation, it is somewhat surprising to learn that he drafted the primary lecture for the tour within the next two weeks. On September 20, he writes M. C. M. Hammond that he is "drudging upon my Northern course, & am nearly exhausted. I have just finished one to be delivered in Boston, on 'South Carolina in the Revolution.'— If they will listen to me!" (*Letters* 3:449). Simms imagines Boston as the site of his lecture, projecting his performance well beyond New York City and secondary cities of New York, but he also imagines an audience that may not give him a hearing. The two images suggest that Simms's desire to carry his historical argument to the very center of New England culture combines uneasily with his doubt that a Northern audience will listen to a Southern speaker.

The doubt proved well founded, although the historical section of "South Carolina in the Revolution" did not cause the most trouble, nor was Boston the site of Simms's defeat. Simms delivered the lecture at Buffalo on 11 November, at Rochester on 13 November, and at New York City on 18 November. On 21 November, having delivered a grand total of four lectures, Simms canceled the rest of his tour; by 1 December, he was back in South Carolina.[19] But it would be utterly wrong to infer that the failed lecturing expedition to the North

18. Sabine, a New England historian, published his attack on South Carolina and the role of slavery in weakening the colony's role in the Revolutionary War in the "Preliminary Historical Essay" to *Biographical Sketches of Loyalists of the American Revolution* (Boston: Little, Brown, 1847). Simms published two long, critical reviews of the book in *SQR* 14 (July, October 1848): 37–77, 261–337, and he later reissued the material as a book, *South-Carolina in the Revolutionary War* (Charleston: Walker & James, 1853). See William L. Welch, "Lorenzo Sabine and the Assault on Sumner," *New England Quarterly* 65 (1992): 298–301.

19. *Letters* 3:424n.; cf. Shillingsburg 191–96. The fourth lecture was "Choice of a Profession," delivered at Syracuse on November 14 (Rochester *Daily Democrat*, 14 November; Buffalo *Commercial Advertiser*, 18 November).

caused Simms to doubt himself as an orator or historian. For much of January, February, and March 1857, Simms was touring the South, delivering his standard lectures "Poetry and the Practical," "The Choice of a Profession," and "Ante-Colonial History of America" to audiences from Baltimore and Washington to Greensboro, North Carolina, and smaller towns in South Carolina (*Letters* 3:484n., 493–94). The climax of the Southern expedition came on 25 May, 27 May, and 1 June 1857, in Charleston. For three evenings Simms lectured in Hibernian Hall, presenting "The Social Moral of the South." The substance of the final lecture, "Antagonisms of the Social Moral, North and South," was Simms's own account of his lecturing expedition to the North. Despite nagging physical ailments, Simms acquitted himself well and was lionized by the Southern press.[20]

Like *Sources of American Independence*, Simms's New York lecture, "South Carolina in the Revolution," is most interesting in the patterned opening and closing.[21] In the exordium, Simms focuses on Sumner's representation of South Carolina as so weakened by slavery as to be unable to defend itself against the British. According to Simms, the revisionary history is extreme, both in method and in conclusions, and he employs disjunctive rhetoric to reduce the historical argument to a choice between two diametrically opposed interpretations. If South Carolina is not angelic, it is demonic.

The strategy of reducing and demonizing the opposing interpretation extends as well to the opposing interpreter. Simms rehearses his extreme version of the Lorenzo Sabine argument and then puts the words into Charles Sumner's mouth. The unnamed Sumner becomes, in Simms's hands, a shocking figure of eloquence, who pours forth his maliciously false history "with a malignant satisfaction . . . to goad and mortify" the South Carolinians. Simms characterizes Sumner's assault as "gratuitously wanton," "hostile," and "grossly subversive." Certainly Simms commits a serious rhetorical error by neglecting even to mention Preston Brooks and the caning of Sumner. Instead, his hyperbolic portrait of a malignant Sumner and an outraged, innocent audience of senators implies a possible excuse for Brooks's actions. The portrait of Sumner, in particular, contrasts too sharply with the well-publicized (and also real) sufferings of the senator.[22] By creating the demonic scene of eloquence, then,

20. For pertinent documents, including newspaper accounts of Simms's lectures, see *Letters* 3:489–503; see especially the Charleston *Mercury* and *Courier* comments on the three lectures in late May and early June, 490n.
21. The text of the lecture appears as an appendix to Simms, *Letters* 3:521–49; all further quotations will be cited parenthetically in my text.
22. See Donald's chapter, "The Vacant Chair," in his *Charles Sumner* (312–47), for the definitive discussion of Sumner's post-traumatic syndrome and long convalescence.

Simms himself ensures that *he* will "goad and mortify" his Northern audience—at least that considerable part of it in sympathy with Sumner. The conceivable, unintended result: Simms becomes a malignant figure of eloquence, while his Northern listeners become the assembled victims of his speech. A more conciliatory stance would require Simms to condemn Brooks's assault, but it would not demand that he accept Sumner's calumnies.

The peroration displays a much more moderate tone than the exordium, and Simms depersonalizes the conclusion by focusing on states rather than individuals. But he cannot resist the temptation to recall Sumner's words:

> The Past of both regions ought to be secure. Let the strifes of the Present be what they may, neither party gains by the brutal defamation of the other. If there is to be strife between our respective countries—if the future is to witness a conflict among ourselves—and this great empire be doomed to the convulsions of Civil War,—let the issues be unmixed; simple, single, unconfounded! If South Carolina, imbecile in the Past—be *now* imbecile—no matter from what cause—there need be no effort to prove the fact by argument. It will prove itself, in action! If imbecile, past and present, how absurd for the brave to go into the discussion! We scorn the imbecile; we do not contend with them! (548)

The suddenness with which Simms changes tone is remarkable. He begins at his most moderate, but the common prophecy of civil war leads to exclamatory rhetoric and to the repetition of Sumner's word "imbecile" four times. In the first three uses of the word, Simms echoes Sumner's charge of "shameful imbecility from Slavery," although he refuses to address the issue of slavery as causing imbecility. Instead, he disputes the very notion of imbecility—if South Carolina is imbecile, why discuss anything with her? The fourth use of the word turns the tables: "we scorn the imbecile" implies that Simms speaks for his entire state, distinguishing their collective self from the multitude included in the term "the imbecile." Although the phrasing suggests that Simms has Sumner and Sabine in mind, it also could be addressed to anyone in the audience who dares to question the speaker's arguments. Thus Simms moves from the conciliatory to the prophetic to the imperious, a dynamic shifting of tones that is surely the opposite of "simple, single, unconfounded."

In the closing sentences of the lecture, Simms maintains his focus on the relationship among the states. He once again softens his tone, describing himself as "standing, here, before you, on a purely Literary Mission" and as "opposed to brutality & violence" (548). But the tone becomes more complicated as he predicts the future destruction of South Carolina:

> If her doom is written, be equally sure, that she will fall no easy victim. With her lithe and sinewy limbs & muscles, she will twine herself around the giant caryatides which sustain the anchor of the great Confederacy, and falling like the strong man of Israel, will bring down with her, in a common ruin, the vast and wondrous fabric, which her own prowess has so much helped to raise. Then, if there shall be one surviving sister, sitting solitary in the desolation, she will remain a monument, more significant of ruin than all the wreck which grows around her—the trophy of a moral desolation, which, by perversity and wrong, by a base selfishness which knew not how to be just, or how to be human, has with fratricidal hand, destroyed all its own securities and hopes—a moral suicide.—Forgive me, my friends, if I have spoken warmly; but you would not, surely, have me speak coldly in the assertion of a Mother's honour! (549)

Simms betrays little of the reluctance that marks the closure of *Sources of American Independence*, but the resulting sense of closure is even more layered and complex than that of the earlier oration. Both noble and tragic, the image of Samson insists upon a biblical, apocalyptic "doom" written into the narrative of sectional conflict. Even though the story of the "great Confederacy" creates a "vast and wondrous fabric," the texture of the passage becomes ever darker as Simms forecasts the aftermath of ruin. The "surviving sister, sitting solitary in the desolation," would in all likelihood be Massachusetts, since that is the only state Simms names in the peroration, and Simms applies terms of absolute opprobrium to her, just as he did to her senator. In casting blame on the "surviving sister" and in predicting her role as a monument to "moral suicide," Simms clearly crosses any supposed boundary dividing the "purely" literary or historical from the "miserable politics of today" (522). The final sentence seeks to apologize and justify at the same time, but it reveals most tellingly the speaker's sense of an immediate and concrete danger—the danger of giving offence.

Simms faces no such danger in the three Charleston lectures, to which he gives the collective title "Our Social Moral."[23] The first lecture, "South Carolina

23. The manuscripts of all three lectures are part of the Charles Carroll Simms Collection, housed in South Caroliniana Library. I quote from my transcriptions. Simms's use of the term *moral*, while per-

in the Revolution," echoes the New York lecture in its title and opening paragraphs, but it differs from the November performance in several ways. Most telling is Simms's developing sense of his relationship to Southern listeners. Throughout the first four sheets of the manuscript, Simms changes all references to "you," "your," and "yourselves" to "we/us," "our," and "ourselves." A proposition such as "You had been living on, in a delightful condition of self-complacency" becomes "We had been living on, . . ." putting the speaker in exactly the same position as the audience. That position is, most fundamentally, the polar opposite of a monolithic Northern "moral."

Second, Simms intensifies the rhetoric of the lecture by his use of vehement invective. Sumner is once again a figure of Satanic eloquence, but Simms demonizes him in more detail and with more likelihood of obtaining a hearing. From the outset, however, Simms regards Sumner as a representative figure rather than a personal enemy or singular cause. So, for instance, he first refers to Daniel Webster speaking in Charleston: "Thus it was that Mr. Webster, in our own city, could tell us with fearless front, that *our* plains had been whitened with the bones of New Englanders perishing in battle." Later, he describes a more general figure of eloquence, a "popular orator" who, "if he speaks to the people . . . is apt to disparage learning & education altogether. He fancies that such terms of disparagement, will be grateful to those to whom education has been denied." The "popular orator" resembles the figure Simms describes in his 1851 review, "Popular Discourses and Orations," but here he figures the orator as ignorant, anti-intellectual, manipulative, and coolly condescending.

The escalating rhetoric brings Simms, not surprisingly, to Sumner himself. Although "one of the best educated and most accomplished men in the Senate," Sumner is "a vain & weak man" and "at best but a fluent rhetorician." Simms's admiration for Sumner is grudging but clear. He seeks to undercut each positive quality with a negative qualification, and even the positive qualities only serve to make Sumner all the more culpable. Simms blames Sumner most directly for abandoning the "language of exhortation & wisdom" in favor of "such language as should defeat their objects—prevent wisdom—baffle counsel—disturb harmony—destroy union." The parallel verb-object phrases build in intensity as they outline the powers of language, culminating in the apocalyptic.

---

haps odd to modern readers, suggests several intriguing interpretations. Most likely is the definition "moral science; moral doctrine; ethics," which is rare. Other now obsolete meanings include "import, meaning, signification"; "a symbolical figure"; "counterpart, likeness"; "(a person's) moral principles or practice" (*OED*). The definition we now associate with the word "morale" also occurs: "the condition (of troops, etc.) with respect to discipline, subordination, and confidence" (*OED*).

Simms next represents Sumner's thoughts and words in an imagined speech delivered to "the insane faction" before the "Crime Against Kansas" speech. Sumner functions as a figure of eloquence, but his eloquence openly serves the ends of "Demagoguerism" and "malignity." The imagined speech has poetic qualities, as in the metrical and syntactic patterning of "I will sting; I will wound; I will fill the wound with venom." Indeed, Sumner's pride rules the passage, and it makes him imagine himself as "like Demosthenes" in his ability to hurl philippics. In language and character, the figure Simms creates recalls villainous and demonic figures such as Iago and Satan, although there is no strict verbal borrowing from Shakespeare or Milton. It would seem, in fact, that Simms seeks to create a generic figure. Thus he summarizes his portrait of Sumner as a "vulgar" figure, a concrete instance of the "popular orator" he scorns.

In contrast to the New York lecture, Simms directly addresses Preston Brooks's caning of Sumner, but he raises the issue in order to interpret the events symbolically:

> The individuals concerned are nothing here to the deep moral issues which they represent. They declare only the gradual progress from words to blows—from speech to action—of that terrible & unhappy strife of sections, which has now been breeding bad blood among us for more than a quarter of a century. We are only reaching a natural result, from the operation of well known causes. It is the beginning of the war. It is a revolution which is already in progress, from the terrible throes of which we are destined to see arise a monstrous phantom, clothed with hissing serpents, breathing the pollution of blood, and speeding, on fiery winds and wings, on its mission of carnage and havoc.

Simms creates a scene of apocalyptic violence, and he adds to that emphasis when he imagines how, "had the chastisement of Sumner taken place in the House, rather than the Senate, the fight would have become pell-mell; and a scene of butchery must have followed, in which the Capital [*sic*], and the Confederacy, would have gone down, in a storm of violence." Sectional conflict is portrayed as necessary, a "gradual progress from words to blows—from speech to action," and it is only by chance that the scene of conflict did not erupt in a general bloodletting. As Simms puts it, "the language which made Brooks fall upon Sumner, would, in like manner, have brought their congregated thousands to blows."

As he closes the first lecture, Simms recurs to the opposition between written and spoken language that he employed in "Popular Discourses and

Orations." Whereas in the review he figured the printed speech as a higher form, rising above the commonplace and appealing to a higher judgment (*SQR* 4:321), Simms focuses here on the relationship between the press and the spoken words of Sumner. In detailing the escalating attacks on South Carolina, Simms delineates a hierarchy of immediacy. Lorenzo Sabine's "fabricated chronicles" are least immediate and therefore elicit little response. Northern newspapers and journals repeat and multiply the fabrications, but they still do not alarm the victims of their assaults. But most immediate and most alarming is "the living voice of the Accuser," which "compels us to hear, and makes us feel that every body else must hear."

The opposition between print and oral cultures controls "Antagonisms of the Social Moral, North and South," the third and most important of the Charleston lectures. Simms notes that he has been asked to explain "why I abandoned, almost at the outset, my tour of lectures in the northern states." His explanation becomes a "moral"—a symbolic narrative: "As straws may be made to show the direction of the winds, so the simple career of an individual, may be made at times, to indicate the courses of the political currents, and especially the ebbs, flows, and overflows, which affect human communities." At the outset of the lecture itself, Simms indicates that the relationship between the press and the lecturing system is fundamental to his story:

> You are to know, my friends, that for several years past, I have had frequent invitations to take part in the Lecture circles of the Northern States; where the Lecture has grown into an institution; is one of the most efficient agencies of popular education, & exercises a vast influence upon the popular mind. Here it is otherwise. But the scene was too remote, my hands were usually too full of other labours, and I felt no adequate motive to compliance, until last year, when an earnest desire to vindicate our State and section from the grievous slanders to which they have recently been subjected, furnished an impulse which proved superior to all personal considerations. These slanders of our past, worked upon my mind, as I fancy, they worked upon yours. I felt that, in a fair field, they were easy of refutation. I had already, thro' the press, done something towards their refutation; but the publications of the South, which hardly circulate at home, still more rarely reach the North; and the Lecturing System of that region seemed to promise a much more ample field. I resolved to avail myself of it—to reopen the old chronicles for the instruction of those who had no opportunity for undertaking the task for themselves.

Simms consistently represents speech as more immediate and effective than the written word; the institution of the lecture or "Lecturing System" becomes the "fair field" or "much more ample field" on which Simms chooses to battle "slanders of our past." The analysis of the relationship strongly recalls Simms's argument in "Popular Discourses and Orations," for in both cases he figures popular oratory as a necessary medium for educating people, North and South. The passage further implies that in delivering the present lecture Simms seeks to create a much more ample field for himself in the South, to "circulate" more freely than print.

At the threshold of his symbolic narrative, Simms recurs to his first Charleston lecture in order to name the villain. If he sees himself as "an advocate," appealing to "thousands who will gladly listen to the truth," he conceives of Sumner as the "Accuser." But in "Antagonisms of the Social Moral," Simms does not at first name his opponent; instead, he uses Sumner's stinging word: "It was especially important that the North should be disabused of the notion that the South *is imbecile*—imbecile because of her slave institutions—imbecile in war—unproductive in letters—deficient in all the proper agencies of civilization,—and so, incapable of defence against assault!" Simms quite correctly phrases Sumner's charge in the present tense, for the charge of "imbecility" relates directly to the present. As in the peroration of the New York lecture, Simms's repetition of the word *imbecile* suggests the repetition of the charge "in every form of phrase, & through every popular medium." Here, too, Simms adds persistent alliteration in order to pound the insistence home. He answers the alliteratively multiplied assault by expanding his statement of purpose from the merely literary and historical to the more broadly cultural and contemporary: "It was somewhat my purpose to do this in my lectures—not merely to vindicate our ancestors, but to show, as indirectly and inoffensively as possible, that we inherit their blood & spirit; their intellect & will—that we are not resourceless in any of the elements that enable a nation to maintain itself in the arena with all other nations;—not imbecile, but particularly powerful, whenever the necessity for conflict shall become sufficiently apparent to compel the exhibition of our strength." Along with the self-aggrandizing but hardly accurate claim that he had "for several years past . . . had frequent invitations," Simms's disingenuous hedging ("somewhat my purpose") casts serious doubt on his sincere desire to speak "as indirectly and inoffensively as possible." But there is nothing disingenuous about the way in which this passage turns from negation to positive defiance.

Nor does Simms wait long before discussing Sumner at some length. After narrating the performance of the first lecture in Buffalo, which he says was attended by more than twelve hundred persons and interrupted "with frequent applause," Simms lists two principal objections made by the Buffalo newspapers. The first refers to comparisons between South Carolina and other states, an objection voiced by the Buffalo *Commercial Advertiser*.[24] The second refers to Simms's near naming of Sumner, and in response Simms calls Sumner nearly every name one might wish. Words like "venomous" and "malignant" pepper the description of Sumner's preparation and delivery of "The Crime Against Kansas." But Simms's grudging admiration for Sumner's eloquence comes through the invective, for he in effect argues that Sumner is a worthy opponent: "He had studied Demosthenes in the preparation of his Philippic; and the thought that all his people looked on longingly to hear his thunders, was the irresistible motive for his eloquence! Why should I forbear him? Because he had been cudgelled? His slanders were on record, and still demanding refutation. His offence was still scored on our chronicles, and would there remain, even when the cudgel marks had faded from his forehead." Simms represents Sumner's eloquence as a verbal version of Brooks's cane, "scoring" the chronicles of South Carolina in order to appeal to "his people." In an equally important figure, Simms himself replaces Brooks by defending South Carolina in the lecture. From Simms's point of view, forbearance would imply that the attack on South Carolina was warranted. The necessity of answering the charge of "imbecility" outweighs any concern for Sumner's physical pain.

An unconscious irony develops from Simms's comparison between Sumner and Brooks, for later in the lecture he blames the "leading abolition papers" of the North for "the studied identification of myself and my objects, with the affair of Brooks and Sumner." After sketching a Northern theory of conspiracy relating to the attack on Sumner, Simms focuses on metaphor: "The same presses described me as seeking to do, in the historical field, what Brooks had done in the physical. I was only another sort of bully, dispatched to hector the Northern people in their own homes. This imputation, as you may well conceive, once put in circulation—& so well calculated to provoke the most

---

24. The review of Simms's lecture appears in the 12 November 1856 issue and runs to nine paragraphs. In the second paragraph, the writer asserts that "Mr. Simms forgot the pithy saying of Mr. [*sic*] Malaprop, that 'comparisons are odorous.' South Carolina was capable of defence upon her own merits. It was unnecessary, and in more than doubtful taste, to build up its fame on a depreciation of the equally earnest and self-sacrificing struggles of the North." The *Commercial Advertiser*, a Democratic newspaper, is in fact rather measured in its criticisms, as is the Buffalo *Evening Post* in its more stinging judgment of the same day. Both periodicals question the appropriateness of delivering "a stump speech instead of a lecture" (*Post*). For selected commentaries from these and other Buffalo newspapers, see Simms, *Letters* 3:456–57n.

unreasoning temper of the people—must be fatal to my mission."[25] One possible implication is that, had Simms continued his tour, the "unreasoning
temper of the people" might have led to violence, and the rhetoric of
identification leads one to infer that Simms might himself be attacked—like
Sumner. Even if that pair of implications goes too far, Simms clearly represents
the Northern press as killing off his lecturing mission and effectively silencing the Southern advocate.

Even though Simms endeavors to show his Charleston audience scenes of
effective eloquence and cooperation in narrating his stay in Rochester and New
York City, the lecture drives home a sense of polarization in public discourse,
as if the languages of North and South were mutually incomprehensible. The
scenes of eloquence and cooperation take place when Simms meets with the
lecture board in Rochester, when the audience in that city receives his speech,
and when the speaker is joined at a reception after the lecture. Likewise, he
describes the eminently reasonable and open-minded members of his committee in New York City—including William Cullen Bryant, George Bancroft,
and Evert Duyckinck—and represents the committee as persuading him to
revise the lecture in order to soften its tone. But the most effective means of
silencing a speaker is to deprive him of an audience, and Simms notes that "but
about 150 persons" attended his New York City lecture. The cause, for Simms,
is immediately apparent:

> I readily conceived the secret. The newspapers had done their work; my
> friends had shown their fears; and, according to every report, the very
> name of South Carolina was everywhere the word of odium; so that I was
> already fully prepared to understand that, even in this great city—this
> Babylon of all races—distinguished by its lenities and lack of character—
> it was easy for a vigorous, powerful, concentrated party, fanatical of mood,
> despotic of will—embodying in its ranks almost the entire mind of the
> community—certainly all the great leading intellects—to coerce the pub-
> lic temper, on all occasions, and, easily, in the case of an individual who
> lacked the *prestige* of party for his support. This was my lack.

25. Several newspapers—not all abolitionist, by any means—did indeed draw the comparison of
Simms to Brooks: *Buffalo Evening Post*, 12 November; *Rochester Daily Democrat*, 14 November; *New York
Daily Tribune*, 19 November. For salient passages from the last of these, see *Letters* 3:462–63n. It should
be noted that the *Tribune* uses Simms as an example of a pervasive, irrational violence in the South; in
the column next to the review of Simms's lecture, an article condemns "the newspaper allies of Preston
S. Brooks in the North" for belittling the Republican party votes for John C. Frémont in the 4
November 1856 election. Like Brooks, Simms is put to political use by the Republican newspaper.

Simms represents the "mind of the community" as subject to the fanatical power of parties, and there is no doubt he means the Republican Party most especially. But the intellectual segment of the North further subjects the "Babylon of all races" to its coercions, so that the potential audience for Simms's lecture is driven away, as it were, from the sound of his voice. The image of Babylon bespeaks a welter of races and languages in exile, but it also implies that the speaker delivers an unheard jeremiad.

Simms's symbolic narrative thus delivers a moral of multiple polarizations. The gap between Southern speaker and Northern audience represents gaps dividing sections, parties, and individuals. In effect, he tells a story of growing, inherent antagonism, one that is fueled by "a power at the North, striding in between the people and all their social influences, which leaves the latter at a woful [*sic*] discount, in the moment of collision. Fanaticism and Politics, in alliance, and in possession of the press, is of so terrible a potency in all the North that Society has ceased to speak, does not decide for itself and dare not act." If we broaden the charge of fanaticism and politics to include the South and its press, Simms's analysis of his own narrative seems quite accurate and telling. But it tells a story of eloquence driven into silence, of words leading to blows, of a society ceasing to speak or to listen. It is altogether fitting, then, that Simms end his triumphant tale of failure with a final, chilling echo of the Sumner-Brooks story:

> While the matter seems doubtful to you, whether the abolitionists mean to be simply funny, or in downright earnest, my advice is that you take them to mean the very things that they avow. They tell you, honestly enough, that they mean to abolish slavery in the South, that it is a war to the knife, and through life with you, until they succeed in their objects. And I believe them. Do you the same, by way of decent precaution, in spite of the politicians. If then,—having destroyed them, having saved yourselves,—you should discover that nothing but fun was meant—then, my friends, I entreat, I implore you, to make the most prompt apology, declare your regrets in the most moving language; I can suppose that a man may, in jest, take his neighbour by the nose or beard, and get himself knocked over for it. But should the violent man find that he who took him by the beard, really meant nothing more than a clever jest, a compliment, or a courtesy, then, I am clear, that this other should make him a very neat apology, in the best English;—but, be sure, that you have first knocked him down!

7

Whitman's Agonistic Arena

1

The evidence from Walt Whitman's manuscripts strongly suggests that the poet considered pursuing a career on the lecture circuit during the 1850s. On his birthday in 1858, for instance, Whitman writes the kind of self-admonition and assessment he usually reserves for his role as a poet, but this year the role is that of eloquent speaker:

> May 31. '58
>
> It seems to me called for to inaugurate a revolution in American oratory, to change it from the excessively diffuse and impromptu character it has, (an ephemeral readiness, surface animation, the stamp of the daily newspaper, to be dismissed as soon as the next day's paper appears.)—and to make it the means of the grand modernized delivery of live modern orations, appropriate to America, appropriate to the world.—(May 31–2) This change is a serious one, and, if to be done at all, cannot be done easily.—A great leading representative man, with perfect power, perfect confidence in his power, persevering, with repeated specimens, ranging up and down The States—such a man, above all things would give it a fair start.—What are your theories?—Let us have the practical sample of a thing, and look upon it, and listen to it, and turn it about for to examine it.—[1]

---

1. *Notebooks and Unpublished Manuscripts*, ed. Edward F. Grier, 6 vols. (New York: New York University Press, 1984), 6:2233–34; hereafter cited parenthetically in my text as *NUPM*.

Whitman's projected revolution should occur in several arenas. Reminiscent of Simms in the same decade, his jeremiad concerning "the excessively diffuse and impromptu" style of current American oratory associates that style with "the stamp of the daily newspaper." So Whitman, himself the editor of the Brooklyn *Times* from spring 1857 to summer 1859, merges spoken and written language, just as the tone of the passage merges public scorn and private dissatisfaction.[2] This double merging leads, in turn, to the figure of a "great leading representative man" who will give "a fair start" to the revolution in oratory. Like the tone of the entire "inaugural address," that figure combines Whitman's personal revolution with the larger revolution he desires for the country. Such a figure of eloquence is exactly what Whitman desires to become, for it is certainly *his* plan to go "ranging up and down The States," delivering "live modern orations, appropriate to America, appropriate to the world." The last two sentences of the passage function as Whitman's direct address to himself, presenting the would-be orator's demands both for "theories" and for "the practical sample of a thing."

Other manuscript notes show Whitman's concern with making his admittedly vague plan concrete and realistic. On one sheet, for example, he defines the revolution:

> "Lectures" or "Lessons."
> The idea of strong live addresses directly to the people, adm. 10 c., North and South, East and West—at Washington,—at the different State Capitols—Jefferson (Mo.)—Richmond (Va.)—Albany—Washington &c—promulging the grand ideas of American ensemble liberty, concentrativeness, individuality, spirituality &c &c. (*NUPM* 6:2234)

Because he chooses "State Capitols" for the addresses, Whitman seems to envision his "Lessons" as teaching the American people his "grand ideas" of American democracy. The ideas he lists in this note are characteristic of Whitman's political and social vocabulary, and most of the words are abstract and general. The one exception is "concentrativeness," originally a phrenological term, which would seem to oppose the diffuse and ephemeral qualities Whitman had attributed to popular oratory and journalism.[3]

---

2. On Whitman's tenure at the *Times*, see Gay Wilson Allen, *The Solitary Singer* (New York: Macmillan, 1955), 208–16, and David S. Reynolds, *Walt Whitman: A Cultural Biography* (New York: Knopf, 1995), 368–75. The most important interpretation of Whitman's interest in oratory and the relationship of oratory to *Leaves of Grass* is C. Carroll Hollis, *Language and Style in "Leaves of Grass"* (Baton Rouge: Louisiana State University Press, 1983), esp. 1–27.

3. The *OED* quotes George Combe's definition of *concentrativeness* as "to maintain two or more powers in simultaneous and combined activity, so that they may be directed towards one object."

The style and content of the manuscript echo a letter that Whitman had written to John Parker Hale, the Free-Soil candidate for president in 1852, in which he admonishes Hale to accept the nomination of the Free-Soilers. Telling Hale to "look to the young men," he proceeds to give the New Hampshire politician advice for winning: "Take two or three occasions within the coming month to make personal addresses directly to the people, giving condensed embodiments of the principal ideas which distinguish our liberal faith from the drag-parties and their platforms. . . . Depend upon it, there is no way so good as the face-to-face of candidates and people—in the old heroic Roman fashion. I would suggest that one of these addresses be delivered in New York, and one in Cincinnati—with a third either in Baltimore or Washington."[4] Whitman's advice to Hale parallels the later advice to himself in one central phrase: "addresses directly to the people." Both in phrasing and in principle, the two texts show that Whitman's ideal orator avoids party politics and indirect means of gaining power in order to speak "face-to-face" to the people, especially to "young men." Nor is it far-fetched to associate "concentrativeness" with the "condensed embodiments of the principal ideas" that Whitman sees as forming an ideal speech. Moreover, the list of "grand ideas" in the manuscript note specifies the "liberal faith" that Whitman professes to Hale. Most important, however, is the way in which both texts elide the distinction between style and substance. For Whitman, the words and the ideas of the address are indistinguishable from one another, and the style of Hale's two or three speeches would be as telling as the speaker's radical ideas. The letter suggests, finally, that in 1852 Whitman saw Hale as potentially the "great leading representative man" he would, in 1858, dream of becoming himself.

Whitman's plans for "ranging up and down The States" take most definite shape in the draft prospectus "Walt Whitman's Lectures," which he drew up in 1858. The two sides of the manuscript feature a mock title-sheet, or cover, and a five-paragraph "Notice" (*NUPM* 4:1436–39). The cover bears two titles and two descriptions of Whitman's plan. In addition to naming the work "Walt Whitman's Lectures," Whitman draws up a large title in the middle of the sheet, "America, A Programme &c."[5] He also includes, in a circle to the left of the first title, the famous quotation from Emerson, "I greet you at the Beginning of a great career. R. W. Emerson," which he had used on the spine of the 1856 edition of *Leaves of Grass*. The first description of his lecturing plan appears

---

4. Walt Whitman, *The Correspondence*, ed. Edwin Haviland Miller, vol. 1 (New York: New York University Press, 1961): 39–40. The letter is dated 14 August 1852.

5. *NUPM* prints a facsimile illustration of the manuscript on the two pages immediately preceding 1436. The illustration shows that the editorial transcription of the second title is not exact.

172 of Culture of Eloquence

between the two titles and develops a general image of employment and audience. The second description presents more concrete economic concerns and reflects on the role of print in educating the audience: "Each Lecture will be printed, with its recitation; needing to be carefully perused afterward, to be understood. I personally sell the printed copies.—" (1437). The two descriptions mix a rather grandiose dream for a new vocation with practical measures for achieving the dream. So Whitman tentatively marks his future as going "by degrees, through all These States" and admits that "some plan I seek, to have the vocal delivery of my lectures free." Both statements combine a grand ideal and a hedging qualification. Similarly, the practical measures combine "vocal delivery" and "printed copies." Whitman imagines his lectures as delivering America a "programme" that needs to be both heard and read, and the prospectus even suggests a price—"One Dime" for the lecture, "15 cents" (1436) for the printed copy. Indeed, the prospectus goes so far as to give the name of the printer who will supply copies of the lectures.[6]

As if to answer potential critics—in his own time as well as in ours— Whitman addresses, on the verso of the prospectus, the relationship of his lecture programme to *Leaves of Grass:*

> *Notice—Random Intentions—Two Branches.*
> Henceforth two co-expressions.—They expand, amicable, from common sources, but each with individual stamp, by itself.—
> First, POEMS, Leaves of Grass, as of *Intuitions*, the Soul, the Body, (male or female) descending below laws, social routine, creeds, literature, to celebrate the inherent, the red blood, one man in himself, or one woman in herself—Songs of thoughts and wants, hitherto repressed by writers.—Or it may as well be avowed, to give the personality of Walt Whitman, out and out, evil and good—whatever he is or thinks, that sharply set down, in a book the Spirit commanding it; if certain outsiders stop puzzled, or dispute, or laugh, very well.-
> Second, LECTURES, as of Reasoning, Reminiscences, Comparison, politics, the Intellectual, the Esthetic, the desire for Knowledge, the sense of richness, refinement, and beauty in the mind, as an art, a sensation— from an American point of view.—Also, in Lectures, the meaning of Religion, as a Statement.—Every thing from an American point of view.

---

6. At the bottom of the title-sheet, after the place and date, "Brooklyn, New York, 1858," Whitman notes, "Trade supplied by De Witt, 162 Nassau st. New York" (1437). This appears to refer to Robert M. De Witt (1827–77), a publisher of songbooks and dime novels (*NUPM* 1:261n.).

Of the above, (so far, only the beginning) both would increase upon themselves.—By degrees to fashion for These States, two athletic volumes, the first to speak for the Permanent Soul, (which speaks for all, materials too, but can be understood only by the like of itself—the same being the reason that what is musical wisdom to one is gibberish to another.) But the second, temporary shall be the speech of the attempts at Statements, Argumentation, Art. Both to illustrate America—illustrate the whole, not merely sections, members—throbbing from the heart, inland, the West, around the great Lakes, or along the flowing Ohio, or Missouri, or Mississippi.

Curious, much advertising his own appearance and views, (it cannot be helped) offensive to many, too free, too savage and natural, candidly owning that he has neither virtue or knowledge—such, en passant, of Walt Whitman, his own way, to his own work—because that, with the rest, is needed—because on less terms how can he get what he has resolved to have, to himself, and to America? (1437–39)

Like the other manuscript texts, this "Notice" insistently employs a combinatory rhetoric. The two projects are called "Two Branches," as if they sprouted from the same tree, and Whitman calls them "co-expressions," "amicable, from common sources." The most important difference between the two has to do with the distinction between "*Intuitions*" in the poems and "Reasoning" in the lectures. Another way of approaching this distinction would be to focus on the "red blood" of the poems, their emotional and spiritual undercurrent, as opposed to "the sense of richness, refinement, and beauty in the mind" that speaks in the lectures. But again, despite these distinctions, Whitman views the two projects as twins, creating "two athletic volumes," both of which "illustrate America—illustrate the whole, not merely sections, members." In addition, the fourth paragraph combines speech and writing as indifferent forms of eloquence, for each volume will "speak" or "be the speech" of its respective faculty or aspect. Finally, the last paragraph finds Whitman reflecting upon himself in the third person. In this "curious . . . advertising" of himself, Whitman becomes both a participant and an observer in his new projecting of himself, and the projecting creates a future result in which Whitman will "get what he has resolved to have, to himself, and to America." As in the birthday message of 1858, Whitman combines his own personal revolution with a larger one that he desires for America.

Other manuscripts provide interesting versions of this same combination and suggest that Whitman's figures of eloquence are more than idle fantasies of a poet frustrated by lack of public attention. On a scrap titled "Friday April 24, '57. True vista before," for example, Whitman develops a timeless, nearly verbless image of the "great leading representative man" he calls for more than a year later. Whitman imagines the "true vista" lying before him—that he will become the "wander-speaker" who will teach America and establish the "mightiest rule over America" by his "powerful words." The combinatory rhetoric creates a rather amazing mixture of raw egotism and bizarre humility. Whitman's figure of eloquence will put aside thoughts of public office or official appointment—the "wander-speaker" will teach America for its own good, not for his advancement. But the dimensions of Whitman's imagination are still vast: "launching at the President, leading persons, Congressmen, or Judges of the Supreme Court." As in the birthday message of 1858, Whitman here imagines a revolution in both public and private life, one that will allow American institutions to remain in place but promises to transfigure them. And the means of transfiguration, in both 1857 and 1858, is "the natural flowing vocal luxuriance of oratory," for eloquence allows the wander-speaker *always to hold the ear of people" (NUPM* 4:1554).

Whitman's figures of eloquence may resemble others in antebellum America, especially in the faith that he places in the power of language to reform American institutions, but they differ from earlier figures in two significant respects. First, Whitman's sense of the political dimensions of language is much more keenly developed than any I have discussed in earlier chapters. Second, his desire to *"hold the ear of people"* suggests his sharp need to create a new, revolutionary space for himself and for an audience. This space he calls, in two different manuscripts, an "agonistic arena" (*NUPM* 6:2224, 2234), in one note giving a terse, incisive portrait of the arena: "Yes the place of the orator and his hearers is truly an agonistic arena. There he wrestles and contends with them— he suffers, sweats, undergoes his great toil and extasy. Perhaps it is a greater battle than any fought by contending forces on land and sea" (2234). In the final sentence of the passage, Whitman makes a point similar to that made in the April 1857 note—that the agonistic arena of public speaking may establish the "mightiest rule," even mightier than that of military forces. The passage adds to Whitman's claim for the power of language by focusing on the "agon" between "the orator and his hearers." It is as if language derived its power from the struggle itself, and Whitman heightens that effect by using dynamic, physical verbs such as "wrestles," "suffers," and "sweats." Moreover, the agonistic arena figures a common, combinatory space for speaker and audience, a space that involves the orator in "great toil" as well as "extasy." As the 1858 advertisement for "Walt Whitman's Lectures" shows, we should add that the audience struggles within this combinatory space, too: "Each Lecture will be printed, with its recitation; needing to be carefully perused afterward, to be understood" (1437). In the agonistic arena, Whitman's imagined audience is as active and exemplary as his imagined wander-speaker.[7]

If the manuscript notes suggest that Whitman's figures of eloquence are more than idle fantasies, they also point toward a configuration of related lecture topics. The "Notice" in "Walt Whitman's Lectures" is quite general, but it does list politics, aesthetics, and religion as three main topics. Other manuscripts show that Whitman never relinquished the idea of treating these three topics in lectures.[8] In addition, he made extensive plans for lectures on slavery (*NUPM* 6:2169–99), German philosophy (2009–18), education (2204–11), and language, also mentioning geography, Elias Hicks, Voltaire, and Emerson as possible topics (2241).[9] The configuration is far from obvious, but the common thread running through Whitman's topics is the power of language—especially the spoken word—to effect social change. The wander-speaker must contend with his hearers and their assumptions in order to create the agonistic arena within which the social questions of antebellum America are to be defined and debated.

Two examples of Whitman's "Lessons" suggest ways in which he connects language and cultural reform. Both *The Primer of Words* and *The Eighteenth Presidency!* date from late 1855 and early 1856 and resemble each other in being neither lectures nor printed texts: neither is the record of an actual performance, although each bears the marks of a script for oral performance. Whitman's remark about *The Primer of Words* could apply to both texts: "It was first intended for a lecture: then when I gave up the idea of lecturing it was intended for a book: now, as it stands, it is neither a lecture nor a book."[10]

---

7. William L. Finkel has shown that a chief source of the agonistic arena passage is Professor Charles Murray Nairne's commencement address of 30 June 1857 at Rutgers College; see Finkel, "Walt Whitman's Manuscript Notes on Oratory," *American Literature* 22 (March 1950): 29–53, especially 38–39.

8. *NUPM*, vols. 4, 5, and 6, includes many pages of notes on all three topics, along with several other study projects, though religion receives the most sustained attention; see 6:2019–107.

9. For the lecture notes on language, see Whitman, *Daybooks and Notebooks*, ed. William White (New York: New York University Press, 1978), 3:728–57; hereafter cited parenthetically in my text as *DN*.

10. *The Eighteenth Presidency!* appears in *NUPM* 6:2119–35; an important earlier edition, with a helpful introduction, is by Edward F. Grier (Lawrence: University of Kansas Press, 1956). *The Primer of Words* appears in *DN* 3:728–57; it was first published in an edited version by Horace Traubel as *An American Primer* (Boston: Small, Maynard, 1904); Whitman's remark to Traubel appears in *American Primer*, ix.

Another language notebook should be mentioned in this connection, since it is also neither a lecture nor a book, though it resembles both. The *Words* notebook contains a host of notes and clippings on language theory, etymologies, definitions, and pronunciation (*DN* 3:664–727); it also features several sheets that contain trial titles for Whitman's lecture series, many of which echo the titles listed in the *NUPM* manuscripts (see *DN* 3:685, 712, 724).

The two texts are also similar in their subtitles, for in each Whitman specifies the audience of his "Lesson." *Eighteenth Presidency* is subtitled "Voice of Walt
Whitman to each Young Man in the Nation, North, South, East and West"
(2120); the *Primer* is more elaborate: "For American Young Men and Women,
For Literats, Orators, Teachers, Musicians, Judges Presidents, &c." (728). The distinction between the two subtitles relates to the difference between votes and
voices. The *Primer* subtitle lists the specific "hearers" who use language in their
cultural work, although at the end of the list Whitman acknowledges the cultural role of government officials. Conversely, the *Eighteenth Presidency* subtitle
figures the "Voice of Walt Whitman" in a direct address to young voters
throughout the country; in that instance, Whitman himself fills the cultural role
of "literat," orator, or teacher. One way of reading the two texts together, then,
is to view the *Primer* as the theoretical background for the practical action of
Eighteenth Presidency. The distinction between theory and practice is by no
means hard and fast, however, and it is equally persuasive to read each text as a
combination of theory and practice. That kind of reading accords, too, with
Whitman's combinatory rhetoric and with his tendency to merge considera-
tions of language and cultural reform.

If the barrage of closely related texts blurs the boundary between theory
and practice, it cannot obscure the connection between language and cultural
reform. In *The Primer of Words*, for example, Whitman writes the following trial
lines for a "Lesson" on language:

> I like limber, lashing—fierce words—I like them applied to myself—and
> I like them in newspapers, courts, debates, congress.—Do you suppose
> the liberties and the brawn of These States have to do only with deli-
> cate lady-words? with gloved gentleman-words? Bad Presidents, bad
> judges, bad clients, bad editors, owners of slaves, and the long ranks of
> Northern political suckers, monopolists, infidels, (robbers, traitors, sub-
> orned,) castrated persons, impotent persons, shaved persons, supplejacks,
> ecclesiastics, men not fond of women, women not fond of men, cry
> down the use of strong, cutting, beautiful rude words- To the manly
> instincts of the People they will forever be welcome. (746)

Whitman begins with his own personal preference for "fierce words," even
when applied to himself, and he contrasts that preference with the decorous
"lady-words" and "gentleman-words" that dominate American culture. The
contrast leads to a litany of those who "cry down the use of strong, cutting,
beautiful rude words," and then Whitman ends the passage by placing his con-

fidence in "the manly instincts of the People." The double contrast thus implies that Whitman's preferences are identical with those of "the People," while the "long ranks" of institutionalized "supplejacks" are the sterile, dehumanized victims of some unnamed puppet master. Perhaps more important, the contrast also implies that Whitman and "the People" will turn the power of their words upon the "Bad Presidents, bad judges," and so on—who may be victims but who also control the People by means of political and social power. What begins as a meditation on language inevitably becomes an agonistic arena that combines, among other things, language and cultural reform.

Eighteenth Presidency develops the same contrast between the People and "Northern political suckers," and that contrast leads either to the kind of "limber, lashing, fierce words" Whitman likes or to a reflection on the ways words are used. In one grand catalog of abusive terms, for instance, Whitman defines the delegates to the presidential party conventions:

WHO ARE THEY PERSONALLY?

Office-holders, office-seekers, robbers, pimps, exclusives, malignants, conspirators, murderers, fancy-men, post-masters, custom-house clerks, contractors, kept-editors, spaniels well-trained to carry and fetch, jobbers, infidels, disunionists, terrorists, mail-riflers, slave-catchers, pushers of slavery, creatures of the President, creatures of would-be Presidents, spies, blowers, electioneerers, body-snatchers, bawlers, bribers, compromisers, runaways, lobbyers, sponges, ruined sports, expelled gamblers, policy backers, monte-dealers, duelists, carriers of concealed weapons, blind men, deaf men, pimpled men, scarred inside with the vile disorder, gaudy outside with gold chains made from the people's money and the harlot's money twisted together; crawling, serpentine men, the lousy combings and born freedom sellers of the earth. (2126)

The fierce humor of this passage derives, I believe, from the chaotic quality of the catalog. Whitman's list is deliberately incoherent, jumbling such relatively benign terms as "post-masters, custom-house clerks, contractors" together with terms of opprobrium such as "robbers, pimps, exclusives." None of these terms is wholly neutral; even the first trio are clearly associated with political appointments and "office-seekers." And that is precisely the point of Whitman's combinatory technique: no one who is at all connected with political parties, no matter how seemingly innocent the person may be, escapes the confines of the catalog. It is as if Whitman were attempting to create a special, hyperbolic hell to which he can consign them.

Hyperbole is merely a polite way of describing the style, which Whitman characterizes more accurately in the *Primer*: "The appetite of the people of These States in popular speeches and writings, is for unhemmed lattitude [*sic*], coarseness, directness, live epithets, explitives [*sic*], words of opprobrium, resistance.—This I understand because I have the taste myself" (741). The figuration parallels the "appetite of the people" with Whitman's own "taste" for fierce, aggressive epithets. One effect of such a catalog of "unhemmed" terms is the combining of pleasure and outrage, for both the speaker/writer and the hearer/reader, in the cathartic act of naming the enemies they hold in common.

In developing the contrast between the people and their representatives, Whitman moves from the language of abuse to the abuse of language:

> Mechanics! A parcel of windy northern liars are bawling in your ears the easily-spoken words Democracy and the democratic party. Others are making a great ado with the word Americanism, a solemn and great word. What the so-called democracy are now sworn to perform would eat the faces off the succeeding generations of common people worse than the most horrible disease. The others are contributing to the like performance, and are using the great word Americanism without yet feeling the first aspiration of it, as the great word Religion has been used, probably loudest and oftenest used, by men that made indiscriminate massacres at night, and filled the world so full with hatreds, horrors, partialities, exclusions, bloody revenges, penal conscience laws and test-oaths. (2127–28)

Whitman attacks two political parties for their abuse of language. The first is the Democratic Party, the "parcel of windy northern liars . . . bawling in your ears the easily-spoken words Democracy and the democratic party." The other is the American or "Know-Nothing" Party, a xenophobic, anti-Catholic movement organized in 1849.[11] Whitman makes no effort to distinguish between the two parties—indeed, he refuses to identify them by name—because they are

---

11. For a recent discussion of this political background in relation to *The Eighteenth Presidency!*, see Betsy Erkkila, *Whitman the Political Poet* (New York: Oxford University Press, 1989), 129–32. See also M. Wynn Thomas, *The Lunar Light of Whitman's Poetry* (Cambridge: Harvard University Press, 1987), 178–85, for a fine discussion of Whitman's troubled relationship to the Democratic Party. The best general introduction to the politics of the 1850s is, to my knowledge, McPherson, *Battle Cry of Freedom*, 6–201; but see also Eric Foner, *Free Soil, Free Labor, Free Men: The Ideology of the Republican Party Before the Civil War* (New York: Oxford University Press, 1970).

alike in their misappropriation of the "solemn and great" words of American English. Such abuse of language hinges upon the hypocrisy of those who wish to gain or maintain power. Hence Whitman uses the analogy of "the great word Religion" to suggest that those who speak the words "democracy" and "Americanism" neither possess nor understand the virtues those words bespeak. The catalog of religious persecutions implies that political persecutions will become a modern version of the age-old abuse of power, but "the masses" are always the victims. Whitman's analogy has an additional resonance in the 1850s: "the great word Religion" is used throughout the period by political parties of every stripe, and issues as diverse as slavery, public education, and temperance are debated in terms of religious belief. In particular, the reactionary quality of the Catholic church during the papacy of Pius IX led to a ground swell of anti-Catholicism.[12] Given the complexities of party politics and social discourse, Whitman's extreme rhetoric disguises, in fact, a rather balanced and dispassionate skepticism. It is as if he refused to decry any one group or faction; instead, he disparages factionalism itself. Whitman thus attempts to combat the twin abuse of language and power by warning his audience of "young men" or "mechanics" to beware of "American craft," for the most telling specimens of craft resound, to Whitman's ears, in native politicians' vicious misappropriation of great words.

The rhetoric of *Eighteenth Presidency* creates a complex weaving together of question and answer, direct address, legal argument, invective, and personal testament. Its thesis is clearly stated at the outset: "At present, the personnel of the government of these thirty millions [of inhabitants], in executives and elsewhere, is drawn from limber-tongued lawyers, very fluent but empty, feeble old men, professional politicians, dandies, dyspeptics, and so forth, and rarely drawn from the solid body of the people; the effects now seen, and more to come" (2120–21). The principal technique for developing that thesis is repetition: by enumerating a host of specific "specimens," Whitman attempts to prove his "theory." In structure, theme, and technique, *Eighteenth Presidency* practices the oratory of Whitman's wander-speaker.

But if the text of *Eighteenth Presidency* acts like the "Voice of Walt Whitman," the writer of that text is never satisfied with his own oratorical performance. Thus Whitman ends with a series of direct addresses to specific "hearers": to John C. Frémont (the Republican Party candidate for president in 1856); to the white workingmen of the fifteen slaveholding states; to the "three hundred and fifty thousand owners of slaves"; to "editors of the independent press, and

12. McPherson, 130–44; Foner, 226–60.

to rich persons." In each section, Whitman creates a figure of eloquence and power, sometimes as an ideal and sometimes as a reproach. So the brief section addressed to Frémont creates the image of a "Redeemer President" (2133), but it is far from clear that Frémont is to be that president. Similarly, the address to the Southern workingmen asks, "Shall no one among you dare open his mouth to say he is opposed to slavery, as a man should be, on account of the whites, and wants it abolished for their sake? Is not a writer, speaker, teacher to be left alive, but those who lick up the spit that drops from the mouths of the three hundred and fifty thousand masters?" (2133). In the third address, however, Whitman names himself as the spokesman for "these fierce and turbulent races" in the "Free States": "From my mouth hear the will of These States taking form in the great cities" (2134). Just as vast as Whitman's own need for holding the ears of the people is his belief that the people need a public teacher or wander-speaker to speak to and for them. Whitman's sense of potential for himself corresponds to his sense "that the best thoughts they have wait unspoken, impatient to be put in shape" (2135). That dual sense creates the dynamic space he calls an agonistic arena.

In the long concluding paragraph of *Eighteenth Presidency*, Whitman presents a final figure of eloquence, one that is both more grand and more impersonal than the Walt Whitman who addresses editors and rich persons. The paragraph is a hymn to modern progress and reform, in many ways a more innocent version of the 1871 poem "Passage to India." Toward the end of the panoramic vision of technological and social "landmarks," Whitman fastens upon a single figure:

> Never was the representative man more energetic, more like a god, than to-day. He urges on the myriads before him, he crowds them aside, his daring step approaches the arctic and the antarctic poles, he colonizes the shores of the Pacific, the Asiatic Indias, the birthplace of languages and of races, the archipelagoes, Australia; he explores Africa, he unearths Assyria and Egypt, he re-states history, he enlarges morality, he speculates anew upon the soul, upon original premises; nothing is left quiet, nothing but he will settle by demonstrations for himself. What whispers are these running through the eastern continents, and crossing the Atlantic and Pacific? What historic denouements are these we are approaching? On all sides tyrants tremble, crowns are unsteady, the human race restive, on the watch for some better era, some divine war. (2135)

The "representative man" in this passage is, to be sure, only in part a figure of eloquence. He encompasses eloquence when he "urges on the myriads before him," and his explorations and speculations are of the type Whitman outlines in the 1858 advertisement. Moreover, he seems to elicit, as well as hear, the "whispers" of change that promise a new future for the human race. Finally, the term *representative man* recalls not only Emerson's "The Poet" and Whitman's 1855 preface to *Leaves of Grass* but also, and perhaps more important here, the 1858 birthday message, in which Whitman calls for "a great leading representative man" to give "a fair start" to the "revolution in American oratory" (2233–34). This is not to say that *Eighteenth Presidency* is only a call for a new American eloquence; the representative man is too large a figure to fit within such a confining formulation. Nevertheless, eloquence is a defining element of the representative man, just as it is a defining element of *Eighteenth Presidency*.

A strong sense of irony has to accompany any attempt to define *Eighteenth Presidency*, of course, for the text exists only as three sets of proofs, printed but never published (2119). Whitman's "Voice" is doubly silent, since it is a printed figure, created by writing, and the printing never reached the intended audience. The agonistic arena that Whitman creates so vividly in *Eighteenth Presidency* remains an imagined space. Just as *The Primer of Words* is "neither a lecture nor a book," so *Eighteenth Presidency* is both a fierce rhetorical performance and an unpublished nonperformance. Both texts occupy a middle ground, with elements that reach—often at one and the same time—toward both speech and writing.

If Whitman's notes on oratory are, as I have been arguing, strongly connected to his hopes for reforming American culture, they are also connected to his study of language theories and historical linguistics.[13] The clearest connection appears in the manuscript notes on oratory, in which Whitman makes the following demands of himself:

> Develop language anew, make it not literal and of the elder modes, but elliptical and idiomatic.
>   . . . elliptical style as not to explain and spread out, not to be afraid of ellipses. An audience of Americans, would they not soon learn to like a hidden sense, a sense only just indicated? As just to indicate what is meant and let the audience find it out for themselves. Whether the whole of the present style of orations, essays, lectures, political speeches

13. For extended discussions of Whitman's study of language, see my *Walt Whitman's Language Experiment* (University Park: Pennsylvania State University Press, 1990), 7–33, 109–38. See also Erkkila, *Whitman*, 79–86; Michael P. Kramer, *Imagining Language in America* (Princeton: Princeton University Press, 1992), 90–115; Tenney Nathanson, *Whitman's Presence* (New York: New York University Press, 1992), 183–245.

&c. is not far below the level of American wants and must not be revolutionized.[14]

The call for a revolution in oratorical style is familiar, although here Whitman broadens the revolution to include many forms of language. In addition, the focus on "elliptical style" corresponds to Whitman's vision of lecturing as an agonistic arena, because the "audience of Americans" will actively seek the meaning of the speaker's "elliptical and idiomatic" language.

Equally important, however, is the way in which this passage echoes Whitman's language manuscripts. The phrase "elliptical and idiomatic" occurs in the *Words* notebook and in the manuscript essay "Our Language and Literature." In the first, Whitman criticizes Lindley Murray's *English Grammar* for failing to understand "those points where the language [is] strongest, and where developements should [be] most encouraged, namely, in being *elliptic* and *idiomatic*" (*DN* 3:666–67). In the second, the essay shows Whitman's oratorical style in making the same point: "I say—The English grammarians have all failed to detect these points where their written speech is strongest, and should be most encouraged—namely in being elliptical and idiomatic, and in expressing new spirits" (*DN* 3:809–10).[15] In all three passages, the phrase suggests Whitman's idea of a revolutionary, utterly new and expressive American language, a "written speech" that will express the "new spirits" of a new American culture. But, like the revolution in oratory called for in the 1858 birthday message, "this change is a serious one, and, if to be done at all, cannot be done easily" (2234).

Whitman's recognition of the difficulties involved in effecting—even in starting—the multiple revolutions he envisions may account for the many false starts and aborted attempts that appear and reappear in the manuscripts throughout his long career. But other factors should also be brought into account. The most important among them is Whitman's theory of a dynamic, ever changing language to express the evolving American spirit. That theory applies equally well to Whitman and to nineteenth-century American culture. As Whitman says in

14. *NUPM* 6:2235–36. The ellipses are not mine. For interesting parallels in Nairne's "Oration," see Finkel, "Manuscript Notes," 49–50.

15. See my *Language Experiment*, 34–42 and "The 'Real Grammar': Deverbal Style in 'Song of Myself,'" *American Literature* 56 (1984): 1–16, for discussions of "Real Grammar" and Murray. Whitman had also responded to British critics of his grammar during his days as the editor of the Brooklyn *Daily Eagle*. In the 5 November 1847 issue, he wrote that "it is well known that a numbskull with a grammar *book* in his hand, but not the least idea of the general philosophy of the science in his head, can pick flaws in any idiomatic sentence, and parade his stupidity by calling incorrect what is frequently the best merit of the composition" (*The Gathering of the Forces*, ed. Cleveland Rogers and John Black [New York: Putnam's, 1920], 2:11).

the advertisement for "Walt Whitman's Lectures," concerning the "two co-expressions" of poems and lectures, "Of the above, (so far, only the beginning) both would increase upon themselves.—By degrees to fashion for These States, two athletic volumes" (1438). Although Whitman can envision the completion of his programme in the form of two books, his words focus more sharply upon the process—"so far, only the beginning"—and the prospect of the two co-expressions growing as they "increase upon themselves." Rather than read the manuscript documents as evidence of failure, we should see them as parts of the agonistic arena Whitman creates whenever he writes or speaks.

2

Whitman's abiding interest in the transforming power of eloquence continues well beyond the 1850s. Even during his busiest time in the military hospitals of Washington, D.C., Whitman could "think something of commencing a series of lectures & readings &c. through different cities of the north, to supply myself with funds for my Hospital & Soldiers visits," and manuscript notes from the same period suggest that he contemplated giving lectures called "The Dead in This War."[16] His projected "Sunday Evening Lectures" on German transcendental philosophy date from the late 1860s and early 1870s, in one case referring directly to the 1871 pamphlet *Democratic Vistas*: "He has read my *Vistas* to little purpose who has not seen that the Democracy I favor (if forced to choose) willingly leaves all material and political successes to enter upon and enjoy the moral, philosophical and religious ones" (*NUPM* 6:2017). Whitman's most extended address on public education dates from September 1872, although we have no record of his actually having delivered it in public (*NUPM* 6:2204–11). Other lectures of the postwar period include "Death of Abraham Lincoln," which Whitman gave nearly a dozen times from 1879 to 1890, and "The Tramp and Strike Questions," subtitled "Part of a Lecture proposed, (never deliver'd.)" Finally, it would be appropriate to add the two essays "Father Taylor (and Oratory)" and "Elias Hicks," both published in the 1888 volume *November Boughs*.[17]

16. The first quotation is from a letter to his mother, dated 9 June 1863 (*Correspondence*, 1:109). The title of the proposed lecture appears in the manuscript "For Lecture" (*NUPM* 4:1376–77). See Karl Adalbert Preuschen, "Walt Whitman's Undelivered Oration 'The Dead in this War,'" *Etudes Anglaises* 24 (1971): 147–51.

17. The texts appear in Whitman, *Prose Works 1892*, ed. Floyd Stovall, 2 (New York: New York University Press, 1964), 497–509, 527–29, 549–52, 626–53; hereafter cited parenthetically in my text as *PW*.

The dimensions of Whitman's agonistic arena grow larger when we consider the many versions of his important essay *Democratic Vistas*. Although this work positions itself in many ways as a postwar document, both because of its publication history and its emphasis on the problems of reconstruction, suffrage, labor, and entrepreneurial capitalism, it also combines Whitman's meditations on the future of postwar America and his retrospective, nostalgic view of an increasingly distant antebellum America.[18] The mixed thematic and temporal elements of the essay reflect its status as both an act of summation and an ongoing act of prophecy. Whitman readily sees the combinatory quality of his *Vistas*; as he says at the outset of the essay, "the passages of it have been written at widely different times, (it is, in fact, a collection of memoranda, perhaps for future designers, comprehenders,)" (*PW* 2:362).

The most interesting example of Whitman's combinatory, cumulative strategy occurs in the "Rough Draft" manuscript for the third section of the essay, originally conceived as a separate essay to be called "Orbic Literature." Two sheets of the manuscript focus on an "appropriate native grand opera," and the first sheet gives a trial title to the memorandum: "Future Music, Savan-Saloons, Oratists, &c. and less Legislation." Then, on the second sheet, Whitman muses upon the music that will be "fully identified with the body and soul of 1856, Mannahatta, Boston, Iowa, the 4th of July, the aversion to poppy-shows in music or any where."[19] The two sheets echo Whitman's *Primer of Words* and *Eighteenth Presidency* in significant ways. The trial title echoes one of Whitman's principal ideas in the "American Theory of Government" section of *Eighteenth Presidency*: "Nine tenths of the laws passed every winter at the Federal Capitol, and all the State Capitols, are not only unneeded laws, but positive nuisances, jobs got up for the service of special classes or persons" (*NUPM* 6:2131). It also echoes the subtitle of the *Primer*, which includes orators and musicians in its list of "hear-

18. The essay was first printed as a pamphlet in 1871, but it consisted of three separate essays composed in 1867–68. The first essay, "Democracy," was published in *Galaxy* 4 (December 1867): 919–33; the second, "Personalism," was published in *Galaxy* 5 (May 1868): 540–47; the third, "Orbic Literature," was never published, although Whitman submitted it to the editors of *Galaxy* on April 30, 1868 (*Correspondence* 2:32–33). For an account of Whitman's activities during this period, see Allen, *Solitary Singer* 388–430; for an excellent discussion of *Democratic Vistas* as a text of the Gilded Age, see Erkkila, 240–59.

19. The two manuscript sheets are [46] and [47] of the "Rough MS.," in Container 20 of the Charles E. Feinberg Collection in the Library of Congress. My quotations are from the manuscript, which to my knowledge has not been edited.

For background on the "Rough MS." and on the language theory in *Democratic Vistas*, see my *Language Experiment* 114–21. For a different description of Whitman's strategy in the essay, see my "Reconstructing Language in *Democratic Vistas*," in *Walt Whitman: Centennial Essays*, ed. Ed Folsom (Iowa City: University of Iowa Press, 1994), 79–87.

ers" (*DN* 3:728). Finally, the 1856 date on the second sheet connects the memorandum to the 1856 *Primer* and *Eighteenth Presidency*.

The "collection of memoranda" becomes yet more intriguing when we consider the material Whitman treats in the "Rough MS." sheets from 1856. After a paragraph devoted to the native grand opera and other musical compositions, Whitman turns to another of his favorite forms of culture:

> Also, a great breed of orators will one day spread over The United States, and be continued. Blessed are the people where, (the nation's Unity and Identity preserved at all hazards,) strong emergencies, throes, occur. Strong emergencies will continually occur in America, and will be provided for. Such orators are wanted as have never yet been heard upon earth. What specimen have we had where even the physical capacities of the voice have been fully accomplished? I think there would be in the human voice, thoroughly practised and brought out, more seductive pathos than in any organ or any orchestra of stringed instruments, and a ring more impressive than that of artillery.[20]

The passage merges past and future in a remarkable way. In the first sentence Whitman predicts the "great breed of orators" to come, while in the second he pronounces a blessing on the "strong emergencies, throes" that the nation has recently survived. In the third, he predicts that such emergencies "will continually occur in America, and will be provided for." The role of the orator in such emergencies parallels that of the wander-speaker that Whitman imagines in 1857. In the final lines of the paragraph, moreover, Whitman confers upon his figure of eloquence the kind of reforming power he imagines elsewhere as the agonistic arena: "Perhaps it is a greater battle than any fought by contending forces on land and sea" (*NUPM* 6:2234).

The figure of Whitman's agonistic arena leads immediately to two passages from *Democratic Vistas*, both of which focus on the role of language in shaping an audience of "hearers." The first, from the introductory section of the essay, strikes the same note of opposition we have heard in the 1856 texts:

---

20. This is the text of the 1871 edition of *Democratic Vistas* (and of the 1876 *Two Rivulets*), as printed in Appendix 4.5 of Stovall's scholarly edition (*PW* 2:755). The manuscript sheets corresponding to the paragraph are [49]–[50]. One suggestive revision: in the manuscript, Whitman predicts "a great race of orators and oratresses" [49]; compare the experiments in suffixes Whitman contemplates in the *Words* notebook (*DN* 3:666, 686), as well as the 1860 poem, "Chants Democratic," 12, later titled "To Oratists" (1871) and eventually Section 1 of "Vocalism."

> To the ostent of the senses and eyes, I know, the influences which stamp
> the world's history are wars, uprisings or downfalls of dynasties, change-
> ful movements of trade, important inventions, navigation, military or
> civil governments, advent of powerful personalities, conquerors, &c.
> These of course play their part; yet, it may be, a single new thought,
> imagination, abstract principle, even literary style, fit for the time, put
> in shape by some great literatus, and projected among mankind, may
> duly cause changes, growths, removals, greater than the longest and
> bloodiest war, or the most stupendous merely political, dynastic, or com-
> mercial overturn. (*PW* 2:366)

The opposition hinges here upon two types of "changeful movements." For
Whitman, the usual version of history focuses on military, political, and economic changes, or upon the "powerful personalities" that have effected such
changes, but he opposes that version of history by claiming that "a single new
thought, imagination, abstract principle, even literary style" can play a "greater"
role in effecting change. Such changes are figured as greater than superlatives
such as "the longest and bloodiest war, or the most stupendous merely political, dynastic, or commercial overturn." Whitman attempts to create his own revolutionary "overturn," then, by giving the greatest power to ideas and their
expression. Both the paragraph on orators and this passage on literary style recall
the following from the 1857 "True Vista Before": "That the mightiest rule over
America could be thus—as, for instance, on occasion, at Washington to be,
launching from public room, at the opening of the session of Congress—perhaps launching at the President, leading persons, Congressmen, or Judges of the
Supreme Court—That to dart hither or thither, as some great emergency might
demand—the greatest Champion America ever could know, yet holding no
office or emolument whatever,—but first in the esteem of men and women"
(*NUPM* 4:1554).

In the second passage from *Democratic Vistas*, Whitman focuses less on the orator or "Champion" and more on the "men and women" who are also part of the
agonistic arena that his eloquence creates. In the paragraph that originally led to
the 1871 passage on orators, Whitman prophesies "new law-forces of spoken and
written language," and the discussion of opera, music, oratory, museums, and lec-
ture-halls amply illustrates the prospects that he sees. In the reduced version of
1882 and thereafter, however, he focuses principally on written language:

> Books are to be call'd for, and supplied, on the assumption that the
> process of reading is not a half-sleep, but, in highest sense, an exercise, a

gymnast's struggle; that the reader is to do something for himself, must be on the alert, must himself or herself construct indeed the poem, argument, history, metaphysical essay—the text furnishing the hints, the clue, the start or frame-work. Not the book needs so much to be the complete thing, but the reader of the book does. That were to make a nation of supple and althletic minds, well-train'd, intuitive, used to depend on themselves, and not on a few coteries of writers. (424–25)

Although Whitman shifts his focus to emphasize the written and textual—the book—he also ensures that we view reading as a version of the agonistic arena. Whitman's "new theory of literary composition" (424) in fact echoes the 1858 advertisement for "Walt Whitman's Lectures": "Each Lecture will be printed, with its recitation; needing to be carefully perused afterward, to be understood. I personally sell the printed copies" (1437). Just as the advertisement combines speaking and writing, and just as the audience must combine listening and reading in order to understand the lecture, so Whitman's text becomes "the hints, the clue, the start or frame-work" for the "gymnast's struggle" of reading. The "gymnast's struggle" itself slantingly echoes "an agonistic arena," although in the latter the orator "wrestles and contends with" his hearers. The same kind of near echo occurs when we compare the "nation of supple and athletic minds" to Whitman's project, in the 1858 advertisement, of fashioning "for These States, two athletic volumes," containing poems and lectures (1438). As I noted in regard to the many "proposed (never deliver'd)" lectures, Whitman is far more interested in the process of reading than in the products of writing. Hence the statement that undercuts any sense of the monumental text: "Not the book needs so much to be the complete thing, but the reader of the book does."

Despite the reduced vistas that Whitman's 1882 revisions deliver, the ways in which he figures reading as a gymnast's struggle lead in two expansive directions. The more obvious of the two is to read the text of *Democratic Vistas* as an agonistic arena in which the reader is engaged to "construct indeed the . . . argument, history, metaphysical essay." Whitman's own statements suggest that the process of construction has no definitive end-product. So, for instance, we should add to previous passages the manuscript title page, in which Whitman calls *Democratic Vistas* "*A Melange*" (*NUPM* 2:868), and the manuscript sketch that Whitman drafted to accompany a photograph, probably as an advertisement for his works: "Besides LEAVES OF GRASS this author has also published a prose work, DEMOCRATIC VISTAS, treating of religious, social, political and artistic topics, with immediate reference to the present and the future of the United

States. It is said that these VISTAS are purposed to be added to by successive accumulations, in the same way as the poems" (2:874). In addition, Whitman clearly views *Democratic Vistas* as on ongoing project in the 28 July 1871 letter to William Michael Rossetti: "My '*Leaves of Grass*' I consider substantially finished, as in the copies I send you. To '*Democratic Vistas*' it is my plan to add much, if I live" (*Correspondence* 2:131). Given these three passages, one may see *Democratic Vistas* as an altered version of the "athletic volume" of lectures Whitman planned in the late 1850s. And it may be equally tempting to note that, like the lecture project, *Democratic Vistas* is not added to "by successive accumulations" but instead remains "the start or frame-work" for a never completed project. In fact, both athletic volumes—poems and prose—are never "substantially finished," for Whitman continues to "add much" as long as he lives.

If this first image of the gymnast's struggle expands beyond the boundaries of my subject, the second also broadens the dimensions of Whitman's agonistic arena. Instead of focusing on the multiple versions of Whitman's texts and their complex combinations of speech and writing, however, I want to emphasize the fact that the agonistic arena is, according to Whitman, the "place of the orator and his hearers" (2234). This place is defined by language, by the orator's eloquence, but also by the audience, the "hearers" who construct the lecture, speech, poem, essay, for the cultural space of eloquence is constructed by the reciprocal relationship of speaker and audience. In Whitman's case, the construction of the agonistic arena leads to a reconstructing of American culture.

One of Whitman's principal targets in *Democratic Vistas* is the crass materialism of postbellum America. In the opening of the "Orbic Literature" section of the essay, for instance, Whitman attempts to pay due respect to "the objective grandeurs of the world," but he also balances that respect in a scale of value: "We must not say one word against real materials; but the wise know that they do not become real till touched by emotions, the mind. Did we call the latter imponderable? Ah, let us rather proclaim that the slightest song-tune, the countless ephemera of passions arous'd by orators and tale-tellers, are more dense, more weighty than the engines there in the great factories, or the granite blocks in their foundations" (*PW* 2:404). The rhetoric of opposition recalls antebellum jeremiads such as *Eighteenth Presidency*, although in this case Whitman's opponents are distinctly creations of postwar America. Equally important, however, is the weight Whitman attributes to "the slightest song-tune, the countless ephemera of passions arous'd by orators and tale-tellers." In the first image, Whitman gives the weight to the "song-tune" itself; in the second, he focuses on the "passions arous'd" by the figures of eloquence. In addition to the more obvious balance between material and spiritual, then, Whitman strikes a second, more subtle balance between the artwork and the audience's response to the artwork. Furthermore, the double balance suggests that the sounds of songs, speeches, and tales will transform the merely material into the real. Or, as Whitman figures the transformation in the next paragraph, the "new creation" would fill the "momentous spaces" of America with "the definitely-form'd worlds themselves, duly compacted, clustering in systems, hung up there, chandeliers of the universe, beholding and mutually lit by each other's lights, serving for ground of all substantial foothold, all vulgar uses—yet serving still more as an undying chain and echelon of spiritual proofs and shows. A boundless field to fill!" (404).

A second way in which the rhetoric of *Democratic Vistas* recalls the strategies of *Eighteenth Presidency* is Whitman's tendency to use particular words as a means of focusing his analysis. For instance, he asserts that "the political history of the past may be summ'd up as having grown out of what underlies the words, order, safety, caste, and especially out of the need of some prompt deciding authority, and of cohesion at all cost" (373) and that the women of America must be "extricated from this daze, this fossil and unhealthy air which hangs about the word *lady*" (389). In these two passages, Whitman does not go so far as to confer absolute power or authority upon language; instead, he reads words as both symbols and causes. So, as he notes in the *Primer of Words*, cultural reform is more than simply a matter of changing the words we use: "But it is no small thing, no quick growth; not a matter of rubbing out one word and writing another.—Real names never come so easily.—The greatest cities, the greatest politics, the greatest physiology and soul, the greatest orators, poets, and literats.—The best women, the freeest [*sic*] leading men, the proudest national character—such, and the like, are indispensable before-hand.—Then the greatest names will follow, for they are results—and there are no greater results in the world" (*DN* 3:755–56).

By figuring words as both causes and effects, Whitman suggests that language and culture exist in a reciprocal, mutually reinforcing relationship. That relationship further implies that cultural and linguistic reform are intimately bound to each other, without either one being granted primary authority or power. Instead of distinguishing between the two, Whitman's discussions tend to combine them: "We have frequently printed the word Democracy. Yet I cannot too often repeat that it is a word the real gist of which still sleeps, quite unawaken'd, notwithstanding the resonance and the many angry tempests out of which its syllables have come, from pen or tongue. It is a great word, whose history, I suppose, remains unwritten, because that history has yet to be enacted. It is, in some sort, younger brother of another great and often-used word, Nature, whose history also waits unwritten" (393). Here, the history of the word and the history of the political realities are indistinguishable, just as the writing and enacting of those histories are indistinguishable. In the case of these great words, as in the case of "Americanism" and "Democracy" in *Eighteenth Presidency*, the "real gist" remains an as yet unwritten meaning, one which has slept despite "the many angry tempests out of which its syllables have come, from pen and tongue."

The most important instance of Whitman's focus on particular words occurs in the "Personalism" section of *Democratic Vistas*, and it once again suggests the reciprocal relationship between language and culture. Fittingly, the word Whitman chooses to focus upon is the word *culture* itself: "Never, in the Old World, was thoroughly upholster'd exterior appearance and show, mental and other, built entirely on the idea of caste, and on the sufficiency of mere outside acquisition—never were glibness, verbal intellect, more the test, the emulation—more loftily elevated as head and sample—than they are on the surface of our republican States this day. The writers of a time hint the mottoes of its gods. The word of the modern, say these voices, is the word Culture" (395). In a paragraph that begins by calling European models "exiles and exotics here," Whitman ends by making postwar America a superficial, unintentional parody of the "Old World." The use of the word "mottoes" is especially telling, since its meaning from heraldry associates it with the "idea of caste." The last two sentences of the passage clearly condemn the modern "gods" whose motto is "the word Culture." For Whitman, the word bespeaks the very idea of caste; even worse, it intimates the inappropriate and insubstantial "surface of our republican States this day." After all, the republic should have nothing to do with the idea or word "caste," since that word evokes "the political history of the past" and is allied with "order, safety," and with "cohesion at all cost" (373).

The word *culture* involves, Whitman claims, "our whole theme," and he calls it "the spur, urging us to engagement." Employing some of the fierce rhetoric of *Eighteenth Presidency*, he calls culture "the enemy" and asks, "As now taught, accepted and carried out, are not the processes of culture rapidly creating a class of supercilious infidels, who believe in nothing?" (395). Although he never becomes so extravagantly abusive as in his 1856 "Voice," Whitman clearly figures the problem of democratic culture as yet another instance of an agonistic arena, a space occupied by both the orator/writer and his audience of hearers/readers. Most significantly, Whitman seeks to reconstruct postwar American culture by reconstructing an audience:

> I do not so much object to the name, or word, but I should certainly
> insist, for the purposes of these States, on a radical change of category,

in the distribution of precedence. I should demand a programme of culture, drawn out, not for a single class alone, or for the parlors or lecture-
rooms, but with an eye to practical life, the west, the working-men, the
facts of farms and jack-planes and engineers, and of the broad range of
the women also of the middle and working strata, and with reference
to the perfect equality of women, and of a grand and powerful moth-
erhood. I should demand of this programme or theory a scope generous enough to include the widest human area. It must have for its spinal
meaning the formation of a typical personality of character, eligible to
the uses of the high average of men—and *not* restricted by conditions
ineligible to the masses. The best culture will always be that of the manly
and courageous instincts, and loving perceptions, and of self-respect—
aiming to form, over this continent, an idiocrasy of universalism, which,
true child of America, will bring joy to its mother, returning to her in
her own spirit, recruiting myriads of offspring, able, natural, perceptive,
tolerant, devout believers in her, America, and with some definite
instinct why and for what she has arisen, most vast, most formidable of
historic births, and is, now and here, with wonderful step, journeying
through Time. (396)

Whitman's combinatory strategy once more works on several levels. First, he
calls for a "radical change" in how the word *culture* is used, for the definition
of the word also involves "the distribution of precedence." Second, the "programme of culture" he calls for combines the plans for "Walt Whitman's
Lectures," also titled "America, A Programme" (*NUPM* 4:1437), with the projected audience of the *Primer of Words* and *Eighteenth Presidency*. In all three of
the texts from 1856–58, as well as in *Democratic Vistas*, Whitman aims to
broaden the audience of the programme of culture so that it will be "not for
a single class alone." Third, the programme seeks to dissolve boundaries of
both class and gender (Whitman is not as consistently generous regarding
race) so as to "include the widest human area." Fourth, the programme and
audience combine individual "personality" with "the high average of men"
to form "an idiocrasy of universalism." Fifth, the word *idiocrasy*, rare after the
seventeenth century (*OED*), is the stylistic enactment of Whitman's paradoxical vision, for it combines the Greek roots for "individual, separate" and
"mixing, mixture." A similar point could be made concerning the phrase
"idiocrasy of universalism" itself. Finally, the passage combines Whitman's
vision of a future democratic culture with his sense of America's past and present. By ending the passage with the image of American culture "journeying

through Time," Whitman suggests his confidence that the programme of culture will one day be realized.

3

If *Democratic Vistas* emerges as a kind of summation of Whitman's lecture schemes of the 1850s, recapitulating and reconstructing some of his most intriguing figures of eloquence, the "Death of Abraham Lincoln" lecture provides a fitting conclusion both to this chapter and to the culture of eloquence as a whole. Most of Whitman's performances were managed with little fanfare, but the 1887 lecture at Madison Square Theatre in New York City was, as David Reynolds puts it, "a Barnumesque event on a high scale" (554). The afternoon lecture was sparsely attended but included such luminaries as James Russell Lowell, Augustus St. Gaudens, John Burroughs, Mark Twain, and William Dean Howells. The evening reception at Whitman's suite in the Westminster Hotel, on the other hand, required "thirty-eight column inches in the next day's New York *Sun* and twenty-six in the *Times* to describe the procession" (Reynolds 555). A member of the afternoon audience described the old man as "half paralyzed, hardly able to walk, leaning with his right hand on a cane, and heavily with his left on that of the poet Stedman. With the aid of his friend he was installed in a great armchair, before papers which he hardly touched, allowing himself to slowly improvise."[21]

Since the text of "Death of Abraham Lincoln" dates from 1879, it is more likely that Whitman recited much of the lecture from memory (*PW* 2:497n.). Despite the exaggerations and contradictory responses by both Whitman and the audience, however, it is clear that the occasion was meant to confer honor upon Whitman as much as to mark the anniversary of Lincoln's death. The elegiac lecture functions as a public farewell—and in several ways. It is of course Whitman's public farewell to Lincoln, but it is also the poet's farewell to the literary public. It is surely, too, the public's farewell to Whitman, as evidenced by the hordes of visitors at the evening reception. Most dramatically, however, Whitman's lecture bids farewell to a culture of eloquence, for the contrast between the numbers who came to hear Whitman and those who came to see

---

21. These are the recollections of Stuart Merrill, quoted in William E. Barton, *Abraham Lincoln and Walt Whitman* (Indianapolis: Bobbs-Merrill, 1928), 211; Barton's account is the least dramatic but most objective I have found; see 187–229.

him bespeaks a new culture of celebrity and spectacle. Whitman's New York performance thus recalls, in its cultural implications, Wendell Phillips's Phi Beta Kappa address at Harvard University in 1881. In both performances the speaker attempts to make antebellum America meaningful to a postbellum American audience.

Whitman's account of Lincoln is most remarkable for what it does not tell. We would expect Whitman's Lincoln to be a figure of eloquence, a representative man, but Whitman's description of the first time he saw Lincoln—in New York City, February 1861, as he traveled to Washington for his first inauguration—is marked not by the sounds of powerful words but by the power of silence:

> He came down, I think from Canal street, to stop at the Astor House. The broad spaces, sidewalks, and street in the neighborhood, and for some distance, were crowded with solid masses of people, many thousands. The omnibuses and other vehicles had all been turn'd off, leaving an unusual hush in that busy part of the city. Presently two or three shabby hack barouches made their way with some difficulty through the crowd, and drew up at the Astor House entrance. A tall figure step'd out of the centre of these barouches, paus'd leisurely on the sidewalk, look'd up at the granite walls and looming architecture of the grand old hotel—then, after a relieving stretch of arms and legs, turn'd round for over a minute to slowly and good-humoredly scan the appearance of the vast and silent crowds. There were no speeches—no compliments— no welcome—as far as I could hear, not a word said. Still much anxiety was conceal'd in that quiet. Cautious persons had fear'd some mark'd insult or indignity to the President-elect—for he possess'd no personal popularity at all in New York city, and very little political. But it was evidently tacitly agreed that if the few political supporters of Mr. Lincoln present would entirely abstain from any demonstration on their side, the immense majority, who were any thing but supporters, would abstain on their side also. The result was a sulky, unbroken silence, such as certainly never before characterized so great a New York crowd. (*PW* 2:499–500)

As he develops this remarkable scene, Whitman notes how the silence differs from the "indescribable human roar and magnetism . . . the glad exulting thunder-shouts of countless unloos'd throats of men" that greeted other visitors to New York: "But on this occasion, not a voice—not a sound" (500). The silence, while threatening, remains unbroken. When Lincoln silently enters the Astor House, the "dumb-show" ends. Whitman's description of the dramatic scene emphasizes the necessity of guarding silence in the face of danger, and in doing so it develops Lincoln as a potential victim rather than a figure of eloquence.

The description of Whitman's first view of Lincoln acts as a prelude to the account of the assassination. As in the New York scene, Whitman frustrates any expectation of eloquence. The scene at Ford's Theatre is replete with ironies, and Whitman focuses especially on the ironic juxtaposition of the parlor drama being performed and the actual assassination. The juxtaposition creates a contrast between the play and "that scene" of assassination, but it also blurs the boundary between play and reality. Whitman describes the stage clearing for a moment and then adds, "At this period came the murder of Abraham Lincoln." The matter-of-fact tone carries over into the description of the "main thing, the actual murder," which "transpired with the quiet and simplicity of any commonest occurrence" (505). As in the scene before the Astor House, Whitman's descriptions counter expectations of sounds and voices. Thus he describes the "muffled sound of a pistol-shot," the "hush" of the audience, and the sudden, dramatic appearance of Booth upon the stage, uttering "in a firm and steady voice the words *Sic semper tyrannis.*" As he closes this portion of the narrative, Whitman pauses to imagine Booth's silent rehearsal of his role: "Had not all this terrible scene—making the mimic ones preposterous—had it not all been rehears'd, in blank, by Booth, beforehand?" (505).

The ensuing description of the response to Lincoln's murder develops a strong sense of chaotic, confused voices and actions, "like some horrible carnival" (506). Mrs. Lincoln's famous cry, "*He has kill'd the President,*" mingles with "the sound, somewhere back, of a horse's hoofs clattering with speed" and "the screams and calls, confused talk—redoubled, trebled." Two hundred soldiers storm the house and drive the crowd outside, but even there chaos reigns: the "infuriated crowd" attempts to lynch a man for no apparent reason. Like the "silent, resolute" policemen who restore order, however, Whitman closes the scene—in a one-sentence paragraph—with his persistent theme of silence: "And in the midst of that pandemonium, infuriated soldiers, the audience and the crowd, the stage, and all its actors and actresses, its paint-pots, spangles, and gaslights—the life blood from those veins, the best and sweetest of the land, drips slowly down, and death's ooze already begins its little bubbles on the lips" (507). Whitman's description does not belittle the tragedy of Lincoln's assassination, but the metonymic figuration ("those veins," "the lips") effectively erases the person of Lincoln from the scene. The "Redeemer President" that Whitman had hoped for in the 1850s becomes the "first great Martyr Chief" (509). Likewise, the figure of eloquence becomes a figure of silence, and the vital agency of speech lapses into deathly "bubbles on the lips." Although Whitman interprets the death of Lincoln as a fortunate fall, predicting that future historians and dramatists will use the event "to mark with deepest cut, and mnemonize, this turbulent Nineteenth century of ours" (509), his interpretation marks most deeply the difference between his postwar ideal—the "genuine homogeneous Union, compact, consistent with itself" (508)—and the actual "turbulence" of antebellum America. Finally, then, Whitman's lecture and the figure of Lincoln silently mark the end of the culture of eloquence.

Index